# Quality Information and Knowledge

## Kuan-Tsae Huang,
## Yang W. Lee
## and Richard Y. Wang

D1444986

Prentice Hall PTR
Upper Saddle River
New Jersey 07458
http://www.phptr.com

ISBN 0-13-010141-9

90000

9 780130 101419

Acquisitions editor: *Mike Meehan*
Editorial/production supervision: *Joanne Anzalone*
Cover design director: *Jayne Conte*
Cover design: *Bruce Kenselaar*
Manufacturing manager: *Alexis R. Heydt*
Editorial Assistant: *Bart Blanken*
Marketing Manager: *Kaylie Smith*

© 1999 by Prentice Hall PTR
Prentice-Hall, Inc.
A Simon & Schuster Company
Upper Saddle River, New Jersey 07458

Prentice Hall books are widely used by corporations and
government agencies for training, marketing, and resale.
The publisher offers discounts on this book when ordered in bulk quantities.
For more information, contact Corporate Sales Department, Phone: 800-382-3419;
FAX: 201-236-7141; E-mail: *corpsales@prenhall.com*
Prentice Hall PTR, One Lake Street, Upper Saddle River, NJ 07458.
All rights reserved. No part of this book may be reproduced, in any form or by any means, without
permission in writing from the publisher.
Printed in the United States of America
10    9    8    7    6    5    4    3    2

ISBN 0-13-010141-9

Prentice-Hall International (UK) Limited, *London*
Prentice-Hall of Australia Pty. Limited, *Sydney*
Prentice-Hall Canada Inc., *Toronto*
Prentice-Hall Hispanoamericana, S.A., *Mexico*
Prentice-Hall of India Private Limited, *New Delhi*
Prentice-Hall of Japan, Inc., *Tokyo*
Simon & Schuster Asia Pte. Ltd., *Singapore*
Editora Prentice-Hall do Brasil, Ltda., *Rio de Janeiro*

*To Lu-Yue, Michael, Stephanie, and Fo*

# Table of Contents

# C h a p t e r   3

# C h a p t e r   4

# C h a p t e r   5

# C h a p t e r   6

# Chapter 7

# Chapter 8

## Network Knowledge Infrastructure     **157**

# C h a p t e r   9

**Prosper in the Digital Economy**                                        **175**

# ACKNOWLEDGMENTS

A book that encompasses the two emerging fields of information quality and knowledge management has many contributors. This book synthesizes our cumulated research results and industrial experiences. Our insights are greatly enriched by executives with whom we interact, colleagues with whom we collaborate, and clients of the IBM Global Services. Furthermore, we benefited greatly from participants of the MIT Total Data Quality Management course and the annual MIT Conference on Information Quality.

We must thank the following special individuals: Professors Stuart Madnick and Ugo Gagliardi for their unreserved support over the last two decades, the late Professor Don Schön for his intellectual guidance that has profoundly influenced our research and practice, and Professor Leo Pipino for his generous help throughout the writing of this book. We are indebted to Tom Maglio and John Maglio, Jr. for their assistance in fulfilling many book requirements such as the glossary, index, and format. Thanks are also due to Professors Don Bollou, Diane Strong, Yair Wand, Peter Chen, Arie Segev, and Beverly Kahn.

We particularly appreciate the IBMers who worked hard to develop and implement the ICM AssetWeb knowledge management methodology and technology that we present in this book. Many IBMers ranging from senior management leadership support, worldwide competency network leaders and their core teams, ICM AssetWeb user communities, and the core ICM team at IBM Global Services contributed significantly to this effort. We list here some of the many people whose efforts have been instrumental: Rock Angier, Richard Azzarello, Dilip Barman, Nancy Brandon, Sacha Clark, Robert Coyne, Christine Engeleit, Faren Foster, Patricia Gongla, Donald Haack, Jessica Hu, Eric Hwang, John Kirby, David Livesey, Renee Marsh, Joseph Movizzo, Chris Newlon, Barbara Osborn, Felicia Paduano, Stephanie Pate, Christine Rizzuto, Barbara Salop, Fred Schoeps, Michael Sinneck, Barbara Smith, David E. Smith, Sunghee Soh, Geng-Wen Su, Theo Van Rooy, Ko-Yang Wang, and Kathy Yglesias.

We must also thank practitioners who have made significant contributions to our intellectual life, most notably Ward Page at DARPA's Command Post of the Future program, Jim McGill at Morgan Stanley, Jim Funk at S. C. Johnson, Mel Bergstein and Alan Matsumura at Diamond Technology Partners, Jim Reardon at the Under-Secretary's Office of the Defense Department for Human Affairs, Chris Firth and Peter Kaomea at Citicorp, Sue Bies at the First Tennessee National Corporation, Rita Kovac at the Information Resources Inc., Col. Lane Ongstad of the U.S. Air Force Surgeon General's Office, Lt. Col. Dave Corey of the U.S. Army Medical Command, and Cambridge Research Group's Jesse Jacobson, Rith Peou, Jason Park, Hyung Kim, and Phil Jun.

In writing this book, we draw a significant amount of materials from our cumulated research results and consulting assignments. We thank IBM, Cambridge Research Group, *Communications of the Association for Computing Machinery*, and *Sloan Management Review* for granting us permissions to incorporate their materials into this book.

Finally, our families have been the source of our joy and support during this project, in particular Lu-Yue, Michael, Stephanie, and Fori. They have endured many late-night rings and wake-up calls.

Kuan-Tsae Huang
North Tarrytown, New York


Yang W. Lee
Brookline, Massachusetts


Richard Y. Wang
Cambridge, Massachusetts

# CHAPTER 1

# Why Quality Information and Knowledge?

$D$o you know who your customers are? Do you know who your competitors are? Do you know how you run your business? Do you know how your partner runs the business when you are not around?

Positive answers to these simple questions may not necessarily be easy for many organizations. There is no shortage of examples of companies that do not manage the quality of information and knowledge that they need to run their business competitively. These problems are exacerbated as more organizations use Web sites as their front gate. Site visitors are potential customers. Presumably the Web site contains information that the firm wishes to convey to its target customers. Clearly, the firm wishes to have high-quality information on its site, as well as collect customer profiles that form the basis of their customer care program—a knowledge-intensive proposition. Unfortunately, too many companies have poor quality information on their Web sites. The *Wall Street Journal* reported that businesses leave "cyberspace increasingly littered with digital debris—Web sites neglected or altogether abandoned by their creators" [6]. This is an example of not managing well the quality of information on the electronic frontier. Information and knowledge constitute the core for important changes and innovations for organizations. This is why the quality of information and knowledge directly impacts the quality of changes and innovations in organizations.

New ways of capitalizing on knowledge have long been the catalysts for the dominant changes in management and industrial movements. Two industrial movements explain why. First, the machine age, punctuated by the industrial revolution, represents how the knowledge held by artisans is captured and restructured for efficient mechanical reproduction. The speed of mass production gained from capitalizing knowledge undoubtedly reduced production time and cost. This increased productivity and efficiency gave the firm a competitive edge. Second, the recent information age, led by the computer revolution, represents how data, information, and organizational knowledge are recorded and transformed for redistribution and reuse. The increased accessibility of information through the networks of systems accelerated distribution of information beyond organizational and geographical boundaries. It fostered extensive communication and collaboration, which revised the conventional notion of how we collect and use information and how we work together as a team [3].

Undoubtedly, today's organizations are operating and competing in the information age. A firm's basis for competition, therefore, has changed from tangible products to intangible information. A firm's information represents the firm's collective knowledge used to produce and deliver products and services to consumers. Quality information is increasingly recognized as the most valuable asset of the firm [9]. Firms are grappling with how to capitalize on information and knowledge. Companies are striving, more often silently, to remedy business impacts rooted in poor quality information and knowledge. The examples come from various business areas and processes.

A telecommunication company suffered a loss of $3 million in their bill collections along with increasing customer complaints. The company suspected poor information quality might have contributed to the problem of not sending out bills to all customers.

The U.S. Army lost confidence in using some of their well-guarded logistics information for decision making and operations.

A global chemical company stopped their data warehousing project upon recognizing that the inconsistent representation of information was tarnishing their global business operation.

A consumer product company lost track of trends in product reorders from their retailers. Their computer order system showed no technical problems.

An eyewear company lost its market share and incurred significant rework on their products and services.

The impacts range from operational inconvenience to ill-informed decision making and even to stoppage of business operations. As in solving any other problems, understanding root causes is the first step for preventing and solving organizational information and knowledge problems.

Many firms assume that when their computer systems are well designed and developed, information will flow seamlessly and business will run smoothly. Market leaders would disagree. Two key assumptions must be examined.

First, information will be used effectively when computer systems are well designed and developed.

Second, knowledge in a company will be shared to produce a common goal for the company when the company has a handful of smart employees.

Market leaders would argue that the above assumptions are fallacies. They would argue that the focus should be on the quality of information and its use, not on the computer systems. They would also argue that the focus should be on organizational knowledge for the company as a whole, not individual knowledge.

How do market leaders win? They adhere to the two principles:

Treat information as a product, not as a byproduct.

Cultivate organizational knowledge as their core intellectual capital, not merely a few smart employees.

Federal Express treats information as a product. Federal Express delivers packages [2]. What makes Federal Express a reliable deliverer? Its reliable information on the state of its processes. Customers as well as anyone at Federal Express can track the company's working processes. Producing, storing, and using this reliable information about its working processes are the company's core knowledge. It gives Federal Express the competitive advantage in the marketplace. Many of their customers use Federal Express not merely for delivery but also for their reliable and accessible information about the delivery process. Customers want recorded evidence that proves when a package is delivered, and to whom.

IBM cultivates organizational knowledge as their core intellectual capital. For example, one consultant at IBM has access to and knowledge about how a similar project in London is designed and implemented along with the project source names and participants whom he can contact for more detailed information. The infrastructure of the networked computer system is necessary but not sufficient for knowledge sharing. The companywide cultural change about sharing knowledge and reward systems has facilitated knowledge sharing in IBM. There is no need to reinvent the wheel.

## TWO PROPOSITIONS

The wealth of information is one of the most revolutionary phenomena that modern organizations have experienced. Firms have installed hundreds of millions of computers to collect, process, and utilize information from various information sources. This trend is continuing relentlessly with the rapid advancement of information technology.

The wealth of information, however, is a double-edged sword. High-quality information benefits firms, whereas poor-quality information hurts firms [8]. For example, Federal Express delivers and tracks the exact location of an overnight package [2]; Lands' End remembers a family's clothing sizes perhaps better than the family can. These competitive advantages increase their profit margins, enhance their corporate images, and strengthen their customer relationships [9]. On the other hand, TRW's credit data unit had so much trouble with the publicity caused by their poor credit data that they decided to discontinue that branch of its business. The first proposition of this book, therefore, is fundamental:

Proposition 1: Firms must create a reservoir of quality information.

Having access to quality information alone is not sufficient. Firms must create new knowledge from quality information and experiences. This knowledge, once captured, must be disseminated throughout the firm to increase productivity and foster innovation. Many companies still operate on the assumption that employees automatically share their knowledge. As these companies expand to operate globally, the assumed opportunities for spontaneous face-to-face exchange of tacit knowledge diminish.

More importantly, modern organizations are increasingly becoming knowledge processing entities whereby employees are the knowledge assets [1, 5, 7, 10]. When a knowledge worker goes home at the end of the day, the knowledge is no longer with the firm. When a knowledge worker retires or resigns from the company, too often the knowledge is lost permanently. Whatever has been learned at the individual level is lost at the organizational level. Our second proposition, therefore, is an extension and utilization of the first:

Proposition 2: Firms must create a wealth of organizational knowledge.

Many best-practice reports witness that information technology alone is not the driver for knowledge management in companies today. We emphasize that information and knowledge experienced by members of an organization should be the focus, not the system or technology per se. Technology and systems, however, are used as facilitators in the production, storage, and use of organizational knowledge.

## CREATE KNOWLEDGE WITH QUALITY INFORMATION

How can firms create organizational knowledge? How can firms develop best practice and distill the core knowledge from their organizational knowledge? We present a solution to these problems. Our solution provides an innovative way to create a new wealth of quality information and organizational knowledge. The essence of the solution, which will be delineated throughout the book, is depicted in Figure 1.1.

Successful corporations excel by exploiting information, not computer systems. The key lies in managing quality information for productive knowledge creation and diffusion. To explain how companies can exploit information and human experiences, we summarize cumulated research results and industrial experiences in the fields of information quality and organizational knowledge.

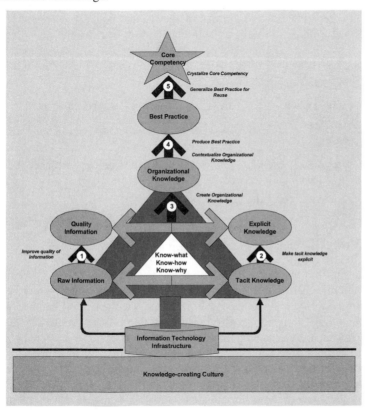

Figure 1.1: Quality Information and Organizational Knowledge

(Source: Cambridge Research Group [4])

Corporations are accustomed to paying attention to protecting their business knowledge as an asset from third-party use. The convention of patents and copyrights has been established and practiced for a long time. To compete more effectively in the global market, however, firms must extend their attention to include information. *Information is a product.* Corporations must define, measure, analyze, and improve the quality of information, treating information as a product.

Creating quality information and organizational knowledge is the prerequisite for any firm to gain competitive advantage. Companies are grappling with creating and reusing organizational knowledge due to the need to compete in the global marketplace. This trend is further accelerated by the presence of enabling technical infrastructures such as groupware, database, and network technology.

In short, capitalizing knowledge will move firms forward. This is the way to prevent and cure organizational Alzheimer's disease. Knowledge production ought to be the focus for any corporation competing in this information age. In this book, we prescribe how to create and diffuse organizational knowledge. The following list highlights the key points:

Transform tacit knowledge to explicit knowledge

Transfer local knowledge to global knowledge

Create organizational knowledge from quality information and human experiences

Establish best practice

Distill core competency

Support organizational knowledge production and reuse process with technological and organizational infrastructures

Foster an environment for creating and sharing knowledge

## Book Organization

This book is organized into two parts: Part I presents how firms should define, measure, analyze and improve information quality. Chapter 2 introduces the fundamental concepts necessary for managing information as a product. Chapter 3 defines information quality. It provides the essential vocabulary for identifying information quality problems. Chapter 4 describes how to measure, analyze, and improve information quality.

Part II prescribes how firms should create and reuse organizational knowledge. Chapter 5 presents the framework for creating organizational knowledge. Chapter 6 illustrates how knowledge management is actually performed in real organizations. Chapter 7 introduces information technologies needed for knowledge creation and reuse. Chapter 8 presents the infrastructure essential for knowledge creation and reuse. Finally, Chapter 9 concludes with a series of concrete actions and future directions.

Throughout this book, anecdotes and case studies are presented, with the information sources footnoted or referenced. Whenever appropriate, we also illustrate our points with industry case studies based on the results of our research and industry experiences. Whenever necessary, the names of the companies are disguised to honor the request for anonymity from the companies. Examples used in the book include BetterCare Company, Computer Company, Data Company, Eyewear Company, Financial Company, GoldenAir Company, HyCare Company, Manufacturing Company, Investment Company, Shipping Company, and Sportswear Company.

## References

[1]  Eisenhardt, K. M. and B. N. Tabrizi, "Accelerating Adaptive Processes: Product Innovation in the Global Computer Industry," *Administrative Science Quarterly,* 1(40), 1995, pp. 84–110.

[2]  Harvind, R., "Federal Express Wins in the Tough Services Category," in *Road to the Baldridge Award: The Quest for Total Quality,* Butterworth-Heinenmann, Stoneham, 1992.

[3]  Lee, Y., *Collective Knowledge: An Institutional Learning Perspective.* Cambridge Research Group, Cambridge, MA, 1997.

[4]  Lee, Y., *Quality Information, Organizational Knowledge, and Core Competency.* Cambridge Research Group, Cambridge, MA, 1997.

[5]  Nass, C., "Knowledge or Skills: Which Do Administrators Learn from Experience?," *Organizational Science,* 4(6), 1994, pp. 38–50.

[6]  Sandberg, J. . "At Thousands of Web Sites, Time Stands Still: Many Web Sites Need Updating," *The Wall Street Journal,* March 11, 1997 p. B1.

[7]  Simonin, B. L., "The Importance of Collaborative Know-How: An Empirical Test of the Learning Organization," *Academy of Management Journal,* 5(40), 1997, pp. 1150–1174.

[8]  Strong, D. M., Y. W. Lee and R. Y. Wang, "Data Quality in Context," *Communications of the ACM,* 40(5), 1997, pp. 103–110.

[9]  Wang, R. Y., Y. L. Lee, L. Pipino and D. M. Strong, "Manage Your Information as a Product," *Sloan Management Review,* 39(4), 1998, pp. 95–105.

[10] Weick, K. E., "Collective Mind in Organizations: Heedful Interrelating on Flight Decks," *Administative Science Quarterly,* 3(38), 1993, pp. 357–381.

Knowledge
Auskunft  Conocimient
Informazione
INDICIUM  지식  Savoir
Informative  インフォーメーシオ
Nozione  Wissen
Information ソウ  SCIENTIA
정보  Información

# Manage Information as a Product

$F$irms believe that quality information is critical to their success — but do they act on this belief? *Barely*. Most Chief Executive Officers (CEOs) have experienced the adverse effects of decisions based on information of inferior quality. Most general managers have experienced the frustration of knowing that data exist in the firm but are not accessible in the integrated form needed. Most Chief Information Officers (CIOs) have experienced the discomfort of explaining why, in light of the costly investment made by the company in information technology, these data are of inferior quality or not accessible. Firms voice the need for quality information. Many strive to satisfy this need. All too often, however, quality information is not delivered or is not accessible to the user. *This does not have to be so.*

Over the last decade, we have investigated information quality problems encountered by organizations. What clearly stands out is the need for firms to treat information as a product, that is, as an end deliverable that satisfies consumer needs. Contrast this approach with the often observed treatment of information as a byproduct. The byproduct approach places its focus on the wrong target, usually the system instead of the end product, the information.

In this chapter, we present social and business impacts of information quality, define the concepts fundamental to the understanding of information quality, and argue for the establishment of the position of the information product manager.

# SOCIAL AND BUSINESS IMPACTS

Across industries such as banking, transportation, insurance, retail, consumer marketing, and health care, firms have been integrating their business processes across functional, product, and geographic lines [22-24]. The integration of these business processes accelerates the demand for more effective application systems in areas such as product development, product delivery, and customer service. Consequently, many business activities require access to a variety of information systems both within and across organizational boundaries. Unfortunately, these information systems may contain poor quality information which can have significant social and business impacts [4, 5, 11, 14, 19-21, 25, 26, 29, 32]. We illustrate the social and business impacts of information quality below.

## Social Impacts

Errors in credit reporting are one of the most striking examples of the social impacts of poor-quality information. The credit industry not only collects financial information on individuals but also compiles employment records. An error on a credit report can be more harmful to an individual than merely the denial of credit. One congressional witness testified that he lost his job when he was reported as having a criminal record, a record that really belonged to a man with a similar name. In light of such testimony, Congress pushed for legislation to require that the credit industry retain accurate information no matter where the information originated.

The *Wall Street Journal* reported that a contact representative for the Internal Revenue Service had access to the IRS database of 200 million tax records of businesses and individuals filed annually. According to a federal jury, he took unauthorized looks at returns of a political opponent and a family adversary. Numerous reports of wrongdoing prompted a sweeping probe of IRS employee browsing, and its sensational results were publicized at a high-profile Senate hearing. As a result, more than 700 IRS employees have been punished for improperly accessing agency information—with penalties ranging from firing to reprimands—and about 20 have faced criminal charges.

"CBS Evening News" further reported that the IRS, after spending more than $4 billion, still failed to provide the adequate mechanism to prevent employees from browsing the taxpayers' records. The IRS also failed to collect more than $200 billion, about the size of this nation's budget deficit.

"NBC News" also reported that "dead people still eat!" It was found that, because of outdated information in government databases, food stamps continued to be sent to recipients long after they died. Food stamps also continued to be sent to convicted criminals while they served their jail terms. Fraud from food stamps cost U.S. taxpayers billions of dollars, according to NBC.

In general, information is gathered on individuals and organizations on a variety of sensitive topics. This includes information on medical, financial, employment, consumption, and legal activities. The organizations creating and using this information may include government agencies, insurance companies, banks, retail organizations, and countless others. It is in the interest of both the collectors and users of this information, as well as the subjects of the information, to keep this information accurate.

# Business Impacts

Delivering quality information to consumers must be viewed as a strategic goal. In managing information as a product, however, firms must answer the following questions: What is the business merit from the general management's perspective? Does it strengthen customer relationships? Does it support managerial decisions? Does it improve the bottom line?

Viewing information as a product extends the scope of customer relationships from external to internal customers. This reinforces the customer orientation of the firm. Quality information leads to improved customer service, customer satisfaction, and stronger customer relationships. If internal users of information are treated as consumers, they will improve performance and increase productivity. Morale will also improve which, in turn, translates into better external customer relationships, increasing the firm's profit margins. In short, it is a self-reinforcing process which leads to improved company performance and increased shareholder value. Below we illustrate these benefits.

## Customer Service

Better information quality leads to better customer service. Shipping Company, for example, is one of the largest providers of international ocean freight services. Formerly, its collection methods for cargo information were highly labor intensive and error prone. Inaccuracies in the information were commonplace. Shipments were often sent to the wrong destination and sometimes lost altogether, resulting in unhappy customers, costly investigative efforts to locate lost goods, and rerouting costs.

By treating their cargo and container information as an information product to be used by both their employees and customers, Shipping Company began installing radio frequency-based tracking mechanisms in their shipping ports to keep track of their containers. The tracking mechanisms are much like bar code scanners in that each container can be uniquely and reliably identified as it moves through checkpoints, with real-time transaction database updates. The end result is that Shipping Company now provides up-to-the-second and correct information to their employees and customers about location and thus delivery schedules for their goods. Many customers consider this a critical factor in choosing Shipping Company as their shipping vendor.

## Management Support

Decision making is an important area where information quality can impact the bottom line significantly. With the proliferation of management support systems [28], more information originates from databases both within and across organizational boundaries. Maintaining the quality of the information which drives these systems is critical.

Financial Company illustrates the financial value of information in such systems. It has a risk management system to gather information documenting all of the securities positions at the firm. With complete and timely information, the system serves as a tool that executives use to monitor the firm's exposure to various market risks. However, when critical information is of poor quality, the system can succumb to major disasters. For example, information availability and timeliness problems caused the risk management system to fail to alert management of an extremely large interest rate exposure. When interest rates changed dramatically, Financial Company was caught unaware and absorbed a net loss totaling more than $250 million. Another problem arose when financial crises occurred in Thailand, Hong Kong, Indonesia, and Korea. During the crises, Financial Company was unable to determine their exposures to firms that had Asian exposures. In scrambling to resolve these problems, Financial Company wasted productive resources and missed opportunities to capitalize on these crises. By treating risk management information as a product, Financial established an information quality program to ensure the quality of information.

## Bottom Line

For more than half a year, direct mail for Investment Company's marketing campaign was sent to wrong target customers, costing millions of dollars and lost market shares. The company spent a significant amount of time debugging the econometric model that determined the target mailing list. The problem, however, was not with the model. By managing the information required for direct marketing as an information product, and beginning an effort that brought together different stakeholders, the root cause of the problem was detected: the company had inadvertently corrupted its personal income and age data database during its migration from traditional mainframe to client/server systems.

Comfortable Flight, a large U.S. airline, further illustrates the problem of focusing on software only and not treating information as a product. While installing some new software, Comfortable Flight inadvertently corrupted its database of passenger reservations due to bugs in the new software. Programmers fixed the software but failed to correct the false reservation information it had made. As a result, planes for several months were taking off partly empty because of phantom bookings, losing significant revenue. Had the information in the reservation system been treated as a product and managed accordingly, the problem would not have occurred.

# FUNDAMENTAL CONCEPTS

We have illustrated the social and business impacts of poor-quality information. But how do executives get their hands around issues related to information quality? We begin with some fundamental concepts useful for understanding information quality.

## Information versus Data

The terms data and information are often used synonymously; in practice, managers differentiate information from data intuitively and describe information as data that have been processed. Unless specified otherwise, this book will use "information" interchangeably with "data."

## From Product to Information Manufacturing

An analogy exists between quality issues in product manufacturing and those in information manufacturing as shown in Figure 2.1 [35]. Product manufacturing can be viewed as a processing system that acts on raw materials to produce physical products. Analogously, information manufacturing can be viewed as a processing system acting on raw data to produce information products [1, 3].

Generally speaking, manufacturing-related activities consist of two parts. The first is the design and development of the product. This is typically performed by a product development group in conjunction with other functional areas. The second is the production and distribution of the product. Typically, the personnel responsible for production manufacture the product based on the specification provided by the designers and engineers. Product quality is a function of both of these two parts: the manufacturing machinery and the methods applied at production time. These two concepts have similar analogies in information manufacturing systems, as discussed below.

|  | Product Manufacturing | Information Manufacturing |
|---|---|---|
| Input | Raw Materials | Raw Data |
| Process | Assembly Line | Information System |
| Output | Physical Products | Information products |

Figure 2.1: Product versus Information Manufacturing

(Source: *Information Technology in Action: Trends and Perspectives* [32])

## Information Manufacturing Systems

We refer to an information manufacturing system as a system that produces Information Products (IPs). The concept of an information product emphasizes the fact that the information output from an information manufacturing system has value transferable to the consumer, either internal or external. We identify four roles in an information manufacturing system:

Information providers are those who create or collect data for the information product.

Information custodians are those who design, develop, or maintain the data and systems infrastructure for the information product.

Information consumers are those who use the information product in their work.

IP managers are those who are responsible for managing the entire information product production process and the information product life cycle.

Each role is associated with a process or task: (1) providers are associated with data-production processes; (2) custodians with data storage, maintenance, and security; and (3) consumers with data-utilization processes, which may involve additional data aggregation and integration.

We illustrate these roles with a financial company's client account database. A broker who creates accounts and executes transactions has to collect from clients the information necessary for opening accounts and executing these transactions, thus is a *provider*. An information systems professional who designs, develops, produces, or maintains the system is a *custodian*. A financial controller or a client representative who uses this system is a *consumer*. Finally, a manager who is responsible for the collection, manufacturing, and delivery of customer account data is an *IP manager*.

Information providers generate information having value to others. For example, retail stores collect and resell point-of-sale data to firms such as Information Resources Inc. (IRI) that specializes in distributing retail data to marketing organizations and investment banks that are interested in promotional effects and market shares of competing firms. IRI collects point-of-sale data from retail stores such as supermarkets, process these data, and resells them. Finally, information consumers acquire information generated externally, for example, consumer marketing firms such as Procter and Gamble or security analysts at investment firms such as Merrill Lynch.

## The Information System Development Cycle

Before we begin to think about managing information as a product, we need to use our manufacturing analogy to consider the development cycle of an information system that encompasses design and implementation to the deployment of the system to the user community, as shown in Figure 2.2.

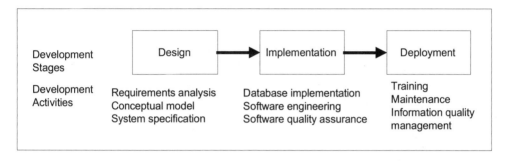

Figure 2.2: Information System Development Cycle

(Source: *Information Technology in Action: Trends and Perspectives* [32])

Because the information produced from the underlying information system is a function of all of the activities at the various stages of the system development cycle, each stage must be carefully considered as a potential target area for information quality improvement. For example, let us consider the following three examples of quality issues related to the development cycle.

The information designed into the system is not the information required by the information consumer as a result of inadequate requirements analysis (design problem).

The testing of the software for the system is incomplete, causing the information manufacturing system to function erratically (implementation problem).

The information custodians are inadequately trained in processing information such as input and retrieval of the information from the system, resulting in corrupted data (deployment problem).

Concepts such as the information manufacturing system and the information system's development cycle form a foundation for managing information as a product. Below we introduce the concepts of the Total Data Quality Management (TDQM) cycle and dimensions of information quality.

## The Total Data Quality Management (TDQM) Cycle

The field of product manufacturing has an extensive body of Total Quality Management (TQM) literature with principles, guidelines, and techniques for product quality [6-9, 13]. In the TQM literature, the widely practiced Deming cycle for quality enhancement consists of *plan*, *do*, *check*, and *act* [15]. By adapting the Deming cycle, we develop the TDQM cycle [31] as Figure 2.3 depicts.

The *definition* component of the TDQM cycle identifies Information Quality (IQ) dimensions. The *measurement* component produces IQ metrics. The *analysis* component identifies root causes for IQ problems and calculates the impacts of poor quality information. Finally, the *improvement* component provides techniques for improving IQ. They are applied along IQ dimensions according to requirements specified by the consumer.

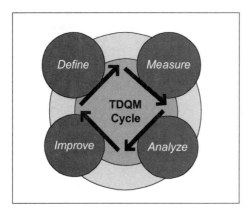

Figure 2.3: The TDQM Cycle

(Source: *Communications of the ACM* [31])

## Dimensions of Information Quality

For a manufacturing firm, the concept of quality encompasses much more than material defects. David Garvin, a knowledge leader in manufacturing quality, proposed an analytic framework [12] encompassing eight dimensions of quality: performance, features, reliability, conformance, durability, serviceability, aesthetics, and perceived quality.

Just as product quality has multiple dimensions, *information quality also has* multiple dimensions. Frequently mentioned dimensions are accuracy, completeness, consistency, and timeliness. The choice of these dimensions is primarily based on intuitive understanding [2], industrial experience [10, 27], or literature review [18]. A comprehensive survey of the literature [35], however, shows that there is no general agreement on information quality dimensions.

Consider accuracy which most information quality studies include as a key dimension. Although the term "accuracy" has an intuitive appeal, there is no commonly accepted definition of what it means exactly. For example, Kriebel [18] characterizes accuracy as "the correctness of the output information." Ballou and Pazer [2] describe accuracy as when "the recorded value is in conformity with the actual value."

Clearly, the notion of information quality depends on the actual use of information. What may be considered good information in one case (for a specific application or user) may not be sufficient in another case. For example, analysis of the financial position of a firm may require information in units of thousands of dollars, whereas auditing requires precision to the cent. This relativity of quality presents a problem. The quality of the information generated by an information system depends on the design of the system. Yet, the actual use of the information is outside the designer's control. Issues such as these will be addressed in later chapters.

## THE INFORMATION PRODUCT MANAGER

Firms must manage information as a product. This is crucial if they are to attain high-quality information. Failure to do so has negative impacts on the firm's relationships with their customers, corporate image, and bottom line. In managing information as a product, firms must follow four principles [33]:

Understand the consumer's information needs

Manage information as the product of a well-defined production process

Manage information as a product with a life cycle

Appoint an information product manager to manage the information product.

We make use of four cases, as shown in Figure 2.4, to illustrate the major principles and concepts of the IP approach.

**Financial Company** is a leading investment bank with extensive domestic and international operations. Its customers need to trade immediately after opening a new account. The new account must be linked to accounts the customer may already have opened and the information in all accounts must be accurate, up to date, and consistent. The company requires real-time account balance information in order to enforce minimum account balance rules across a customer's multiple accounts. Failures in this area of operations expose the company to potentially large monetary losses. By statute, the company has to close all the accounts of a customer when informed by federal authorities of criminal activities on the part of the customer. To do so requires timely, integrated information on a customer's accounts.

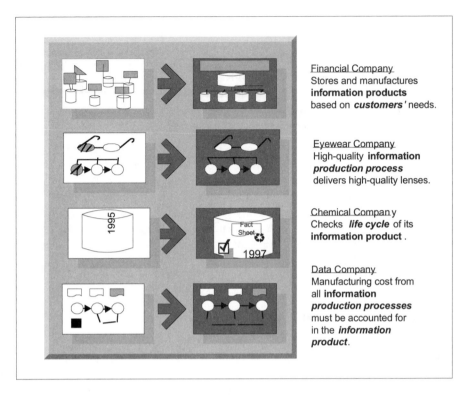

Figure 2.4: Four Case Studies in Managing Information as a Product

(Source: *Sloan Management Review* [33])

**Eyewear Company** sells eyewear products at its retail outlets throughout the country. For its eyeglass products, specifications were generated at the retail outlet and forwarded to one of four laboratories for grinding the lens to specification. Twenty-five thousand eyeglass orders were received by these laboratories each week. The ability to produce eyeglasses that met consumer needs depended heavily on the quality of information provided to the grinders at the laboratories. If the grinder's information needs were not met, the production of lenses was adversely affected.

**Data Company**'s primary business is the capture of data from hundreds of millions of transactions a week generated by tens of thousands of retail stores. Clients purchase information refined from the raw data collected from these retail stores. Data Company had built sufficient intelligence into their systems to provide high-quality information. It had been using neural networks for several years and had built an imputation process that estimated any missing data. For example, this system had enabled the company to correct data that were corrupted by failed or bad transmissions.

   **Chemical Company** is a major presence in the petrochemical industry and a Fortune 500 company. For each of its chemical products, Chemical Company is required by law to produce a Material Safety Data Sheet (MSDS) that identifies the potential hazards of the product, the symptoms of the hazard, and the actions to be taken should a symptom be observed. Because of the extremely high product liability costs of not reporting potential hazards, the company has every incentive to provide accurate, complete, timely, and understandable MSDSs. Chemical Company has a well-defined process for creating MSDSs. When a new chemical is developed, the MSDS group contacts experts who contribute to the specifications of the MSDS.

## Managing Information as a Product — The Four Principles

*Companies must understand their consumers' information needs.* In our analysis of Financial Company, it became clear that the company had to specify the needs of two types of consumer: the external customer of the firm and the internal information consumer. For its external customers, Financial Company must open new accounts quickly, maintain up-to-date customer risk profiles, and know all accounts related to a particular customer. Investments at inappropriate customer risk levels cause major customer dissatisfaction and potential indemnification to customers for losses. For its internal consumers, Financial Company must provide real-time information about any changes in customers' account balances.

   Eyewear Company provides an additional example of what can happen when this principle is violated. Satisfying the needs of Eyewear's customers translates into providing the proper lenses. Delivering the appropriate lenses is predicated on the correct lens specifications being transmitted to the factory. A lack of understanding of the information needs of the lens grinders (the internal customer) by the writers of the lens specifications, the opticians, resulted in the rework of many lenses. Regrinding lenses resulted in additional costs of rework and time delays which negatively affected customer satisfaction.

   *Companies must manage information as the product of a well-defined information production process.* Financial Company maintained a centralized customer account database. Transactions, which occurred throughout the day, were posted nightly to the database, and customer account balances updated. Other customer information was updated on an ad hoc basis, when convenient. This is an effect of treating information solely as the *byproduct* of a physical event, rather than as the product of a well-defined information production process.

   Managing information as a byproduct will fail to meet consumers' needs. In Financial Company, customer account information was perceived by the internal consumers as error prone and insecure. As one vice-president joked, "everyone but the consultant has update privileges to customer account information." The desire to solve these information quality problems coupled with the tendency toward local control led individual departments to develop home-grown customer account databases. The result was a proliferation of local customer databases with inconsistencies among them. These local databases were tailored to the specific needs of each department and contained more current information on the department's customers than did the central database. Each department collected and processed information as a byproduct of its local operations, independent of the corporation's need for integrated customer account information.

*Companies must manage the life cycle of their information products.* Adapting the classical marketing notion of product life cycle [17], we define the information product life cycle as the stages through which information passes from introduction to obsolescence. The life cycle can be divided into four stages: introduction (creation), growth, maturity, and decline. Chemical Company provides an example of not following this principle. The company's well-defined process for creating MSDSs did not extend to maintaining the quality of this information over time — over the life cycle of the information product. As a consequence, information on new hazards, based on accumulated experiences with the product and most recent scientific evidence, was incorporated into a product's MSDS erratically. In short, the quality of the information deteriorated over time.

At Financial Company, changes in the operating environment called for updated production processes to improve the company's information products. Financial Company, however, did not manage the life cycle of their customer account information for the new global, legal, and competitive environment. The company was not poised to leverage customer account information in its global operations. For example, customers with sufficient credit across accounts could not trade or borrow on their full balance. Tracking customer balances for individual and multiple accounts, closing all accounts of a customer because of criminal activities, and ensuring an accurate customer risk profile could also not be accomplished without significant, error-prone, human intervention. All of these presented the company with potentially huge problems and considerable missed opportunities.

*Companies should appoint an information product manager to manage their information processes and resulting products.* In the case of Financial Company, the information product manager would be responsible for monitoring and capturing consumer needs on a continual basis, reconciling these varied needs, and transforming this knowledge into a process of continuous improvement. Without an information product manager, Financial Company established few information process measures or controls. For example, there were no controls to ensure that customer risk profiles were updated on a regular basis [34]. The account creation process was not standardized or inspected. Consequently, no metrics were established to measure how many accounts were created on time, and whether customer information in those accounts was updated. Because management focused on the revenue generating operations such as trading, the Information Technology (IT) department found itself responding reactively to ad hoc requests from the trading department for updated customer account information. Had IT been allowed to manage its customer account information as a product, Financial Company would have had better risk management and customer service — two critical success factors for companies in the financial industry.

Financial Company hired a new IT director who was knowledgeable about information quality concepts, process engineering, and business applications. This began the company's transition toward an IP perspective. The director began to institute a cross-functional approach and acted as a de facto information product manager. With support from the CIO, he constructed a work-flow model of the customer account information production process that integrated client services, business operations, and the IT department. The process of producing high-quality customer account information, the foundation of Financial Company's business, had begun.

Data Company provides a second example of a company rapidly moving toward managing information as product. The company currently manages the entire information delivery system in an integrated fashion. It provides a contrasting example to Financial Company in that Data Company distributed the responsibilities of the information product manager to two individuals.

## Managing Information as a Byproduct Will Not Work

Information can always be viewed as the byproduct of a physical event and managed as such. From the information consumer's perspective, however, the information is a product, not a byproduct. This notion of information as a product cannot be overemphasized. Contrast the byproduct approach to the information-as-product approach. Five factors should be analyzed: What is managed? How is it managed? Why manage it? Who manages it? and What is considered success? (See Table 2.1.)

### What Is Managed?

Organizations commonly focus on managing the life cycle of the hardware and software that produce the information instead of the life cycle of the information product. Although this focus is the norm, it is an inappropriate norm. The focus should be on the end product, information. Solely managing the hardware and software is insufficient to capture the additional knowledge necessary to achieve meaningful information quality. For example, in Eyewear Company, the grinding instructions are distinct from, and as important as, the actual lenses. If the instructions are not correct, there is no way that the lenses will be correct. The instructions, however, are considered a byproduct of selling eyeglasses to a customer.

Table 2.1   Manage Information as a Product versus Byproduct

|  | Product | Byproduct |
|---|---|---|
| What is managed? | Information<br>Information product life cycle | Hardware and software systems' life cycles |
| How is it managed? | Integrated, cross-functional approach<br>Encompass information suppliers, manufacturers, and consumers | Integrate stove-pipe systems<br>Control of individual components<br>Cost controls |

| Why manage it? | Deliver quality information products to consumers | Implement quality hardware and software system |
|---|---|---|
| What is success? | Quality information product continuously delivered over the product life cycle! No Garbage-In-Garbage-Out (GIGO)! | The system works! No bugs! |
| Who manages it? | CIO Information Product Manager | CIO IT director and database administrators |

(Source: *Sloan Management Review* [33])

## How Is It Managed?

In the byproduct approach, because the focus is on the hardware and software systems' life cycles, the means becomes the end. The system is managed by attempting to control individual components and establishing cost controls on the various components. The focus is placed on components in isolation instead of the components as an integrated whole.

The previously cited example of Eyewear Company serves as a clear case of what can happen when the organization focuses purely on the components. When asked for lens rework figures, the IT director stated that, "We know we have 15 percent errors." He left unstated the assumption that all errors were attributed to the grinding machines. No one questioned this assumption. Focus was on the hardware and software components of lens production, not on the lens specifications. It took outside observers to recognize that communication problems between opticians and grinders resulted in information quality problems. Approximately 3 percent of the lens specifications sent to grinders had information quality problems that caused lens regrinding. Many of these problems were due to mismatches between how opticians wrote orders and how grinders read these orders. For example, opticians used special instruction lines on the form to add information. The grinders ignored this information because they did not expect grinding specifications in those lines. Lack of communication between opticians and grinders contributed to this problem. IT also contributed to the problem. The MIS director primarily focused on upgrades of hardware and software. The necessary cross-functional view was absent.

Failing to treat lens specifications as an information product, whose consumer was the grinder, resulted in regrinding approximately 40,000 lenses per year. The problem had existed for a long period of time and was costing the company more than $1 million annually. This was an estimate of rework costs alone; it did not include other costs such as those associated with customer dissatisfaction. In short, Eyewear Company was not treating the opticians and grinders, in their roles as information suppliers and consumers, as part of one integrated system.

Financial Company presents a further illustration of the misplaced focus on individual components. Databases were optimized at the local level and were not truly integrated. The account managers, who were the internal information consumers, had local information for local needs. These managers did not have access to the integrated, global information required to exploit emerging opportunities. The quality of the information that account managers received affected their ability to manage risk, improve service, and increase revenue.

## Why Is It Managed?

The byproduct view is reflected in the conventional approach to information management. Too often, the IT department emphasizes improving the quality of the delivery system and its components as opposed to focusing on optimizing the quality of the information product delivered to the consumer [16]. The latter requires a thorough knowledge of the consumer's information needs and the consumer's quality criteria.

Eyewear Company illustrates the stress on component improvement. The opticians' insertion of information in the special instruction section of the order forms was an example of "improving" the order writing component as opposed to improving the quality of information supplied to the grinder. It made the opticians' task easier at the consumers' (grinders') expense.

In contrast, Data Company was rapidly evolving toward managing information as a product. It provided an example of some success in managing information as a product. The company was beginning to manage the entire information delivery process as an integrated system. It recently adopted a companywide Total Quality Management (TQM) program [6, 8, 9] and invested in modernizing its technology infrastructure. The company worked with its information suppliers to produce better information. It instituted procedures that enabled information consumers to report information quality problems directly. Because the company tailored its information products to individual clients, it recognized the need to proactively partner with its clients.

Even with all this attention to an integrated production process, some communication problems remained. For example, Data Company had problems pricing its product because fixed costs were not communicated well within the company. The cost data were accurate. They, however, were not represented in a manner useable by the marketing department. For example, data such as management overhead was not appropriately communicated to the sales force. As a result, Data Company's sales force did not believe the cost data provided by the IT department and continued to ignore the management overhead in their contract bidding pricing. This prompted the marketing executive vice-president to state, "I may not price strictly based on cost, but I need to know the cost." Consequently, the company's profit margins remained low despite its predominant position in a competitive market.

## What Is Success?

Employing an information-as-product approach as opposed to a byproduct approach changes the measures of success from a delivery system focus to an information end-product focus. Instead of judging success of the computer system on the basis of "no bugs," companies should measure the quality of the information end product as its fitness for use to the consumer.

Chemical Company's experience with the quality of their MSDSs over time, which was mentioned earlier, provides a good example of not recognizing the need to deliver a quality information product to consumers over the product's life cycle. Although the information quality of the MSDSs was initially high, it deteriorated over time. As the company's chemical products were used, evidence of new hazards arose from accumulated experience in using the products and new scientific discoveries that confirmed new hazards. The company was expected to update its MSDSs as new evidence became available. It often failed to do so. To Chemical Company, success was measured by the quality of its initial MSDS. The life cycle of the MSDS product, however, is not necessarily the same as the life cycle of the chemical product. A truer measure of success would account for this difference and assess the quality of the MSDS over its life cycle.

## Who Manages It?

If companies take an information product approach and manage across functions, management structure must be adapted to this environment. A product manager of information is needed. We refer to such a function as the information product manager. The positions of information product manager and CIO are not identical. The CIO exists in most modern organizations. Among the CIO's responsibilities is the management of the firm's data repositories. A subordinate function reporting to the CIO, that of Database Administrator (DBA), is typically assigned this management task. In the four cases as shown in Figure 2.5, solutions to their information quality problems require intervention on the part of management. Our research suggests that the agent of this intervention should not be the DBA. The traditional focus of the DBA is to control what enters the databases. The DBA does not focus on the production and delivery of information as a cross-functional, integrated system involving information suppliers, information producers, and information consumers.

What is striking about the companies in the cases is their intuitive sense that such a position as information product manager is necessary. Although they do not formally recognize the need as such, Financial Company, Chemical Company, and Data Company all have evolved to the point where each has an individual performing duties that we would associate with those of an information product manager. The companies have taken an information-as-product view and have begun to manage information with this view in mind.

## Appoint the Information Product Manager

The position of information product manager is necessary to ensure that relevant, high-quality information products are delivered to information consumers. The information product manager's key responsibility is to coordinate and manage the three major stakeholder groups: the supplier of raw information, the producer or manufacturer of the deliverable information, and the consumer of the information. To do so, the information product manager must apply an integrated, cross-functional management approach. The information product manager orchestrates and directs the information production process during the product's life cycle in order to deliver quality information to the consumer (see Figure 2.5).

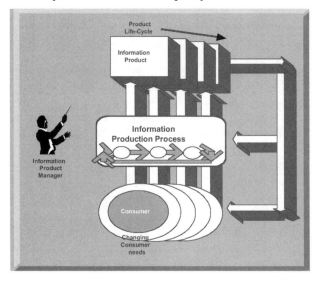

Figure 2.5: **Managing Information as a Product**

(Source: *Sloan Management Review* [33])

## The De Facto Information Product Manager

As indicated previously, companies have an intuitive, if not clearly articulated, sense of how the information product should be managed. In the case of Financial Company, its IT director served as a de facto information product manager. In Data Company, the functions of the information product manager were shared by the IT director and a Senior vice-president who reported to the CIO. Together, they oversaw and managed the company's information suppliers, the in-house information production, and the clients who were consumers of their information products. Chemical Company also had an information product manager in the making. This manager was assigned to create the necessary cross-functional approach to ensure that an MSDS met high-quality standards throughout the life cycle of the corresponding chemical product, and, as such, throughout the life cycle of the MSDS.

## Information Product Manager's Responsibilities

The information product manager must incorporate the requirements of the three stakeholders (the information consumer, the information manufacturer, and the information supplier) at each stage of the information product life cycle. Each stakeholder group, however, may have more than one constituent. Financial Company had many sources of raw information that are used in developing their final information products, hence, multiple constituents in the information supplier stakeholder group. Financial Company also services multiple information consumers. The same information, however, might be a different product to each of these consumers.

In eliciting the stakeholders' requirements and integrating these into the information product, the tasks faced by the information product manager will change over the course of the life cycle. During the introductory stage, the primary task is design and development, an engineering effort. During the growth stage, emphasis is placed on improving and monitoring the information product. As the information product matures, the main task is maintenance which emphasizes the monitoring aspect. Attention to these major tasks over the life cycle is critical. For example, Chemical Company ensured proper development and production of its information product, the MSDS, during the introductory stage. Its legal liability problems arose because insufficient attention was paid to the maintenance of the MSDSs after their initial production.

As part of the monitoring process, the information product manager must continually measure the product's production and use it to detect when product modification is necessary. Indeed, even "old" physical products require a product manager to keep them "new and improved." The emerging information quality assessment tools can provide the mechanisms to measure and monitor the process. Periodic reassessments can determine whether the quality of information is improving — both objectively and as perceived by information consumers.

Having a set of standards is of critical importance to the monitoring process. Standards that define the goodness of information along all the important quality dimensions of the information consumer must be available. Furthermore, these standards should be continuously reviewed and improved to ensure that the quality of information itself is continuously improved. Analysis of any variances between the quality of the information products and the quality expectations of consumers provides the basis for improvement.

The information product manager uses knowledge obtained by monitoring to initiate changes to the product — the  continuous improvement process. Continuous improvement should start as soon as the information product is developed. As analyses during monitoring reveal gaps, improvement is undertaken. Because the standards are continuously improved, gaps between the standard and the actual will continue to exist. Such differences drive the information quality improvement effort. The information product manager's task is to set new quality goals based on evolving information consumer needs and to translate these goals into improvements in the raw information provided and the information production process that delivers information products to consumers.

The information product manager's duties are, in essence, process management and coordination. Traditionally, information process management was performed by the IT function, if it was performed at all. The IT function, however, has seldom viewed information consumers as part of the process they managed, even in IT organizations with a strong consumer focus. The lack of quality in organizational information is commonly caused by the lack of coordination and shared knowledge among information consumers, producers, and suppliers [30]. Thus, the role and responsibilities of the information product manager are critical for delivering information that is fit for use by information consumers.

The information product manager does not replace the CIO. The leadership of the IT function, and its agenda, rests with the CIO. The information product manager reports to the CIO and is charged with implementing and managing the integrated IP approach — the keystone of providing quality information throughout the organization.

## Establish an Information Quality Program

To establish an information quality program, the information product manager can adapt classical TQM principles. As presented earlier, an analogy exists between product manufacturing and information manufacturing. In the manufacturing world, improvements in productivity and customer service have resulted in significant reductions in the total cost of quality. Since most IT departments have few, if any, formal methods for information quality management, the opportunities to improve information quality management are numerous and the economic gain for so doing will be immense. In many cases, such improvement may not be achievable without significant change. Adapting the TQM literature, five tasks should be undertaken:

>*Articulate an IQ Vision in Business Terms.* In order to improve quality, one must first set standards. At the highest levels, standards are set by users: the external and internal customers for the information produced by information systems. Such standards are expressed in business terms. In this manner, the first step toward implementing an IQ improvement plan is for the information product manager to clearly articulate an information quality vision in business terms. The following example from Financial Company's report illustrates this principle very well: *"Customer service and decision making at Financial Company will be unconstrained by the availability, accessibility, or accuracy of information held in automated form on any strategic platform."* Since leadership is crucial in the early stages of any quality improvement program, the information quality vision must be clearly identified with top-level management. At this stage, top-management's goal is to begin organizational awareness of information quality problems. Toward this end, the CIO must make it clear to the entire organization that information quality has become a top priority.

*Establish Central Responsibility for IQ Within through the IPM.* Once a vision has been articulated, the organization needs to establish central responsibility for information quality. Ultimately, this responsibility rests with the CIO, but the information product manager needs to be given day-to-day responsibility for information quality. Many organizations are tempted to proclaim that information quality is "everybody's responsibility," but in practice this approach leads to confusion and inaction. Implementing an information quality improvement program requires significant organizational change as well as the adoption of new management techniques and technologies. For these reasons, an information product manager must be given explicit responsibility and authority for ensuring information quality. Our case studies illustrate the variety of approaches organizations are taking to assign responsibility for information quality. For example, Data Company has outlined a Customer Information Delivery initiative centered around the creation of an information product management team. This team is responsible for the development and delivery of zero-defect information products to their clients.

*Educate Information Product Suppliers, Manufacturers, and Consumers.* Once central responsibility for an information quality manager has been established, the stage is set to begin educating key people in the organization who will take charge of continuous improvements of information quality. Within IT, these people are the project and systems managers. These managers must learn the relationship between quality and productivity so that they consider investing the time and resources appropriate to improve information quality. Beyond this, they must learn specific methods of information quality improvement that are relevant to their projects or systems. For project development managers, this means learning to view information quality as a fundamental objective. For systems managers, it means learning to apply the quality control principles to monitor systems.

*Teach New IQ Skills.* Responsibility for the successful development and continuous improvement of an information product over its life cycle belongs to all the constituents of an information product, which include information suppliers, information manufacturers, and information consumers. Hence, all the constituents must learn the skills required to put information quality improvement programs into place. The skills required by an individual will vary according to his or her responsibilities. In general, they fall into one or more categories of the TDQM cycle.

*Institutionalize Continuous IQ Improvement.* Once the entire organization has received the necessary training and information product improvement plans have been put into action, it is necessary for top management to ensure that the information product improvement process becomes institutionalized. This requires leadership from the CIO and other top management in the form of visible continuous interest in information quality activities. For example, regular meetings, presentations, and reporting structures should be established to track the organization's progress in meeting information quality goals. Additionally, information product improvement projects need to become a regular part of the budgetary process.

## CONCLUSION

The twenty-first century will witness only two kinds of companies: those that exploit IT and those that are out of business. But exploiting IT for what purpose? *To deliver quality information*. Until firms treat information as a product and manage it accordingly, quality information will not be delivered to consumers consistently and reliably. The results will be lower margins, missed opportunities, and tarnished images.

The path to an information product approach begins with the initiation of a strong customer orientation. Meeting the customer's needs for quality information is foremost. Top management must commit to the IP approach and support the information product manager function. The information product manager is the agent for the transition to an IP approach. With the proper focus and commitment in place, the information product manager can properly frame the information quality problem and develop innovative solutions within the context of the firm.

Much is at stake. In an increasingly networked world, information of different quality levels is being aggregated for business use. In this new world, information quality is a paramount concern. Senior management's course of action is clear: view information as a product, manage information as a product, and deliver information as a product.

## References

[1]   Arnold, S. E., "Information Manufacturing: The Road to Database Quality," *Database,* 15(5), 1992, pp. 32.

[2]   Ballou, D. P., and H. L. Pazer, "Modeling Data and Process Quality in Multi-input, Multi-output Information Systems," *Management Science,* 31(2), 1985, pp. 150–162.

[3]   Ballou, D. P., R. Y. Wang, H. Pazer, and G. K. Tayi, "Modeling Information Manufacturing Systems to Determine Information Product Quality," *Management Science,* 44(4) April, 1998, pp. 462–484.

[4]   Bulkeley, W., "Databases Are Plagued by Reign of Error," *Wall Street Journal,* May 26, 1992, p. B6.

[5]   Courant, H., "Data Quality Problems," *San Jose Mercury News,* December 27, 1992, Section 3.

[6]   Crosby, P. B., *Quality Without Tears.* McGraw-Hill Book Company, New York, 1984.

[7]   Cykana, P., A. Paul, and M. Stern, "DoD Guidelines on Data Quality Management." In *Proceedings of The 1996 Conference on Information Quality.* Cambridge, MA; pp. 154–171, 1996.

[8]   Deming, E. W., *Out of the Crisis.* Center for Advanced Engineering Study, MIT, Cambridge, MA, 1986.

[9]   Feigenbaum, A. V., *Total Quality Control.* 3rd ed. McGraw-Hill, New York, 1991.

[10]  Firth, C. P., and R. Y. Wang, *Data Quality Systems: Evaluation and Implementation.* Cambridge Market Intelligence Ltd., London, 1996.

[11]  Gartner, "Data Pollution Can Choke Business Process Re-engineering," *Insider GartnerGroup,* 1993, p. 1.

[12]  Garvin, D. A., "Competing on the Eight Dimensions of Quality," *Harvard Business Review,* 65(6), 1987, pp. 101–109.

[13]  Garvin, D. A., *Managing Quality-The Strategic and Competitive Edge.* 1st ed. The Free Press, New York, 1988.

[14]  Hardjono, H., "A Case Study of the Business Impact of Data Quality in the Airline Industry." Sloan Fellow Thesis, MIT Sloan School of Management, 1993.

[15]  Ishikawa, K., *What is Total Quality Control?—The Japanese Way.* Prentice Hall, Englewood Cliffs, NJ, 1985.

[16]  Kahn, B. K., D. M. Strong, and R. Y. Wang, "Information Quality Benchmarks:  Product and Service Performance," *Communications of the ACM,* Accepted for publication.

[17] Kinnear, T. C., and K. Bernhardt, *Principles of Marketing*. 3rd ed. Scotts, Foresman/Little Brown, Glenview, IL, 1990.

[18] Kriebel, C. H., "Evaluating the Quality of Information Systems," In *Design and Implementation of Computer Based Information Systems,* N. Szysperski and E. Grochla, eds. 1979, Sijthtoff & Noordhoff, Germantown, PA, 1979.

[19] Lai, S. G., *Data Quality Case Study — "Optiserv Limited"*. Master Thesis, MIT Sloan School of Management, Cambridge, MA, 1993.

[20] Liepins, G. E., "Sound Data Are a Sound Investment," *Quality Progress*, 22(9), 1989, pp. 61–64.

[21] Madnick, S., and R. Y. Wang, *Introduction to Total Data Quality Management (TDQM) Research Program* (No. TDQM-92-01). Total Data Quality Management (TDQM) Research Program, MIT Sloan School of Management, 1992

[22] Madnick, S. E., ed. *The Strategic Use of Information Technology*. 1987, Oxford University Press: New York. 206 pages.

[23] Madnick, S. E., "Integrating Information from Global Systems: Dealing With the "On- and Off-Ramps" of the Information Superhighway," *Journal of Organizational Computing*, 5(2), 1995, pp. 69–82.

[24] Madnick, S. E., "Database in the Internet Age," *Database Programming and Design,* 1997, pp. 28–33.

[25] McGee, A. M., *Total Data Quality Management (TDQM): Zero Defect Data Capture* (No. TDQM-92-07). Total Data Quality Management (TDQM) Research Program, MIT Sloan School of Management, Cambridge, MA, 1992

[26] Percy, T., "Business Re-engineering: Does Data Quality Matter?," *Insider GartnerGroup*, 1993, p. 1.

[27] Redman, T. C., *Data Quality: Management and Technology*. Bantam Books, New York, 1992.

[28] Rockart, J. F., and J. E. Short, "IT in the 1990s: Managing Organizational Interdependence," *Sloan Management Review,* 30(2), 1989, pp. 7–17.

[29] Sandberg, J., "At Thousands of Web Sites, Time Stands Still: Many Web Sites Need Updating," *The Wall Street Journal,* March 11, 1997 p. B1.

[30] Strong, D. M., Y. W. Lee, and R. Y. Wang, "Data Quality in Context," *Communications of the ACM,* 40(5), 1997, pp. 103–110.

[31] Wang, R. Y., "A Product Perspective on Total Data Quality Management," *Communications of the ACM,* 41(2), 1998, pp. 58–65.

[32] Wang, R. Y., and H. B. Kon, Toward Total Data Quality Management (TDQM), In *Information Technology in Action: Trends and Perspectives,* R. Y. Wang, Ed., 1993, Prentice Hall, Englewood Cliffs, NJ, 1993.

[33] Wang, R. Y., Y. L. Lee, L. Pipino, and D. M. Strong, "Manage Your Information as a Product," *Sloan Management Review,* 39(4), 1998, pp. 95–105.

[34] Wang, R. Y., Y. W. Lee, and D. Strong, "Can You Defend Your Information in Court?" In *Proceedings of the 1996 Conference on Information Quality*. Cambridge, MA: 1996, pp. 53–64.

[35] Wang, R. Y., V. C. Storey, and C. P. Firth, "A Framework for Analysis of Data Quality Research," *IEEE Transactions on Knowledge and Data Engineering,* 7(4), 1995, pp. 623–640.

# Define Information Quality

*I*n their commitment to improve Information Quality (IQ), firms have established an evolving management function to oversee the effort. New positions such as vice-president of data quality, value of information quality program manager, supervisor of information quality, and data quality manager at major corporations are examples toward the trend. To manage information as a product effectively, however, the concept of IQ must be well understood.

Conventionally, IQ has been described as how accurate the information is. Our research and practice over the last decade indicate otherwise. Indeed, we have found that both researchers and practitioners define IQ to be beyond accuracy. They identify IQ as encompassing multiple dimensions. Some of the dimensions are objective while others subjective; some are context independent and others context dependent. Furthermore, no standard information quality definition exists today.

In this chapter, we present three approaches that have been used in the literature and in business practice to study IQ:

Intuitive

System

Empirical

An intuitive approach is taken when the selection of IQ attributes in a specific study is based on the individual's experience or intuitive understanding about what attributes are important. Many IQ studies fall into this category. The cumulative effect of these studies is a small set of IQ attributes that are commonly selected. For example, many IQ studies include *accuracy* as either the only one or one of several key dimensions [2, 14, 17].

A system approach to IQ focuses on how information may become deficient during the information manufacturing process. Although system approaches are often recommended, there are few research examples. One such study uses an ontological approach in which attributes of IQ are derived based on data deficiencies, which are defined as the inconsistencies between the view of a real-world system that can be inferred from a representing information system and the view that can be obtained by directly observing the real-world system [19].

The advantage of using an intuitive approach is that each study can select the attributes most relevant to the particular goals of that study. The advantage of a system approach is the potential to provide a comprehensive set of IQ attributes that are intrinsic to an information product. The problem with both of these approaches is that they focus on the information product in terms of development characteristics instead of use characteristics. They are not directed to capturing the voice of the consumer.

An empirical approach analyzes information collected from information consumers to determine the characteristics they use to assess whether information is fit for use in their tasks. The advantage of the empirical approach is that it captures the voice of customers. Furthermore, it may reveal characteristics that researchers and practitioners have not considered as part of IQ. The disadvantage is that the correctness or completeness of the results cannot be proven based on fundamental principles.

The intuitive approach to defining IQ is conceptual and dependent on the specific domain applications. While this approach has its merits, it is difficult to be rigorous. In the remainder of this chapter, we present a system definition that is anchored in an ontological logical foundation and an empirical approach that defines IQ from the information consumer's perspective. As noted in Chapter 2, unless specified otherwise, we will use "information" interchangeably with "data."

## THE INFORMATION SYSTEM PERSPECTIVE

We begin by making a distinction between the external and internal views of an information system [19].The external view is concerned with the use and effect of an information system. It addresses the purpose and justification of the system and its deployment in the organization. In the external view, an information system is considered a given, that is, a "black box" with the functionality necessary to represent the real-world system. Indeed, the empirical approach is based on this assumption.

In contrast, the internal view addresses the construction and operation necessary to attain the required functionality, given a set of requirements which reflect the external view. System construction includes design and implementation. System operation includes activities involved in producing the information such as data capture, data entry, data maintenance, and data delivery. For simplicity, we assume perfect implementation since a faulty implementation is equivalent to a faulty design with a perfect implementation.

The system approach concentrates on the internal view and is oriented toward system design and data production. This has two important implications. First, since the internal view is use independent, it supports a set of definitions of dimensions of IQ that are comparable across applications. Hence, these dimensions can be viewed as being intrinsic to the data. Second, this view can, in principle, be used to guide the design of an information system with certain IQ objectives.

The distinction between the external and internal views should not be interpreted as a sequential systems development process. Rather, the distinction is intended to establish that the designer, having no control of user requirements, should take the requirements as given at any time during development. It is possible that system designers and users will cooperate in an iterative design process as needed.

In the system approach, IQ is based on the fundamental notion that the role of an information system is to provide a representation of an application domain (also termed the real-world system) as perceived by the user. Representation deficiencies are defined in terms of the difference between the view of the real-world system as inferred from the information system and the view that is obtained by directly observing the real-world system. From various types of representation deficiencies, a set of IQ dimensions is derived.

To base IQ concepts on the role of an information system as a representation, it is necessary to define

What is directly observed in the real-world system.

How an information system acts as a representation of the real-world system.

"What is in the world" is the subject of ontology. In the *Dictionary of Philosophy*, Angeles defines ontology as "that branch of philosophy which deals with the order and structure of reality in the broadest sense possible" [1, p. 198]. Hence, the formalization is based on ontological concepts.

## Data Deficiency

Ontologically, a data deficiency is defined as an inconformity between the view of the real-world system that can be inferred from a representing information system and the view that can be obtained by directly observing the real-world system (Figure 3.1).

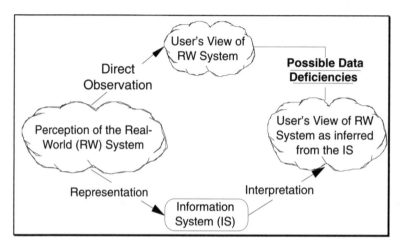

Figure 3.1:  Possible Data Deficiencies

(Source: *Communications of the ACM* [19])

We identify the criteria for a real-world system to be properly represented by an information system. Based on this, we identify possible representation deficiencies that can occur during system design and data production. These deficiencies are used to define intrinsic IQ dimensions.

Let $RW_L$ denote the lawful state space of a real-world system, and $IS_L$ that of an information system representing this real-world system. For a real-world system to be properly represented, two conditions must hold (Figure 3.2). First, every lawful state of the real-world system should be mapped to at least one lawful state of the information system (a real-world state can be mapped into multiple information system states). Second, it should be possible, in principle, to map an information system state back to the "correct" real-world state.

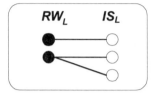

Figure 3.2: Proper Representation

(Source: *Communications of the ACM* [19])

We formalize this in the following definition for proper representation.

Definition 3.1 A real-world system is said to be properly represented if (1) there exists an exhaustive mapping, Rep: $RW_L \rightarrow IS_L$, and (2) no two states in $RW_L$ are mapped into the same state in $IS_L$ (i.e., the inverse mapping is a function).

Our analysis of data deficiencies is based on deviations from the conditions of Definition 3.1. We distinguish deviations due to system design flaws from those due to data production (system operation) flaws.

## Design Deficiencies

Based on Definition 3.1, we identify three generic categories of design deficiencies: incomplete representation, ambiguous representation, and meaningless states. For an information system to properly represent a real-world system, the mapping from $RW_L$ to $IS_L$ must be exhaustive (i.e., each of the states in $RW_L$ is mapped to $IS_L$). If the mapping is not exhaustive, there will be lawful states of the real-world system that cannot be represented by the information system (Figure 3.3). We term this incompleteness. An example is a customer information system design which does not allow a non-U.S. address (a lawful state of the real-world system) to be recorded.

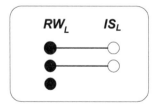

Figure 3.3: Incomplete Representation

(Source: *Communications of the ACM* [19])

For a proper representation no two states of the real-world should be mapped into the same state of the information system. If several states in $RW_L$ are mapped into the same state in $IS_L$, there is insufficient information to infer which state in $RW_L$ is represented. We term this situation ambiguity (Figure 3.4). A typical case of ambiguity is when there is an insufficient number of digits to represent some states of the real-world system. This is usually viewed as a precision problem. However, we consider it a special case of ambiguity which is more general as it relates to any type of data, not just to numeric values. For example, a system design may allow for only one telephone number, without indicating whether it is the office or home telephone.

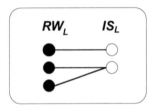

Figure 3.4: Ambiguous Representation

(Source: *Communications of the ACM* [19])

It is not required that the mapping from $RW_L$ to $IS_L$ be exhaustive with respect to $IS_L$. However, when this situation exists, there are lawful states in $IS_L$ that cannot be mapped back to a state in $RW_L$ (Figure 3.5). Such states are termed meaningless states. An information system design with meaningless states can still represent a real-world system properly. However, it is not a good design as it allows, in principle, meaningless data. For such meaningless data to materialize, some operational failure will have to occur.

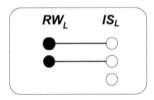

Figure 3.5: Meaningless State

(Source: *Communications of the ACM* [19])

We have identified two main design deficiencies, corresponding to the two conditions of proper representation in Definition 3.1:

The representation mapping (from $RW_L$ to $IS_L$) is not exhaustive.

The representation mapping is many to one.

We also identified a potential deficiency when the mapping does not exhaust $IS_L$. Consider the fourth case: the representation mapping is one to many. Having multiple representations of a real-world situation may or may not be detrimental, depending on the user's cognitive style, and on the purpose of the system. These issues are not subject to a designer's decisions and therefore we do not consider this a design deficiency.

## Operation Deficiencies

At operation time, a state in $RW_L$ might be mapped to a wrong state in $IS_L$. We refer to this as garbling, and distinguish between two cases.

If there exist meaningless states of the information system, the mapping might be to a meaningless state.

The mapping might be to a meaningful, but incorrect, information system state.

In the first case the user will not be able to map back to a real-world state (Figure 3.6). In the second case the user will be able to infer back, but to an incorrect state of the real world (Figure 3.7). Typically, garbling occurs due to incorrect human actions during system operation (e.g., erroneous data entry, or failure to record changes in the real world).

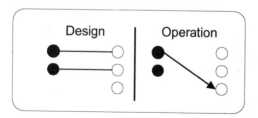

Figure 3.6:  Garbling (Mapping to a Meaningless State)

(Source: *Communications of the ACM* [19])

Our analysis of design and operational flaws does not encompass the case where the user perceives a "wrong" state of the real world (either by error or due to malicious intent).

This is because the information system is only required to enable mapping into perceived states, not "real" states.

Based on the analysis of the representation mapping from states of the real-world system to states of the information system, we identified four potential representation deficiencies. As a consequence of these deficiencies, information system states can be incomplete, ambiguous, meaningless, or incorrect. In this view, inconsistency is not treated as a separate dimension, as it is manifested as ambiguity, lack of meaning, or incorrectness resulting from decomposition. Accordingly, we propose a set of four intrinsic IQ dimensions as shown in Table 3.1.

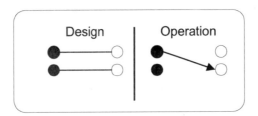

Figure 3.7:  Garbling  (Mapping to a Wrong State)

(Source: *Communications of the ACM* [19])

Table 3.1: Intrinsic IQ Dimensions

| Dimension | Nature of Associated Deficiency | Source of Deficiency |
|-----------|--------------------------------|----------------------|
| complete | Improper representation: missing *IS* states | Design failure (Figure 3.3) |
| unambiguous | Improper representation: multiple *RW* states mapped to the same IS state | Design failure  (Figure 3.4) |
| meaningful | Meaningless *IS* state and garbling (mapping to a meaningless state) | Design failure  (Figure 3.5) and Operation failure (Figure 3.6) |
| correct | Garbling (mapping to a wrong state) | Operation failure (Figure 3.7) |

(Source: *Communications of the ACM* [19])

## Some Implications of Information Systems Design

We identified four intrinsic dimensions of IQ. Accordingly, we identify four generic types of data problems that can be observed in using an information system as shown in Table 3.2. The generic IQ dimensions were derived by analyzing possible failures of the representation transformation. Based on this analysis, we can identify the types of design actions that can be used to avoid or correct these problems (Table 3.3). The first two deficiencies—loss of information and insufficient information (ambiguous data)—require modifications to the lawful state space of the information system or to the mapping into this space. Such decisions are, in principle, under a designer's control. In contrast, meaningless and incorrect data result from operational failures (usually due to human actions). However, meaningless data can only occur when there exist meaningless states of the information system. The designer can reduce such states through the application of information system controls such as integrity constraints [4, 5, 7, 15].

**Table 3.2: Generic IQ Problems**

| Dimension | Mapping Problem | Observed Information Problem |
|---|---|---|
| Complete | Certain $RW$ states cannot be represented. | Loss of information about the application domain. |
| Unambiguous | A certain $IS$ state can be mapped back into several $RW$ states. | Insufficient information: the data can be interpreted in more than one way. |
| Meaningful | It is not possible to map the $IS$ state back to a meaningful $RW$ state. | It is not possible to interpret the data in a meaningful way. |
| Correct | The $IS$ state may be mapped back into a meaningful state, but the wrong one. | The data derived from the $IS$ do not conform to those used to create these data. |

(Source: *Communications of the ACM* [19])

**Table 3.3: Data Deficiency "Repairs"**

| Observed Problem | Reasons for Deficiency | Repair |
|---|---|---|
| Loss of information | Missing lawful states of the information system. | Modify $IS_L$ to allow for missing cases. |
| Insufficient information (ambiguous data) | Several states of the real world mapped into same state of information system. | Change the mapping from $RW_L$ to $IS_L$. This may require adding states to $IS_L$. |
| Meaningless data | There are information system states that do not match the realworld, and garbling. | Reduce $IS_L$ to include only meaningful states. This can be done by adding integrity constraints. |
| Incorrect data | Garbling. | Design to reduce garbling. This might be done by adding some controls. |

(Source: *Communications of the ACM* [19])

The situation is more complicated for incorrect data, as they result from incorrect mapping into meaningless information system states. However, automated mechanisms may still be used to reduce this problem. Assume the state space of the information system was increased by adding a large number of meaningless states. Then the probability that incorrect operation will result in a meaningless state rather than a meaningful state would increase. Meaningless states can be controlled by integrity constraints. Thus, some garbling might be prevented by artificially increasing the possible state space of the information system and adding controls. This approach is usually implemented by increasing the possible state space of the information system without increasing the lawful state space. Specific examples are the addition of a check digit to identification codes, and the use of control totals for transaction batches.

We have analyzed IQ based on inconformities between two views of the real-world system: the view obtained by direct observation and the view inferred from the information system. The analysis generated four intrinsic (i.e., system-oriented) IQ dimensions. These dimensions specify whether data are complete, unambiguous, meaningful, and correct. Each of these dimensions is well defined in terms of a specific deficiency in the mapping from real-world system states to information system states. Therefore, they can be used to reason about IQ. Such reasoning can be done for the purpose of improving IQ. Conversely, there are cases when low-quality data can be advantageous. An example would be preventing an adversary from knowing true real-world states in national defense or commercial competition situations. Knowing the sources of the generic deficiencies can help plan for intentionally low-quality data.

## THE INFORMATION CONSUMER PERSPECTIVE

The concept of fitness for use is widely adopted in the TQM literature. It emphasizes the importance of taking a consumer viewpoint of quality because ultimately it is the consumer who will judge whether a product is fit for use or not [8, 9, 12, 13]. Garvin, for example, has stressed the importance of looking at quality from the consumer's viewpoint: "To achieve quality gains, I believe, managers need a new way of thinking, a conceptual bridge to the consumer's vantage point. Obviously, market studies acquire a new importance in this context. . . . One thing is certain: high quality means pleasing the consumer, not just protecting them from annoyances" [11, p. 104].

In this view, *IQ* should not be defined by providers or custodians of information, such as IT departments, but instead, by information consumers. Information quality, defined from this perspective, can be used by researchers and practitioners to direct their efforts for information consumers instead of the IS professionals.

## Fitness for Use

In the empirical approach, the consumer viewpoint of "fitness for use" is taken to conceptualize the underlying aspects of IQ. Following the general quality literature, *IQ* is defined as *information that is fit for use by information consumers*. In addition, an *IQ dimension* is defined as a set of IQ attributes that represent a single aspect or construct of IQ.

This approach implicitly assumes that information is treated as a product. It is an appropriate approach because an information system can be viewed as an information manufacturing system acting on raw information input to produce output information or information products. While most information consumers are not purchasing information, they are choosing to use or not use information in a variety of tasks.

## Dimensions of IQ

We have conducted a series of comprehensive empirical studies [6, 18, 20] and developed a framework with four IQ categories (Table 3.4). Intrinsic IQ denotes that information has quality in its own right. *Accuracy* is merely one of the four dimensions underlying this category. Contextual IQ highlights the requirement that IQ must be considered within the context of the task at hand; that is, information must be relevant, timely, complete, and appropriate in terms of amount so as to add value. Representational IQ and accessibility IQ emphasize the importance of the role of systems. The system must be accessible but secure. It must present information in a way that is interpretable, easy to understand, and concisely and consistently represented.

**Table 3.4: IQ Categories and Dimensions**

| IQ Category | IQ Dimensions |
|---|---|
| Intrinsic IQ | Accuracy, objectivity, believability, reputation |
| Contextual IQ | Relevancy, value-added, timeliness, completeness, amount of information |
| Representational IQ | Interpretability, ease of understanding, concise representation, consistent representation |
| Accessibility IQ | Access, security |

(Source: *Journal of Management Information Systems* [20])

As mentioned earlier, the disadvantage of the empirical approach is that the correctness or completeness of the results cannot be proved based on fundamental principles. However, the underlying information systems must be sound in order to produce quality information, much as a car assembly line must be correctly built in order to produce zero-defect cars. Thus, it is also important to understand the information manufacturer's perspective, or the information system's perspective.

## Define IQ in Organizational Context

Organizational databases reside in the larger context of information systems. The term "information system" is often referred to as a database or a computer system, including hardware and software. We use the phrase "larger information system's context" to cover the organizational processes, procedures, and roles employed in collecting, processing, distributing, and using data. Within this larger context, data are collected from multiple data sources and stored in databases. From these stored data, useful information is generated for organizational decision making. IQ problems may arise anywhere in this larger IS context.

Using qualitative analysis, we examined 42 IQ projects from three leading-edge organizations and identified common patterns of IQ problems. These patterns emerged because we used a broader conceptualization of IQ as shown in Table 3.4. Based on these patterns, we developed recommendations to improve IQ from the perspective of data consumers.

We define an IQ problem as any difficulty encountered along one or more IQ dimensions that renders data completely or largely unfit for use. We define an IQ project as organizational actions taken to address an IQ problem given some recognition of poor IQ by the organization. We intentionally include projects initiated for purposes other than improving IQ. For example, during conversion of data to a client/server system, poor IQ may be recognized and a project for IQ improvement initiated.

### Method

To examine IQ problems in practice, we studied 42 IQ projects from three data-rich organizations: GoldenAir, an international airline; BetterCare, a hospital; and HyCare, a Health Maintenance Organization (HMO). In terms of industry position, attention to IQ, and information systems, these three firms are leaders, yet they exhibit sufficient variation for investigating IQ projects (Table 3.5). All have identified significant IQ problems and are actively attending to them. This contrasts with many organizations that fail to address their IQ problems.

We applied qualitative data collection and analysis techniques [3, 16, 21, 22]. The IQ projects at each organization form an embedded case design with each IQ project serving as a minicase [22]. Here we refer to a case study as an empirical inquiry that investigates a contemporary phenomenon within its real-life context. It has been argued that case studies are the preferred strategy when "how" or "why" questions are being posed and when "the investigator has little control over events" [22, pp. 1–13]. In embedded case study designs, attention is given to subunits within each case, allowing examination of specific phenomena in operational detail within the context of each case [22, pp. 41–44].

**Table 3.5: Organization Characteristics**

| Organization Name & Industry | Attention to IQ | IS Organization | Hardware and Software Environment |
|---|---|---|---|
| GoldenAir Airline | IS Development | IS is essentially a service bureau. | IBM-compatible mainframe with IMS databases and Material Management System. |
| BetterCare Hospital | IQ Administrator | Centralized IS organization reporting to finance VP in a centralized, functional firm. | PC-based client server environment with TRACE, a MUMPS-based database system. |
| HyCare HMO | Total Quality Management Initiatives | Powerful, centralized IS organization in a decentralized, divisional firm. | Heterogeneous hardware and software across divisions. |

(Source: *Communications of the ACM* [18])

We collected data about these projects via interviews of data producers, custodians, consumers, and managers. We organized each IQ project in terms of three problem-solving steps: (1) problem finding (how the organization identified an IQ problem); (2) problem analysis (what the organization determined the cause to be); and (3) problem resolution which includes changing processes (changing the procedures for producing, storing, or using data) and changing data (updating the data value). Four example projects (Table 3.6) represent the richness and variety of our 42 IQ projects.

**Table 3.6: Synopsis of Four Example IQ Projects**

| GoldenAir Data for a New Info. System | BetterCare Recording of Disease Types | BetterCare Recording of Medical Procedures | HyCare Recording of Medical Procedures |
|---|---|---|---|
| (1) Problem Finding | (1) Problem Finding | (1) Problem Finding | (2) Problem Analysis |
| Materials Management at GoldenAir realized the need to physically count inventory so that the new computerized inventory system would have accurate data.<br><br>What should be done about the expected significant discrepancies between the manual | While running routine mid-month reports, BetterCare's TRACE IQ administrator (IQA) noticed a large increase in infectious disease patients. Such an increase was not likely.<br><br>What caused this problem?<br><br>(2) Problem Analysis<br><br>The IQA, who knew that diseases were assigned based on the specialty of | A BetterCare TRACE analyst producing an ad hoc requested report noticed that some female babies had procedure codes indicating male circumcision.<br><br>Were these babies actually male or was this procedure not performed?<br><br>(2) Problem Analysis<br><br>If TRACE received the | A study of the data production process internal to HyCare found that during data entry of the claims data, the system rejected the submitted codes.<br><br>The system was set up to accept CPT4 procedure codes, the codes used by physicians, but most of the input data had ICD9 codes, the |

| | | | |
|---|---|---|---|
| records and the warehouse count?<br><br>(2) Problem Analysis<br><br>Materials and IS managers decided that the negative discrepancies (lower warehouse counts) represented misplaced parts, not missing parts, while positive discrepancies were the result of miscounts in the manual records.<br><br>(3) Problem Resolution<br><br>Process Changes<br><br>None.<br><br>Data Changes<br><br>In the computer system, created two warehouses: the first, representing the physical warehouse, contained the actual physical count of parts.<br><br>The second, labeled "Warehouse 99," was a fictitious warehouse existing only in the computer system. It recorded all the misplaced parts. | the admitting doctor, guessed that an infectious disease doctor was assigned to the emergency room that month and the emergency room personnel failed to override this default. The IQA called the director of admissions to confirm this cause and it was confirmed.<br><br>(3) Problem Resolution<br><br>Process Changes<br><br>Emergency room personnel were further trained in the appropriate procedures. In addition, admissions quality control procedures were reassessed, and QC personnel were made aware of this type of problem.<br><br>Data Changes<br><br>Admissions and IS worked together to change the incorrect data because these data were reported externally. | billing record before it received the patient record, it assigned its default sex of female. Receiving the billing record first could only occur when the elapsed time between admitting a patient and billing after patient release was less than one week. This was rare (much less than 1 percent of the cases), but the hospital improved its billing efficiency. Also, since TRACE's sex field could not be changed, use of the default was permanent.<br><br>(3) Problem Resolution<br><br>Process Changes<br><br>The TRACE system was fixed so this problem would not re-occur. In addition, the sex field was made updatable.<br><br>Data Changes<br><br>A search was made for all such records in TRACE, and their sex field was changed. | procedure codes used by hospitals.<br><br>(3) Problem Resolution<br><br>Process Changes<br><br>In the short term, the codes were input into a free-form field, and IS changed processing to use data from this field.<br><br>In the longer term, the vendor will fix this problem in the next software release.<br><br>Data Changes<br><br>The process change fixed new data; the missing data remained missing. |

(Source: *Communications of the ACM* [18])

Each project was analyzed using the dimensions of IQ (Table 3.4) as content analysis codes [16, 21]. We then examined relationships among these IQ dimensions within and across projects. First, the overriding IQ issue of each IQ project was assessed as one of the four IQ categories (Table 3.4). Interestingly, representational IQ did not appear as a primary issue; instead representational dimensions were the underlying causes of accessibility issues articulated by data consumers. Second, we identified common patterns and sequences of dimensions attended to during IQ projects (Table 3.7). The resulting patterns of dimensions are discussed below.

Table 3.7: IQ Patterns in IQ Projects

| IQ issue | Pattern 1: Intrinsic IQ | Pattern 2: Accessibility IQ | Pattern 3: Contextual IQ |
|---|---|---|---|
| If problem not resolved | Data not used | Barriers to accessibility | Data utilization difficulties |
| Subpatterns: underlying causes of IQ problems | (1) Multiple, inconsistent data sources (2) Data production requires judgment (e.g., coding) | (1) Computing resources lacking (2) Data are confidential (3) Uninterpretable representation, (4) Unanalyzable form of representation, (5) Too much data, timeliness | (1) Operational data production problems: incomplete data (2) Changing needs, especially changing needs for aggregation (3) Distributed system incompatibilities |
| Problem and Solution Focus | Data producers, data production processes | Technical issues, computer systems, data storage | Data consumers, data utilization processes |
| Context of Needed Changes | Data production processes are generating inaccurate, incomplete, or inconsistent data. | IS provides accessibility; however, data consumers view other problems (e.g., timeliness, interpretability) as accessibility problems. | The basic data units, as perceived by data consumers, change over time. Databases must support this changing view of data. |
| Lessons and Solution | Change both the process and supporting computer systems. Either by itself is not sufficient for long-term IQ improvements. | Understand and remedy the underlying causes of perceived poor accessibility. | Structure data around fundamental business entities so that changes in basic data units can be accommodated by actual/stored data units. |

(Source: *Communications of the ACM* [18])

## Intrinsic IQ Pattern

Problem Pattern

Mismatches among sources of the "same" data are a common cause of intrinsic IQ concerns. Initially, data consumers do not know the source to which quality problems should be attributed; they know only that data are conflicting. Thus, these concerns initially appear as *believability* problems. The italics signifies that *believability* is an IQ dimension. This convention will be used in the remainder of this chapter to highlight the interaction of IQ dimensions in an IQ project.

Over time, information about the causes of mismatches accumulates from evaluations of the *accuracy* of different sources, which leads to a poor *reputation* for less *accurate* sources. (A *reputation* for poor quality can also develop with little factual basis.) As a *reputation* for poor-quality data becomes common knowledge, these data sources are viewed as having little *added value* for the organization, resulting in reduced use (subpattern 1, Figure 3.8).

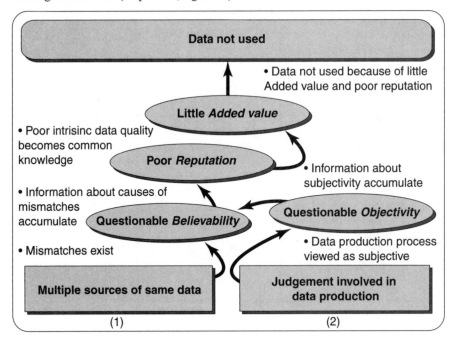

Figure 3.8: Intrinsic IQ Problem Pattern

(Source: *Communications of the ACM* [18])

Judgment or subjectivity in the data production process is another common cause (subpattern 2). For example, coded or interpreted data are considered to be of lower quality than raw, uninterpreted data. Initially, only those with knowledge of data production processes are aware of these potential problems, which appear as concerns about data *objectivity*. Over time, information about the subjective nature of data production accumulates, resulting in data of questionable *believability* and *reputation* and thus of little *added value* to data consumers. The overall result is reduced use of these suspect data.

Intrinsic IQ subpattern 1 was exhibited at all three research sites. GoldenAir has a history of mismatches between their inventory system data and physical warehouse counts. Warehouse counts serve as a standard against which to measure the *accuracy* of system data, that is, the system data source is *inaccurate* and not *believable* and is adjusted periodically to match actual warehouse counts. The system data gradually develop mismatches, however, and their *reputation* gradually worsens until the data are not used for decision making.

At BetterCare, this subpattern occurred between TRACE and STATUS. TRACE is a database containing historical data extracted from the hospital's information and control system for use by managers making longer-term decisions and by medical researchers. STATUS is an operational system that records a snapshot of daily hospital resources. Some data, for example, daily hospital bed utilization, are available from both systems. Nevertheless, they frequently have different values. Over time, TRACE has developed a *reputation* as an *accurate* source, and the use of STATUS has declined.

At HyCare, inconsistent data values occur between internal HMO patient records and bills submitted by hospitals for reimbursement. For example, when the HMO is billed for coronary bypass surgery, the HMO patient record should indicate active, serious heart problems. Mismatches occur in both directions: hospital claims without HMO records of problems, and HMO records of problems without corresponding hospital claims. Initially, HyCare assumed the external (hospital) data were wrong; HMO staff perceived their data to be more *believable* and have a better *reputation* than those of hospitals. This general sense of the quality of sources, however, was not based on factual analysis.

Subpattern 2 occurred at both BetterCare and HyCare. Using doctors' and nurses' notes about patients, BetterCare's medical record coders designate ICD9 (diagnosis and procedure) codes and corresponding DRG (Diagnosis Related Groups [10]) codes for billing. Although coders are highly trained, some subjectivity remains. Thus, these data are considered to be less *objective* than raw data.

Data-production forms also contribute to reduced *objectivity* of data. At HyCare, doctors using preprinted forms with checkboxes for specifying procedure codes generated a reduced range of procedures performed, as compared to doctors using free-form input. This variance affects the *believability* of these data.

## Problem Analysis and Solutions

The three organizations developed the following solutions for handling subpattern 1:

> GoldenAir continues their cycle of physically counting inventory and adjusting system values whenever the mismatch becomes unacceptably large.

BetterCare is rewriting STATUS. They are also designating single data production points for data items and improving computerized support for data production.

HyCare's analysis of the causes of mismatches between hospital and internal data found problems with both sources. They fixed an edit check problem with their internal computer systems, fixed a data production problem in doctors' designation of active, serious problems for internal HMO records, and initiated joint IQ projects with associated hospitals.

These solutions manifest two different approaches to problem resolution: changing the systems or changing the production processes. GoldenAir focused on computer systems as the solution and ignored their data production processes. As a result, their processes continue to produce poor quality data that increase data *inaccuracies*. In contrast, BetterCare's and HyCare's solutions involve both data production processes and computer systems, resulting in long-term IQ improvements.

BetterCare's efforts to designate single data production points deserve further discussion. Systems developed for different purposes sometimes require the "same" data, for example, an indicator of patient severity in intensive care units in both STATUS and TRACE database systems. For TRACE system, a specialist examines the patient immediately before intensive care. For STATUS systems, an intensive-care nurse observes the patient during intensive care. These two observations can be different. To designate a single source, definitions and indicators of severity were agreed upon and both systems were changed to support this single data production source.

BetterCare's decision to rewrite STATUS illustrates *reputation* development. Like accounting systems that prohibit changes once the accounting period is closed, STATUS prohibits changes to the "official" daily record. STATUS's data are *consistent* across time, whereas TRACE's data are *accurate* because they are updated as needed. Although both systems are viewed as containing the "correct" data, TRACE developed a *reputation* as the system with high-quality data, whereas STATUS's data were considered to be suspect. As a result, STATUS is being rewritten with update routines.

## Accessibility IQ Pattern

Problem Pattern
Accessibility IQ problems were characterized by underlying concerns about (1) technical accessibility (subpatterns 1-2, Figure 3.9), (2) data representation issues interpreted by data consumers as accessibility problems (subpatterns 3-4), and (3) data volume issues interpreted as accessibility problems (subpattern 5).

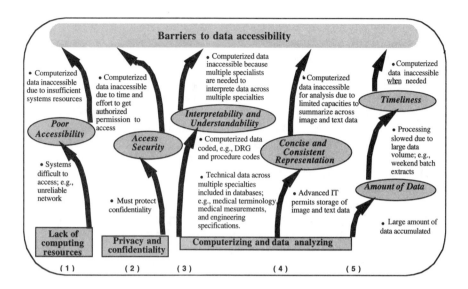

Figure 3.9: Accessibility IQ Problem Patterns

(Source: *Communications of the ACM* [18])

GoldenAir provides a simple example of subpattern 1. When GoldenAir moved to its new airport, its computing operations remained at the old airport with *access* to data via unreliable data communications lines. Since reservations had priority, the unreliable lines resulted in inventory data *accessibility* problems. This in turn contributed to GoldenAir's inventory *accuracy* problems because updating took lower priority than other data-related tasks.

BetterCare had an accessibility IQ concern related to the confidential nature of patient records (subpattern 2). Data consumers realized the importance of *access security* for patient records, but they also perceived the permissions as barriers to *accessibility*. This in turn affected the overall *reputation* and *value* of these data. In addition, data custodians became barriers to *accessibility* because they could not provide data *access* without approval.

Subpattern 3 addresses concerns about *interpretability* and *understandability* of data. Coding systems for physician and hospital activities at BetterCare and HyCare are necessary for summarizing and grouping common diagnoses and procedures. The expertise required to interpret codes, however, becomes a barrier to *accessibility*; these codes are not *understandable* to most doctors and analysts. At HyCare, analyzing and interpreting across physician groups are problems because they use different coding systems.

Medical data in text or image form also present an *interpretability* problem (subpattern 4). Medical records include text written by doctors and nurses and images produced by medical equipment, for example, X-rays, EKGs. These data are difficult to analyze across time for individual patients. Furthermore, analyzing trends across patients is difficult. Thus, data *representation* becomes a barrier to data *accessibility*. These data are *inaccessible* to data consumers because they are not in a *representation* that permits analysis.

Subpattern 5 addresses providing *relevant* data that *add value* to tasks in a *timely* manner. For example, HyCare serves hundreds of thousands of patients resulting in several million patient records tracking medical history. Analyses of patient records usually require weekend data extraction. In addition, companies purchasing HMO options are increasingly demanding evaluations of medical practices, resulting in an increased need for these analyses at HyCare. This pattern of a large *amount of data* leading to *timeliness* problems are interpreted as *accessibility* problems.

Problem Analysis and Solutions
Subpattern 1 has straightforward, though possibly costly, solutions. For example, Golden Air is moving its computing facility to the new airport to avoid unreliable data communication lines. Subpattern 5 is also relatively easy to solve. For example, BetterCare's HICS generates 40 gigabytes of data per year. From this, TRACE extracts the most relevant data (totaling 5 gigabytes over 12 years) for historical and cross-patient analyses.

Subpatterns 3 and 4 are more difficult to solve. Although HyCare completely automated its medical records, including text and image data, to solve *accessibility* problems for individual patients, problems with analyzing data across patients persist. At BetterCare, data consumers and custodians believe that an automated *representation* of text and image data would not solve their analyzability problems; thus, they have partially automated their patient records.

## Contextual IQ Pattern

Problem Pattern
We observed three underlying causes for data consumers' complaints that available data do not support their tasks:

missing (*incomplete*) data

inadequately defined or measured data

data that could not be appropriately aggregated

To solve these contextual IQ problems, IQ projects were initiated to provide *relevant* data that *add value* to the tasks of data consumers.

Subpattern 1 in Figure 3.10 addresses *incomplete* data due to operational problems. At GoldenAir, *incomplete* data in inventory transactions contributed to inventory data *accuracy* problems. For example, mechanics sometimes failed to record part numbers on their work activity forms. Because transaction data were *incomplete*, the inventory database could not be updated, which in turn produced *inaccurate* records. According to one supervisor, this was tolerated because "the primary job of mechanics is to service aircraft in a timely manner, not to fill out forms."

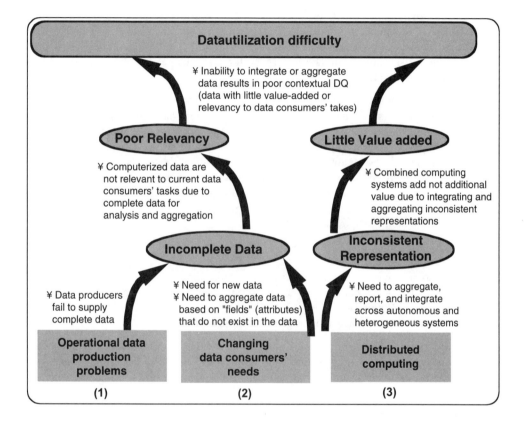

Figure 3.10: Contextual IQ Problem Pattern

(Source: *Communications of the ACM* [18])

BetterCare's data were *incomplete* by design (subpattern 2), whereas GoldenAir's data were *incomplete* due to operational problems. By design, the *amount* of data in BetterCare's TRACE database is small enough to be *accessible* but *complete* enough to be *relevant* and *add value* to data consumers' tasks. As a result, data consumers occasionally complained about *incomplete* data.

Subpattern 3 addresses problems caused by integrating data across distributed systems. At HyCare, data consumers complained about inconsistent definitions and data representations across divisions, for example, Diagnosis Related Group (DRG) codes stored with decimal points in one division and without in another. Furthermore, basic utilization measures, for example, hospital days per thousand patients, were defined differently across divisions. These problems were caused by autonomous design decisions in each division.

Problem Analysis and Solutions
GoldenAir is considering bar code readers as data input mechanisms (subpattern 1). BetterCare's decision about the data to include in TRACE is being reassessed as data consumers request additional data (subpattern 2), for example, health care proxy and living will information were added.

This reassessment of TRACE data in the context of their *relevance* and *value* to data consumers goes beyond missing data. As health care reimbursement systems move from payments for procedures performed (fee for service) to payments for diagnosed diseases (prospective payment) to possibly payments for yearly care of patients (capitated payment), the basic unit of analysis for managerial decision making in hospitals has changed from procedures, to hospital visits, to patients. When BetterCare tracked data by procedures, for example, they could answer questions about costs of blood tests, but not costs of treating heart attacks. Such analyses became necessary when hospital reimbursement changed to a fixed amount for treating each disease.

TRACE was developed in response to this anticipated change to prospective payments. Such a reimbursement system began in 1983 for Medicare. By 1983, TRACE had the capability to aggregate across patient visits for similar diagnoses. Currently, the ability to aggregate across all in- and out-patient medical services delivered to each patient per year is being anticipated by BetterCare. Thus, TRACE is being extended with out-patient data and quality indicators because management anticipates these changes.

HyCare initiated IQ projects to develop common data definitions and representations for cross-divisional data (subpattern 3). The comprehensive data dictionary and corresponding data warehouse are their next steps.

## Implications for IS Professionals

Our findings provide generalizable implications for IS professionals about solving intrinsic, accessibility, and contextual IQ problems.

Intrinsic IQ
Conventional IQ approaches employ control techniques (e.g., edit checks, database integrity constraints, and program control of database updates) to ensure IQ. These approaches have improved intrinsic IQ substantially, especially the accuracy dimension. Attention to accuracy alone, however, does not correspond to data consumers' broader IQ concerns. Furthermore, controls on data storage are necessary but not sufficient. IS professionals also need to apply process-oriented techniques such as IS auditing to the processes that produce these data.

Accessibility IQ

Data consumers perceive any barriers to their access of data to be accessibility problems. Conventional approaches treat accessibility as a technical computer systems issue, not as an IQ concern. That is, data custodians have provided access if data are technically accessible (e.g., terminals and lines are connected and available, access permission is granted, and access methods are installed). To data consumers, however, accessibility goes beyond technical accessibility; it includes the ease with which they can manipulate these data to suit their needs.

These contrasting views of accessibility are evident in our study. For example, advanced forms of data (e.g., medical image data) can now be stored as binary large objects (blobs). Although data custodians provide technical methods for accessing this new form of data, data consumers continued to experience these data as inaccessible. They need to analyze these data the way they analyze traditional record-oriented data. Other examples of differing views of accessibility include (1) data combined across autonomous systems are technically accessible, but data consumers view them as inaccessible because similar data items are defined, measured, or represented differently; (2) coded medical data are technically accessible as text, but data consumers view them as inaccessible because they cannot interpret the codes; and (3) large volumes of data are technically accessible, but data consumers view them as inaccessible because of excessive accessing time.

IS professionals must understand the difference between the technical accessibility they supply and the broad accessibility concerns of data consumers. Once this difference is clarified, technologies such as data warehouses can provide a smaller amount of more relevant data, and graphical interfaces can improve ease of access.

Contextual IQ

Data consumers evaluate IQ relative to their tasks. At any time, the same data may be needed for multiple tasks that require different quality characteristics. Furthermore, these quality characteristics will change over time as work requirements change. Therefore, providing high-quality data implies tracking an ever-moving target. Conventional approaches handle contextual IQ through techniques such as user requirements analysis and relational database query capabilities. They do not explicitly incorporate the changing nature of data consumers' task context.

Because data consumers perform many different tasks and the data requirements for these tasks change, contextual IQ means much more than good data requirements specification. Providing high-quality data along the dimensions of value and usefulness relative to data consumers' task contexts places a premium on designing flexible systems with data that can be easily aggregated and manipulated. The alternative is constant maintenance of data and systems to meet changing data requirements.

In addition to theory building, studies of IQ solutions could use the IQ problem patterns identified in this research as solution objectives. For example, known IQ problems will focus the search for organizational mechanisms that solve these problems. Finally, this research should be replicated in organizations for which data are their primary product, such as financial firms.

## CONCLUSION

It cannot be overemphasized that IQ has many dimensions. Some dimensions are objective, and others are subjective. Because of these distinct characteristics, we have found incongruities in the understanding of the quality of information between the IT department and other functional areas in virtually all of the cases we studied. IT departments by and large focus on the objective dimensions that can be quantified, whereas functional departments attend to subjective dimensions that are important in the context of their tasks at hand. To define IQ correctly, therefore, it is critical to understand both the information consumer's subjective perspective and the information manufacturer's objective perspective.

Without a good understanding of what IQ means, the firm will not be in a position to identify IQ problems. This, in turn, will inhibit it from systemically creating a new wealth of quality information. This chapter has defined the concepts of IQ objectively and subjectively. It provides the essential vocabulary for identifying IQ problems. These research-grounded definitions form the foundations for measuring, analyzing, and improving information quality in a continuous cycle.

## References

[1]   Angeles, P. A., *Dictionary of Philosophy*. Harper Perennial, New York, 1981.

[2]   Ballou, D. P., and H. L. Pazer, "Modeling Data and Process Quality in Multi-input, Multi-output Information Systems," *Management Science*, 31(2), 1985, pp. 150–162.

[3]   Benbasat, I., D. K. Goldstein, and M. Mead, "The Case Research Strategy in Studies of Information Systems," *Management Information Systems Quarterly* (MISQ), 11(3), 1987, pp. 369–386.

[4]   Brodie, M. L., "Data Quality in Information Systems." *Information and Management*, (3), 1980, pp. 245–258.

[5]   Codd, E. F., *The Relational Model for Database Management: Version 2*. Addison-Wesley, Reading, MA, 1990.

[6]   CRG, *Information Quality Assessment Survey: Administrator's Guide*. Cambridge Research Group, Cambridge, MA, 1997.

[7]   CRG, *Integrity Analyzer: A Software Tool for TDQM*. Cambridge Research Group, Cambridge, MA, 1997.

[8]   Deming, E. W., *Out of the Crisis*. Center for Advanced Engineering Study, MIT, Cambridge, MA, 1986.

[9]   Dobyns, L., and C., Crawford-Mason, *Quality or Else: The Revolution in World Business*. Houghton Mifflin, Boston, MA, 1991.

[10] Fetter, R. B., "Diagnosis Related Groups: Understanding Hospital Performance," *Interfaces*, 21(1), 1991, pp. 6–26.

[11] Garvin, D. A., "Competing on the Eight Dimensions of Quality," *Harvard Business Review*, 65(6), 1987, pp. 101–109.

[12] Juran, J. M., *Juran on Leadership for Quality: An Executive Handbook*. The Free Press, New York, 1989.

[13] Juran, J. M., and F. M. Gryna, *Quality Planning and Analysis*. 2nd ed. McGraw Hill, New York, 1980.

[14] Laudon, K. C., "Data Quality and Due Process in Large Interorganizational Record Systems," *Communications of the ACM*, 29(1), 1986, pp. 4–11.

[15] Lee, Y. W., D. M. Strong, L. Pipino, and R. Y. Wang , *A Methodology-based Software Tool for Data Quality Management* (No. TDQM-97-02). MIT TDQM Research Program, 1997.

[16] Miles, M. B., and A. M. Huberman, *Qualitative Data Analysis: A Sourcebook of New Methods*. Sage Publications, Newbury Park, CA, 1984.

[17] Morey, R. C., "Estimating and Improving the Quality of Information in the MIS," *Communications of the ACM*, 25(5), 1982, pp. 337–342.

[18] Strong, D. M., Y. W. Lee, and R. Y. Wang, "Data Quality in Context," *Communications of the ACM*, 40(5), 1997, pp. 103–110.

[19] Wand, Y., and R. Y. Wang, "Anchoring Data Quality Dimensions in Ontological Foundations," *Communications of the ACM*, 39(11), 1996, pp. 86–95.

[20] Wang, R. Y., and D. M. Strong, "Beyond Accuracy: What Data Quality Means to Data Consumers," *Journal of Management Information Systems* (JMIS), 12(4), 1996, pp. 5–34.

[21] Weber, R. P., *Basic Content Analysis*. 2nd ed. Sage, Newbury Park, CA, 1990.

[22] Yin, R. K., *Case Study Research: Design and Methods*. 2nd ed. Sage, Thousand Oaks, CA, 1994.

# Measure, Analyze, and Improve IQ

$T$o manage effectively, one must measure and analyze. To measure, however, one must first define what to measure. Defining what Information Quality (IQ) means, therefore, is crucial in managing information as a product. In the process of defining what IQ means, the participants will engage in problem identification and problem solving in the context of their own organizational setting. They must identify the necessary organizational processes and technical solutions for managing the information product. Toward that goal, the Information Product Manager (IPM) [10] must develop the corresponding IQ metrics, upon defining IQ dimensions, to measure and analyze the quality of the information product and improve it accordingly. This chapter addresses these issues.

## MEASURE IQ

Invariably, companies concerned about IQ pose three basic questions:

How good is the quality of information in my databases, data warehouses, or customer information systems?

How does the quality of my information compare to that of others in my industry? Is there a set of benchmarks that we can use as a basis of comparison?

Is there a useable, single, aggregate IQ measure, similar to stock market indicators, such as the Dow Jones Industrial Average?

To answer these questions, the IPM must develop a suitable set of metrics to perform the necessary measurements. The requirement to measure is inextricably intertwined with the needs to analyze and improve IQ. Unfortunately, there is no one universal, invariant set of metrics that can be used by everyone. There is no "one size fits all" set of metrics or, for that matter, no one universal number that measures IQ. An aggregate, weighted function can be developed, but this will be specific to one company and reflect subjective assignment of the weights.

In developing IQ metrics, it is important to recognize the many factors that should be considered. All too often, however, firms develop their IQ metrics based on their intuition or previous experience. As a result, sustainable long-term improvement is not achieved. This is particularly unfortunate after millions of dollars have been invested in implementing a software system for improving IQ, and tens of millions more dollars are required to maintain and modify the system. A negative consequence is that these firms become cynical when their IQ initiatives fail to achieve the planned objectives.

Based on the cumulative body of IQ research and practice, we propose three complementary classes of metrics that the IPM must recognize and use when assessing IQ metric needs. Specifically, the IPM must obtain an accurate assessment of the perception of IQ from the key organizational functional units. The IPM must have a set of application-independent baseline measures of the quality of the information—the necessary conditions for IQ. Lastly, the IPM must develop a set of application-dependent measures that reflect specific requirements and business rules of the organization. In other words, the IPM must have three classes of metrics:

Metrics that measure an individual's subjective assessment of IQ (how good do people in our company think the quality of our information is)

Metrics that measure IQ quality along quantifiable, objective variables that are application independent (how complete, consistent, correct, and up to date the information in our customer information system is)

Metrics that measure IQ quality along quantifiable, objective variables that are application dependent (how many clients have exposure to the Asian financial crisis that our risk management system cannot estimate because of poor quality information)

Used in combination, metrics from each of these classes provides fundamental information that goes beyond the static IQ assessment to the dynamic and continuous evaluation and improvement of information quality. Each class measures something different. The metrics that provides subjective evaluations relates to one individual's perception of the quality of information. The application-independent metrics transcends specific applications and is context independent. The application-dependent metrics has meaning and relevance to a specific application and is context dependent [8].

By approaching the development of IQ metrics from the perspective of these three classes, the IPM can diagnose the current status of IQ, develop the required metrics, link these metrics to the organization's goals and objectives, and conduct cost-benefit analyses allowing management to make informed decisions regarding initiatives to improve the quality of information.

## Subjective IQ Metrics

Subjective IQ metrics measure an individual's subjective assessment of IQ. That is, how good do people in our company think the quality of our information is? Two types of subjective IQ measures can be established. The first type measures the dimensional IQ, while the second measures the level of IQ knowledge in the firm.

### Dimensional IQ Assessment

Based on the 16 IQ dimensions [11] presented in the previous chapter, we can generate a set of questions (questionnaire) to determine the perception of the state of IQ in an organization. Such a questionnaire has been developed based on the cumulated research conducted at MIT's TDQM program [3]. A complete copy of this questionnaire is shown in the appendix at the end of this chapter. Each question is rated using a Likert-type scale on a scale from 0 to 10 where 0 indicates "not at all" and 10 "completely." A sample question to assess the dimension on completeness is: "This information is sufficiently complete for our needs."

This questionnaire has been used effectively in both public and private sectors. For example, IS managers in one investment firm thought they had perfect IQ (in terms of accuracy) in their organizational databases. However, following their completion of the questionnaire, they found deficiencies such as,

additional information about information sources was needed so that information consumers could assess the reputation and believability of the information

information downloaded to servers from the mainframe was not sufficiently timely for some information consumers' tasks

the currencies ($, £, or ¥) and units (thousands or millions) of financial information from different servers were implicit so information consumers could not always interpret and understand this information correctly

The questionnaire can be used to measure perceived IQ. It can be used as a diagnostic tool to evaluate the quality of information from a much broader perspective than the limited perspective of information accuracy only. Information obtained during this diagnostic phase provides the motivation to develop methods for improving the quality of information as perceived by information consumers. Such methods could include users. Aside from its diagnostic uses, the framework and associated questionnaire are valuable aids when used as checklists during information requirement analysis.

In addition to the assessment of IQ, a number of questions are included to assess the degree to which a company has in place mechanisms to ensure the quality of information. These mechanisms include TQM programs, IQ software tools, and an IQ administration function. A complete copy of this questionnaire is shown in Section 3 of the Appendix. Each question is rated using a Likert-type scale using values from 1 to 10 where 1 indicates "very small extent" and 10 "very large extent." A sample question is: "In this company, there are people whose primary job is to assure the quality of information." Analysis of the degree to which these mechanisms have been instituted helps the firm to plan, execute, and monitor the firm's IQ program.

## IQ Knowledge Assessment

The previous discussion focused on the assessment by the information consumer of the current quality of information, and the mechanisms that the firm deploys to assure high-quality information. To maintain a viable total IQ program in the firm, knowledge of the system in place to manage IQ must also be assessed.

Three aspects of knowledge pertinent for shaping organizational IQ capabilities have been identified [5]. This perspective explicitly includes aspects of knowledge that probe underlying reasons and axiomatic assumptions behind the work practice in organizations. Specifically, *IQ-related "know-what" knowledge* is the accumulated understanding of the activities and procedures involved in producing, storing, and utilizing information. *IQ-related "know-how" knowledge* is the accumulated skills for applying routine procedures to known IQ problems. *IQ-related "know-why" knowledge* is the ability to analyze and discover previously unknown IQ problems or solutions. This type of knowledge is gained from experience and understanding of the objectives and cause-effect relationships underlying the activities involved in collecting, storing, and utilizing information. These three types of knowledge apply to each of the three information manufacturing processes: information production, storage, and use.

To assess the state of these three types of IQ knowledge in the firm, a separate questionnaire has been developed. The questions are intended to assess the level of IQ knowledge in the firm. Each question is rated using a Likert-type scale using values from 1 to 10 where 1 indicates "very small extent" and 10 "very large extent." A sample question is: "I know which group collects this information."

The responses from the IQ knowledge questionnaire can be analyzed to identify problem areas and to develop corresponding solutions. Repeated applications of these questionnaires in companies in different industries will eventually lead to the establishment of a representative data set. These standards provide IQ benchmarks for individual organizations in different industries. The results of these questionnaires will be used to analyze and improve the IQ.

## Objective, Application-Independent Metrics

Objective, application-independent metrics measures IQ quality along quantifiable, objective variables; for example, how complete, consistent, correct, and up to date the information in our customer information system is. These metrics are based on established theory for controlling the quality of information entering the system. Systems for which these controls are not in place at the time of information acquisition can still use the measures to assess the degree to which the existing information meets the standard.

Most database systems have been designed from a systems perspective. Mechanisms such as integrity constraints and normalization theories [1, 2, 7] used to maintain the integrity and consistency of information are necessary, but not sufficient, to attain quality information as demanded by information users.

Dr. Edgar F. Codd proposed five integrity rules that must be followed by any true relational database management system. Although developed specifically for the relational model, the integrity rules are very useful in many contexts ranging from the relational database systems to network database systems to flat files. Indeed, many of the corporate databases are just beginning to be migrated to the relational database environment such as IBM's DB2 from the decade-old CICS hierarchical database management systems. Moreover, much of current-day information is stored in either spreadsheets or groupware such as Lotus Notes. Ensuring the quality of information in these databases requires a methodological approach, and integrity rules proposed by Codd present such an approach.

Even in the relational environment, many present-day relational databases are not integrity compliant for many reasons.

The specific relational database implementation does not have an integrity facility to enforce integrity.

Although the integrity facility is available, the DBA does not provide the specifics.

While the edit checks are programmed into the database management system, the user by necessity often overrides the rules when under time pressure.

As the business environment changes, so do the business rules that must be enforced on the underlying data.

Simply put, Codd's integrity rules ensure data meet the specifications demanded by the designer and the user. An IQ tool developed based on Codd's integrity rules, therefore, offers a rigorous method to define, measure, analyze, and improve the quality of information. Below we recap the five kinds of integrity Codd proposed.

Domain Integrity — All the values of a field must be of the same domain.

Column Integrity — specifies the set of acceptable values for the column.

Entity Integrity — No component of a primary key is allowed to have a missing value of any type. No foreign key is allowed to have a missing and inapplicable value.

Referential Integrity — For each distinct foreign key in a relational database, there must exist in the database an equal value of a primary key from the same domain. If the foreign key is composite, those components that are themselves foreign keys must exist in the database as components of at least one primary key value drawn from the same domain.

User-Defined Integrity — This captures business rules and company regulations and operations that should be reflected in the database. User-defined constraints are used not only to ensure the state of the database is valid but also to trigger specific actions when specified conditions arise in the database.

## Application-Dependent IQ Metrics

Application-dependent metrics measure IQ quality along quantifiable, objective variables that are domain specific and require domain experts' participation. Some application-dependent metrics are relatively intuitive and easy to develop whereas others may be very involved. Below we illustrate these problems and opportunities in a financial company case study.

Financial Company is a leading investment bank with extensive domestic and international operations. The nature of its business requires the company to have an accurate and up-to-date representation of each customer's risk profile. Investments at inappropriate customer risk levels cause major customer dissatisfaction and potential indemnification to customers for losses. The company was not poised to leverage customer account information in its global operations. For example, customers with sufficient credit across accounts could not trade or borrow on their full balance. Tracking customer balances for individual and multiple accounts, closing all accounts of an investor because of criminal activities, and ensuring an accurate investor risk profile also could not be accomplished without significant, error-prone human intervention. All of these presented the company with potentially huge problems and many missed opportunities.

The company established a few information process measures or controls. For example, there were no controls to ensure that customer risk profiles were updated on a regular basis. The account creation process was not standardized or inspected. Consequently, no metrics were established to measure how many accounts were created on time, and whether customer information in those accounts was updated. Managing its customer account information as a product would provide Financial Company with better risk management and customer service — two critical success factors for companies in the financial industry.

In the client account database, for example, the following IQ metrics could be applied:

the percentage of incorrect client address zip code found in a randomly selected customer accounts (*inaccuracy*)

an indicator of when client account information was last updated (*timeliness* or *currency* for database marketing and regulatory purposes)

the percentage of nonexistent accounts or the number of accounts with missing values in the industry-code field (*incompleteness*)

the number of records that violate referential integrity (*consistency*)

At a more complex level, there are business rules that need to be observed. For example, the total risk exposure of a client should not exceed a certain limit. This exposure needs to be monitored for clients who have many accounts. Conversely, a client who has a very conservative position in one account should be allowed to execute riskier transactions in another account. For these business rules to work, however, the firm needs to develop a proper linking method to link the accounts.

There are also information-manufacturing-oriented IQ metrics. In the client account system, for example, the firm needs to track

which department made most of the updates in the system last week

how many unauthorized accesses have been attempted (*security*)

who collected the raw data for a client account (*credibility*)

Another example is Financial Company's mission-critical Capital Markets System. Consider its account reconciliation which is conceptually similar to balancing a checkbook. For a checkbook, one may

record all checks for completeness

inspect checks for accuracy

adjust the beginning balance with checks issued during the period for internal consistency with the end balance

compare the checkbook balance with bank balance for external validity

monitor large checks and control possible overspending in certain categories

improve the check balancing process as necessary

Account reconciliation in the Capital Markets System, however, is more complicated than balancing a checkbook. It involves thousands of transactions drawn on hundreds of accounts stored in computer and manual systems around the world. Each account has a one-to-one relationship with a ledger. An item in a ledger, which is the bank's record of payments made and expected, could be a payment of £6 million to an Exxon office in London. These items need to be matched with items in statements from hundreds of other banks in which this international bank has accounts. Tens of billions of U.S. dollars are reconciled each day.

Many IQ problems arise during reconciliation. For example, a statement may not be received in time for reconciliation or could have items with wrong account numbers. The sources of poor IQ could be recording, transmission, or simply missing information. Some example causes are

> An operator delayed sending a statement or entered wrong data.

> Instead of paying £6 million to Exxon, London directly, three separate items were created: pay £1 million to Ford, £2 million to GM, and £3 million to Chrysler.

For operational and regulatory reasons, it is critical to minimize the number of items, called open items, not reconciled. Based on results from this research, an IQ monitor is being developed in the bank to minimize open items. Open items that do not match are prioritized according to the number of days since initially identified as an open item.

To verify internal consistency, an IQ monitor adds all the candidate items in statements for an account (e.g., Exxon) to the beginning balance in a ledger to see if they match the ending balance. If the result is inconsistent, the candidate items are listed as open items.

To verify cross consistency, an IQ monitor matches items in a ledger with those in a statement (and vice versa). Candidate item-pairs are compared to see if the account number, amount, debit/credit, date, and so on are consistent. Those with no match are listed as open items. Efforts are made to reconcile these problems by, for example, calling the party who produced the items. Credibility of information source is also important in reconciling open items; some banks are notorious for poor-quality information in their statements, and therefore, items from those statements are often checked first during reconciliation.

In addition to the above relatively obvious IQ issues, there are business-oriented rules. For example, it is important to keep track of items that are more than $10,000 and remain open for more than 10 days.

## ANALYZE IQ

We have presented three classes of IQ measures and argued that when used in combination, these measures provide fundamental information that goes beyond the static IQ assessment to the dynamic and continuous evaluation and improvement of information quality. To perform the necessary IQ analysis efficiently and effectively, however, it would be useful to have some computer-based tools to facilitate the analysis. In this section, we present such a software implementation and illustrate how these tools can be applied.

# IQ Assessment (IQA)

The *IQ Assessment* ™ (IQA) Survey consists of three sections. Section 1 collects the characteristics of the information source being assessed. The subject is required to answer four questions in this section.

Question 4 elicits the role the subject plays in activities involved in this database. The four primary roles are information producer, information consumer, information manufacturer, and manager of these positions. Our experience shows that often a subject will declare multiples roles of involvement. In this case, the IQA Survey administrator should ask the subject to focus on the primary role played for purposes of completing the questionnaire. The department in which a subject is employed often determines the primary role. For example, a subject who works in the MIS department is most likely to be an information manufacturer, an information vendor representative such as one from Reuters or Dun & Bradstreet is an information producer; and a marketing manager whose is responsible for a direct market campaign is most likely to be an information consumer.

The IQA software instrument is developed to collect the survey data electronically, following the principle that the quality of information will be high if entered by subjects themselves (the very information source). We illustrate the electronic questionnaire below using question 2. As shown in the appendix at the end of this chapter, the subject would respond to question 2 by selecting the appropriate numerical response from 1 to 10. The response that the subject has chosen will also be displayed to the left of the selection buttons. If the subject wishes, the responses can be typed in directly in the box to the left of the button. Section 2 of the IQA assesses the dimensional quality of the information. It would be completed in the same manner as Section 1 except that the screen contains more than one question. The subject would select the desired numerical rating for each question. Figure 4.1 illustrates the screen for Section 2.

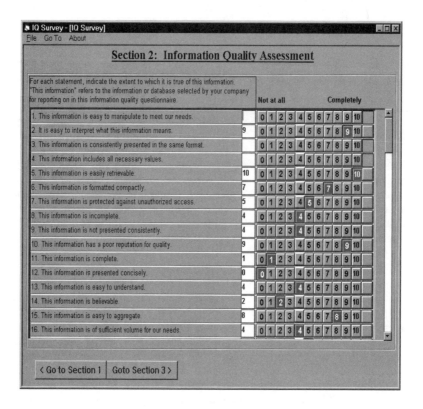

Figure 4.1 Sample IQA Screen
(Source: *Cambridge Research Group* [3])

For most of the questions, the subject can simply use the mouse to click a button to indicate the response. Alternatively, the subject can respond to the questions using the keyboard. In that case, the subject will use the tab key to position the cursor in the appropriate box, enter the desired numerical rating, and tab again to move to the next question.

Section 3 of the IQA collects the contextual quality. It is completed in the same manner as Section 2. Note, however, that in Section 3 a response of N/A is permissible because specific questions on context will not apply to all organizations.

As mentioned earlier, the questions are repetitive and some are reverse coded to ensure the validity of the questionnaire. Survey results that violate the validity are excluded from further analysis. Although the IQ Survey software is developed for the subject to enter responses electronically, a subject can complete a hard copy version of the questionnaire instead of using the IQ Survey software. In that case, the administrator can enter the results directly with the software's survey administrator function.

IQA Survey Administration

In preparing for the administration of the IQ Assessment Survey, the survey administrator works with key stakeholders of an IQ project to pick an information system whose information is (mission) critical to the firm and for which IQ improvement is important to the firm. Before administering the IQA survey, the survey administrator should emphasize to the subjects that

The survey is not a test. There is no correct answer to each of the questions. The subject serves as an informed representative in answering the survey questions.

Survey questions are repetitive and some are reverse coded, again, to verify the validity of the results.

It takes about 8 minutes to complete the survey.

There is no need to check previous answers for consistency.

## Survey Results Analysis: A Case Study

After the IQA Survey results have been collected and entered into the IQA Survey Master Database, the analysis task can take place. The results of analysis will vary depending on the many contextual factors in an IQ project. Accordingly, expertise in IQ management and familiarity with the project are essential in developing insightful results. Statistical packages such as SPSS, SAS, and Minitab can be applied to facilitate the analysis of the survey results. A proprietary software tool to analyze results of the survey has also been developed [3]. Below, we present a case study illustrating the use of this tool to conduct an analysis.

Appliance Company sells personal computers, home office products, consumer electronics, entertainment software, major appliances and related accessories through its retail stores. The company generates billions of dollars of revenue annually. Prior to the year we investigated the quality of information in the company, net income fell 100 percent compared to the previous year. Revenues reflect the opening of new stores. Earnings were offset by the inability to leverage certain components of its fixed costs, and an increase in interest expense.

To compete more effectively, senior management demanded more accurate, timely, and relevant snapshot reports. As part of a mission-critical thrust to meet the demand, consultants were called upon to assess the IQ of the underlying databases from which these reports are produced. Following the survey administration process as presented above, data points were collected from various functional areas that encompass information producers, information manufacturers, information consumers, and those who are responsible for managing the production of the reports as an information product.

Analysis of the survey results provided answers to the following questions:

Q1: How is Appliance Company's IQ?

Q2: Which IQ dimensions are of high/low quality?

Q3: How do different groups assess high/low quality information?

To answer the first question, an unweighted, aggregate IQ index was computed, yielding a score of 6.77 out of 10. As with many other self-assessment questionnaires, this overall score is merely an index that reflects the participants' views of Appliance's IQ (similar to that of Dow Jones Industrial Average as an index to the U.S. equity market).

The answer to the second question is shown in Table 4.1. Overall, the data from snapshot reports rate high along the intrinsic quality category, which includes the dimensions of believability and reputation. Poor quality shows up in the contextual and representational IQ categories. In order for Appliance Company to improve IQ, it needs to focus on improving completeness of information so as to reflect and plan its business performance. It also needs to improve ease of manipulation so that information can easily be adapted for analysis and other business purposes.

**Table 4.1: Overall Information Quality**

|  | **High-quality IQ Dimensions\*** | **Low-quality IQ Dimensions\*\*** |
|---|---|---|
| Overall | H1. Believability H2. Reputation H3. Relevancy | L1. Ease of manipulation L2. Security L3. Appropriate amount of data L4. Completeness |

\*   These IQ dimensions are evaluated as high by the survey participants.

\*\*   These IQ dimensions are evaluated as poor by the survey participants.

To answer the third question, the survey results are aggregated by the roles the subjects assumed. The results of analyzing the responses for perceived quality as a function of the role of the respondent are depicted in Figure 4.2. It is evident that information custodians (mostly MIS department) view the information as very timely, but information consumers disagree. Information consumers in all groups view information from snapshot reports as not easy to manipulate for their business purposes, but information custodians disagree [9].

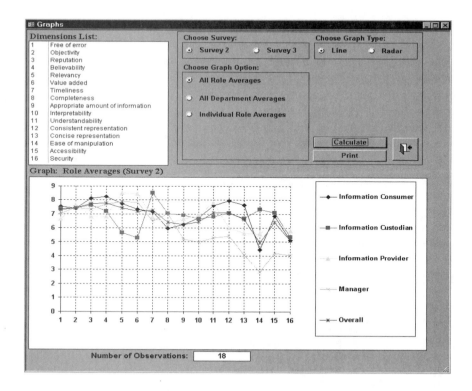

Figure 4.2  IQ Assessment across Roles

(Source: *Cambridge Research Group* [3])

We have presented the IQA Survey software tool and illustrated, through the Appliance Company case study, an analysis based on the survey results collected from Appliance. This survey, along with interviews, can diagnose critical areas and directions for IQ improvement. Moreover, these qualitative IQ assessment results can be combined with the results of both system-based and application-based metrics. The combination of results from the IQ Survey, system-based metrics, and application-based measurements contribute to the development of a comprehensive picture of a company's overall level of IQ. We present a software implementation below.

## Integrity Analyzer™

An outgrowth of research from MIT's Total Data Quality Management (TDQM) research, the *Integrity Analyzer™* (IA) embeds a TDQM methodology that combines the principles of the TDQM cycle with the principles of integrity constraints in relational databases, as shown in Table 4.2 [4, 6]. Each column of Table 4.2 represents one of the five integrity constraints defined by Codd: domain, entity, referential, column, and user-defined integrity. Domain integrity requires that all values in a column of a table must be drawn from the same domain. Entity integrity requires that every entity (table) must have a primary key consisting of one or more columns. The primary key must be unique and have no missing values. Referential integrity requires that, for each distinct foreign key in a relational database, there must exist in the database an equal value of a primary key from the same domain. Column integrity further restricts the values that can be drawn from the domain for that particular column. In short, column integrity specifies the set of acceptable values for the column. These values can be specified in the form of uniqueness requirement, nonnull requirements, a range of acceptable values, or a list of acceptable values. User-defined integrity specifies additional business rules that column values must meet. These rules often involve conditions dependent on values of other fields. The four actions, *define*, *measure*, *analyze*, and *improve,* for IQ constitute the rows of Table 4.2. These four actions can be applied to achieve domain, entity, referential, column, and user-defined integrity. The cells in Table 4.2 represent the application of an IQ action to a type of integrity.

**Table 4.2: A TDQM Methodology for Integrity Analyzer**

|         | Domain Integrity | Entity Integrity | Referential Integrity | Column Integrity | User defined Integrity |
|---------|------------------|------------------|-----------------------|------------------|------------------------|
| Define  | Define the domains used in the database. For each column, specify its associated domain. | For each table, specify the primary key, and any candidate keys. | Specify all foreign keys. For each, specify its associated primary key. | For each column, specify the rules for acceptable values. | Specify any business rules not captured in entity, referential, and column integrity. |
| Measure | Check for violations, i.e., values in a column that are not drawn from the appropriate domain. | Check for violations, i.e., keys that are null or non-unique. | Check for violations, i.e., foreign key values that have no corresponding primary key value. | Check for violations, i.e., column values that have unacceptable values, e.g., out of range. | Check for violations, i.e., record instances that do not satisfy the business rules. |
| Analyze | Examine the measurement | Examine the measurement | Examine the measurement | Examine the measurement | Examine the measurement |

| | statistics nu-merically or graphically. | statistics nu-merically or graphically. | statistics nu-merically or graphically. | statistics numerically or graphi-cally. | statistics numeri-cally or graphi-cally. |
|---|---|---|---|---|---|
| Improve | View the vi o-lation records and change values as ap-propriate. | View the viola-tion records and change values as appropriate. | View the vi o-lation records and change values as ap-propr iate. | View the violation records and change val-ues as appro-pr iate. | View the viola-tion records and change values as appropriate. |

We illustrate the IA's functionality by using the example of an international bank that is migrating legacy files to a relational database. This problem typifies a problem that companies face when migrating data from legacy systems or spreadsheet files to a relational database or data warehouse. All too often, the quality of the information in the source files is poor. This state occurs, in part, because integrity constraints were not applied when the data were originally entered. Our example consists of five files that have been migrated: the customer file, the account file, account type file, transactions file, and type of transaction file. Figure 4.3 shows an entity-relationship diagram for this example.

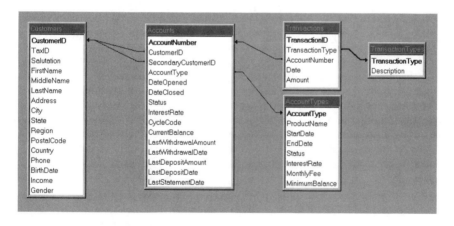

Figure 4.3: An Entity-Relationship Diagram for a Sample Financial Application

(Source: *Cambridge Research Group* [4])

To illustrate the use of the IA, we first assume that the data have been migrated but an IQ assessment has not been conducted. A user would typically assess the soundness of the database structure, that is, assess primary and foreign key quality.

the quality of the data in nonkey attributes.

that data conform to the business rules of the firm.

In this example, we focus on the sequence of events and the user-system interface for achieving these objectives.

At the start of a session, the IA gives the user the choice of either opening an existing project file or creating a new project file. For a new project file administrative information such as the name and location of the database and a name for the improvement project is obtained. Information in the project file is maintained throughout the life of the project and consists of administrative information on the project, definitions of the structures, and any quality measurements previously made. The user can then select any of the four integrity functions by pulling down the *data integrity* menu and making the desired choice. To perform the frequency check the user would pull down the *tools* menu and select the desired function.

## Data Integrity

The entity integrity function checks that all primary and candidate keys for each table are unique and nonnull. The referential integrity function checks that all foreign keys have corresponding primary key values.

To check entity integrity, the IA user selects entity integrity from the data integrity pull-down menu and selects the Define tab. In the Define list box the user selects the fields that are primary and candidate keys for each table. Next the user selects the Measure tab and asks the system to measure the number of violations to entity integrity. After the assessment has been completed, the user can select the Analyze tab and have the violation statistics displayed in numerical, graphical, or report form. Selecting the Improve tab produces a data object that displays the violation instances. The Referential integrity check works in a similar manner.

Exhibits of the screens corresponding to the functions of defining, measuring, analyzing, and improving entity integrity are shown in Figure 4.4

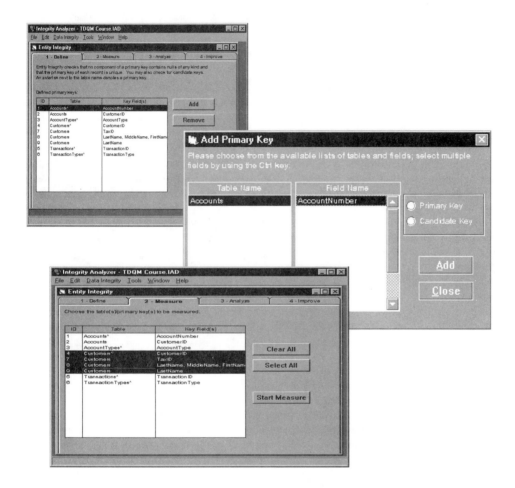

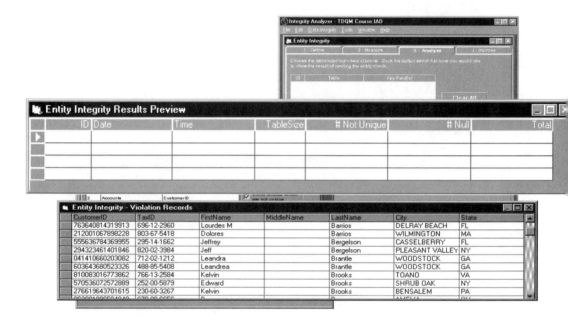

Figure 4.4: Entity Integrity Implementation

(Source: *Cambridge Research Group* [4])

The example we use to illustrate the features of column integrity is the checking of the values in the gender field of the customer record. The values should be either M or F and not null. After choosing column integrity, the user specifies the table, the column, the type of data, and one or more checks with the Define function. In our example, the user has selected the Customers table, the Gender field whose data type is text, and the "Check Null" and "Check List" options. The appropriate test for the list is constructed by using the condition button adjacent to the Check List selection window and specifying the desired values in the adjacent space provided. In the example shown in Figure 4.5, "Is Not" has been selected and the specific values are "M" and "F."

Selecting the Measure tab initiates the execution of the assessment. A number of different reports can be displayed by using the Analyze feature. Selecting the Improve tab will produce a listing of records in violation of the condition (or more precisely meeting the conditions specified which is the same as the specification of the violation being checked). Two conditions are shown in Figure 4.5: records with values other than "M" or "F" and records with null values.

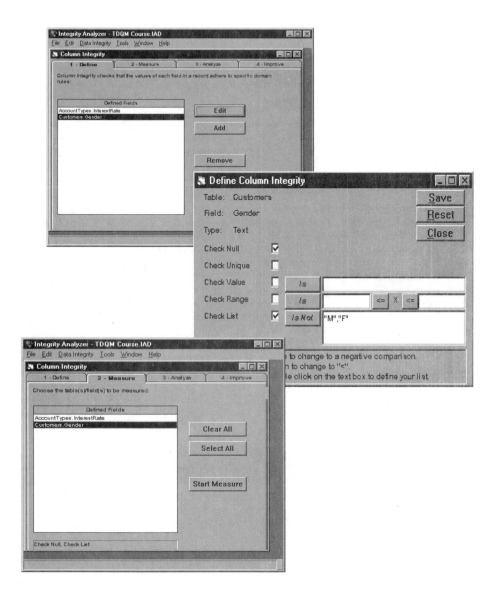

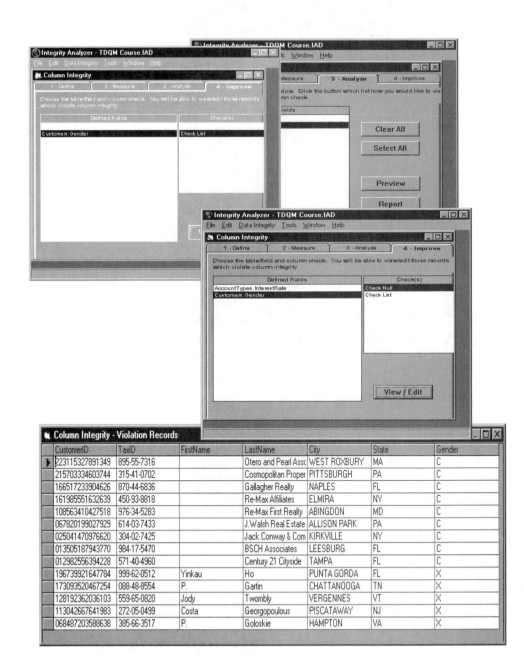

| CustomerID | TaxID | FirstName | LastName | Gender |
|---|---|---|---|---|
| 230668642988558 | 687-28-2269 | Trisha | Zuttermeister | |
| 227975365788383 | 835-12-9100 | Malcolm | Beauvais | |
| 227150953439037 | 290-44-2507 | David | Montanaro | |
| 184602008525293 | 941-81-0176 | William | Hite | |
| 245870493877225 | 536-84-9957 | Juan | Sosa | |
| 165109872007520 | 399-37-0799 | Gerard | O'Connor | |
| 499035950495443 | 370-58-8098 | Chris | Higgins | |
| 136765020596559 | 742-84-5074 | Llen | Boemer | |
| 139278952089574 | 961-38-0655 | Michael | Norgard | |

Figure 4.5: Column Integrity Implementation

(Source: *Cambridge Research Group* [4])

User-defined integrity captures rules that are application dependent. Typically, these would be specific business rules. Examples of such rules are

A student account does not accrue interest.

ATM transactions will incur a fee beginning January 1, 1997.

A senior account holder should be more than 65 years old.

When a customer turns 65 years old, a "senior account" status should be offered.

A customer with an average balance of $1M should be flagged for new business opportunities.

These business rules range from strict integrity constraints to rules that support marketing and customer support functions. The IA functionality for user-defined integrity is demonstrated below for the first example, a student account does not accrue interest.

Having chosen the User-Defined Integrity function, the user is presented with a display of conditions that have been defined. The user can now edit an existing condition or add a new user-defined rule. If the user selects add, the system displays a Define window that elicits the information necessary to define a condition. The user defined rule is that student accounts do not accrue interest, that is IF Account type = Student, THEN Interest rate =0.

As in the previous examples, selection of the Measurement function evaluates the database for violation of this rule. Selection of the Analysis function displays the results of the assessment. Selection of the Improvement function will result in a display of the records that violate the condition.

### Frequency Checks

Several additional tools to support IQ analysis are provided with the IA. A particularly useful one is frequency checks, which reports the values and frequencies of each value in a column. Frequency checks is often used in combination with column integrity. Consider the gender field we checked for M and F values with column integrity. The results of integrity checking show many violations. As demonstrated in Figure 4.6, frequency checks can provide information to further analyze these violations.

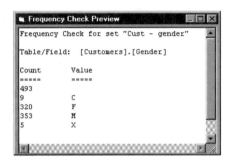 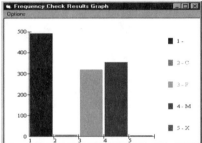

Figure 4.6:  Frequency Check

(Source: *Cambridge Research Group* [4])

As in the examples of previous features, the user can define one or more specific frequent checks or edit a previously defined frequency check specification. By selecting the Measure function, the user initiates a specific frequency check. The user can display results of the assessment by selecting the Analyze option. The results of a frequency check on the gender field of the Customer table are shown in Figure 4.6.

The *Integrity Analyzer* supports both Codd's formally defined integrity constraints and his user-defined constraints. Assessment of domain integrity, column integrity, entity integrity, and referential integrity is invariant across applications. All relational database management systems, ideally, should abide by these rules. All databases, regardless of subject matter, should adhere to the rules represented by these constraints.

The user-defined constraints, however, are application dependent. They vary from application to application, and from industry to industry. Furthermore, these application-dependent constraints evolve over time. The *Integrity Analyzer* can be customized for a specific company within a specific industry by coding these user-defined rules in the software.

We note that the integrity analyzer is more than simply an implementation of Codd's integrity constraints in relational database software. Unlike the standard, commercial Relational Data Base Management Systems (RDBMS) packages which check for adherence to

Codd's constraints when data are entered into the database, the *Integrity Analyzer* is a diagnostic tool which can assess the degree to which existing databases adhere to all the constraints defined by Codd as well as application-dependent user-defined rules. As a diagnostic tool, the analyzer delivers an analysis of the data repository's current quality state and suggests where improvements must be made.

By using the IQA and the integrity analyzer software tools, an analyst can assess the consumer's perceptions of IQ and specific objective states of IQ. These assessments will form the basis for improvement in the overall IQ of the firm.

## IMPROVE IQ

It is important that both technical solutions and organizational processes be introduced, disseminated, and institutionalized in the organization over time in order to sustain long-term improvement of organizational information quality. By managing information as a product, an information product management team is established to define what an information product is, and how to manage the information product or information product line over its life cycle. Techniques and methods developed in many disciplines can be applied to the various phases of the TDQM cycle and the information product cycle, for example, statistical process control in production, record tracing and auditing in accounting, and product services in marketing.

Depending on the organizational context, the technical solutions can range from data scrubbing to integrity enforcement to dummy record tracing to data dictionary standardization to complete an information system's overhaul. Similarly, because information quality requirements evolve over time, the organizational processes must capture and monitor the shifting demand of information quality requirements of soundness, useability, usefulness, and dependability. An encoded file that is accurate is sound but not usable if the consumer can not decode it. The information is not useful if does not add value to the consumer's tasks. The IQA instrument can be applied to monitoring the evolving changes of IQ requirements. For example, an organization began its corporatewide IQ initiative. As part of the initiative, more than 30 executives participated in the IQA survey. As shown in Figure 4.7, the results from 28 observations indicate that accessibility is more of a concern than accuracy.

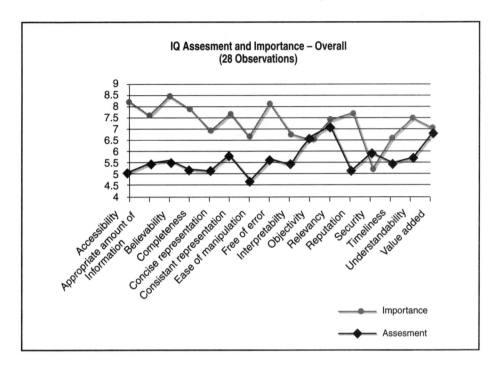

Figure 4.7: IQ Assessment and Importance Ratings

(Source: *Cambridge Research Group* [3])

A weighted rating, based on the distance between the assessment of a dimension and the ideal score times the importance of the dimension, provides a better indication of how to prioritize the tasks. This is illustrated in Figure 4.8. Note that over time when the accessibility problem has been addressed, an IQA survey of the participants would show another dimension such as timeliness as the primary concern. Furthermore, as with the quality of a physical product, such as a car, the consumer's expectation becomes higher as they become more sophisticated. Information previously considered as accurate, timely, or accessible may not be so as time goes by because of a higher expectation.

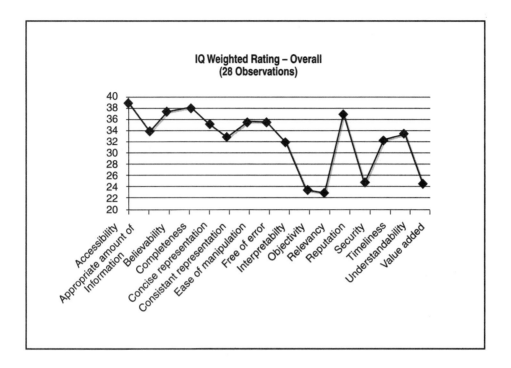

Figure 4.8: Weighted Ratings for Prioritizing IQ Tasks

(Source: *Cambridge Research Group* [3])

## CONCLUSION

We have presented an innovative methodology for managing the quality of organizational information beyond conventional approaches that are limited to the adaptation of TQM techniques to the IQ arena or some specific software tools that scrub data, match names, or reconcile data semantics. Central to our methodology is the concept of managing information as a product. In substantiating the methodology, we developed fundamental concepts such as the TDQM cycle and the information manufacturing system. We also developed a comprehensive set of dimensions to capture the essence of information quality based on rigorous field studies that premised on the belief that information quality needs to be defined as information that is fit for use by information consumers, as well as a set of ontologically grounded IQ dimensions that established a basis for the rigorous development ultimately of a theory for information quality. With the concept and principles of information quality well defined, we developed tools, methods, and techniques for measuring, analyzing, and improving information quality.

The road to information quality can be bumpy. To facilitate the process, we have presented many cases to illustrate how firms go about launching an information quality initiative, such as introducing, disseminating, and institutionalizing their organizational IQ processes and system solutions. Properly managed, the information product will meet or exceed the expectations of the various stakeholders of the product, and in the long term become part of the organizational culture. Sound, useable, useful, and dependable information is quality information. It is the keystone for organizational knowledge management, the subject that we will present in depth based on IBM's experience and success in developing and deploying their Intellectual Capital Management (ICM) solutions.

# APPENDIX: IQA SURVEY

Information Quality Study

This study is being conducted in cooperation with your company and MIT's Total Data Quality Management (TDQM) Research Program. We ask you to assess the quality of your organization's information along many dimensions of quality. These quality dimensions all relate in some way to whether the information is "fit for use" in organizational tasks and decision making. We also ask you to characterize your company in terms of its quality activities.

Before filling out this questionnaire, you will be told which information to respond to. This set of information was selected because its quality is important to your company.

Your participation in this study is voluntary. If you object to any questions, you may choose not to respond. However, your cooperation is strongly desired and appreciated. This study can only be successful if you carefully and honestly answer the questions.

©Wang, Strong, and Lee, 1996–1997

Please do not duplicate or distribute the questionnaire without explicit consent of the authors.

---

*Section 1: Characteristics of the Information*

---

For the information you are reporting on in this questionnaire, indicate:

1. The primary type of this information (check one):

____Financial or Accounting Data
____Human Resources Data
____Production or Manufacturing Data
____Customer, Client, or Patient Data
____Marketing or Sales Data
____Clinical Data
____Other: _____

2. Rate the complexity of the activities for collecting, storing, and using this information.

**Very Simple**                              **Very Complex**

   1   2   3   4      5   6       7   8   9   10

3. Your department (check one):

____Finance, Accounting
____Information Systems (MIS)
____Production, Manufacturing
____Legal
____Marketing, Sales
____Strategic Planning
____Human Resources
____Senior Executive
____Field Operations

4. Your main role relative to this information.  Do you <u>primarily</u> (check one):

____Collect this information
____Manage those who collect this information
____Use this information in tasks
____Manage those who use this information in tasks
____Work as an information systems
____Manage information systems professionals

## Section 2: Information Quality Assessment

| For each statement, indicate the extent to which this information is true:<br><br>"This information" refers to the information or database selected by your company for reporting on in this information quality questionnaire. | Not at All     Avg.     Completely |
|---|---|
| 1. This information is easy to manipulate to meet our needs. | 0 1 2 3 4 5 6 7 8 9 10 |
| 2. It is easy to interpret what this information means. | 0 1 2 3 4 5 6 7 8 9 10 |
| 3. This information is consistently presented in the same format. | 0 1 2 3 4 5 6 7 8 9 10 |
| 4. This information includes all necessary values. | 0 1 2 3 4 5 6 7 8 9 10 |
| 5. This information is easily retrievable. | 0 1 2 3 4 5 6 7 8 9 10 |
| 6. This information is formatted compactly. | 0 1 2 3 4 5 6 7 8 9 10 |
| 7. This information is protected against unauthorized access. | 0 1 2 3 4 5 6 7 8 9 10 |
| 8. This information is incomplete. | 0 1 2 3 4 5 6 7 8 9 10 |
| 9. This information is not presented consistently. | 0 1 2 3 4 5 6 7 8 9 10 |
| 10. This information has a poor reputation for quality. | 0 1 2 3 4 5 6 7 8 9 10 |
| 11. This information is complete. | 0 1 2 3 4 5 6 7 8 9 10 |
| 12. This information is presented concisely. | 0 1 2 3 4 5 6 7 8 9 10 |
| 13. This information is easy to understand. | 0 1 2 3 4 5 6 7 8 9 10 |
| 14. This information is believable. | 0 1 2 3 4 5 6 7 8 9 10 |
| 15. This information is easy to aggregate. | 0 1 2 3 4 5 6 7 8 9 10 |
| 16. This information is of sufficient volume for our needs. | 0 1 2 3 4 5 6 7 8 9 10 |
| 17. This information is correct. | 0 1 2 3 4 5 6 7 8 9 10 |
| 18. This information is useful to our work. | 0 1 2 3 4 5 6 7 8 9 10 |
| 19. This information provides a major benefit to our work. | 0 1 2 3 4 5 6 7 8 9 10 |
| 20. This information is easily accessible. | 0 1 2 3 4 5 6 7 8 9 10 |
| 21. This information has a good reputation. | 0 1 2 3 4 5 6 7 8 9 10 |
| 22. This information is sufficiently current for our work. | 0 1 2 3 4 5 6 7 8 9 10 |
| 23. This information is difficult to interpret. | 0 1 2 3 4 5 6 7 8 9 10 |
| 24. This information is not protected with adequate security. | 0 1 2 3 4 5 6 7 8 9 10 |
| 25. This information is of doubtful credibility. | 0 1 2 3 4 5 6 7 8 9 10 |
| 26. The amount of information does not match our needs. | 0 1 2 3 4 5 6 7 8 9 10 |
| 27. This information is difficult to manipulate to meet our needs. | 0 1 2 3 4 5 6 7 8 9 10 |
| 28. This information is not sufficiently timely. | 0 1 2 3 4 5 6 7 8 9 10 |
| 29. This information is difficult to aggregate. | 0 1 2 3 4 5 6 7 8 9 10 |
| 30. The amount of information is not sufficient for our needs. | 0 1 2 3 4 5 6 7 8 9 10 |
| 31. This information is incorrect. | 0 1 2 3 4 5 6 7 8 9 10 |
| 32. This information does not add value to our work. | 0 1 2 3 4 5 6 7 8 9 10 |
| 33. This information was objectively collected. | 0 1 2 3 4 5 6 7 8 9 10 |
| 34. It is difficult to interpret the coded information. | 0 1 2 3 4 5 6 7 8 9 10 |
| 35. The meaning of this information is difficult to understand. | 0 1 2 3 4 5 6 7 8 9 10 |

| Section 2: Information Quality Assessment (continued) |
|---|

| | |
|---|---|
| 36. This information is not sufficiently current for our work. | 0 1 2 3 4 5 6 7 8 9 10 |
| 37. This information is easily interpretable. | 0 1 2 3 4 5 6 7 8 9 10 |
| 38. The amount of information is neither too much nor too little. | 0 1 2 3 4 5 6 7 8 9 10 |
| 39. This information is accurate. | 0 1 2 3 4 5 6 7 8 9 10 |
| 40. Access to this information is sufficiently restricted. | 0 1 2 3 4 5 6 7 8 9 10 |
| 41. This information is presented consistently. | 0 1 2 3 4 5 6 7 8 9 10 |
| 42. This information has a reputation for quality. | 0 1 2 3 4 5 6 7 8 9 10 |
| 43. This information is easy to comprehend. | 0 1 2 3 4 5 6 7 8 9 10 |
| 44. This information is based on facts. | 0 1 2 3 4 5 6 7 8 9 10 |
| 45. This information is sufficiently complete for our needs. | 0 1 2 3 4 5 6 7 8 9 10 |
| 46. This information is trustworthy. | 0 1 2 3 4 5 6 7 8 9 10 |
| 47. This information is relevant to our work. | 0 1 2 3 4 5 6 7 8 9 10 |
| 48. Using this information increases the value of our work. | 0 1 2 3 4 5 6 7 8 9 10 |
| 49. This information is presented in a compact form. | 0 1 2 3 4 5 6 7 8 9 10 |
| 50. This information is appropriate for our work. | 0 1 2 3 4 5 6 7 8 9 10 |
| 51. The meaning of this information is easy to understand. | 0 1 2 3 4 5 6 7 8 9 10 |
| 52. This information is credible. | 0 1 2 3 4 5 6 7 8 9 10 |
| 53. This information covers the needs of our tasks. | 0 1 2 3 4 5 6 7 8 9 10 |
| 54. Representation of this information is compact and concise. | 0 1 2 3 4 5 6 7 8 9 10 |
| 55. This information adds value to our tasks. | 0 1 2 3 4 5 6 7 8 9 10 |
| 56. The measurement units for this information are clear. | 0 1 2 3 4 5 6 7 8 9 10 |
| 57. This information is objective. | 0 1 2 3 4 5 6 7 8 9 10 |
| 58. Information can only be accessed by people who should see it. | 0 1 2 3 4 5 6 7 8 9 10 |
| 59. This information is sufficiently timely. | 0 1 2 3 4 5 6 7 8 9 10 |
| 60. This information is easy to combine with other information. | 0 1 2 3 4 5 6 7 8 9 10 |
| 61. This information is represented in a consistent format. | 0 1 2 3 4 5 6 7 8 9 10 |
| 62. This information is easily obtainable. | 0 1 2 3 4 5 6 7 8 9 10 |
| 63. This information comes from good sources. | 0 1 2 3 4 5 6 7 8 9 10 |
| 64. This information is quickly accessible when needed. | 0 1 2 3 4 5 6 7 8 9 10 |
| 65. This information has sufficient breadth and depth for tasks. | 0 1 2 3 4 5 6 7 8 9 10 |
| 66. This information presents an impartial view. | 0 1 2 3 4 5 6 7 8 9 10 |
| 67. This information is applicable to our work. | 0 1 2 3 4 5 6 7 8 9 10 |
| 68. This information is sufficiently up to date for our work. | 0 1 2 3 4 5 6 7 8 9 10 |
| 69. This information is reliable. | 0 1 2 3 4 5 6 7 8 9 10 |

Section 3: IQ Context Assessment

| | | |
|---|---|---|
| 1. This company has adopted a TQM approach. | N/A | 1  2  3  4  5  6  7  8  9  10 |
| 2. This company has tools that identify deficiencies with this information. | N/A | 1  2  3  4  5  6  7  8  9  10 |
| 3. In this company, there are people whose primary job is to assure the quality of information. | N/A | 1  2  3  4  5  6  7  8  9  10 |
| 4. This company has tools to assure the consistency of this information. | N/A | 1  2  3  4  5  6  7  8  9  10 |
| 5. In this company, employees view continuous quality improvement as a part of their job. | N/A | 1  2  3  4  5  6  7  8  9  10 |
| 6. This company uses TQM to control process quality. | N/A | 1  2  3  4  5  6  7  8  9  10 |
| 7. This company has a specific position or group responsible for information quality. | N/A | 1  2  3  4  5  6  7  8  9  10 |
| 8. This company solves quality problems using one of the popular quality improvement methods such as developed by Deming, Juran, or Crosby. | N/A | 1  2  3  4  5  6  7  8  9  10 |
| 9. In this company, there are designated people whose job is to solve information quality problems. | N/A | 1  2  3  4  5  6  7  8  9  10 |
| 10. This company has tools to assure the completeness of this information. | N/A | 1  2  3  4  5  6  7  8  9  10 |
| 11. In this company, there are designated people who are responsible for the quality of information. | N/A | 1  2  3  4  5  6  7  8  9  10 |
| 12. In this company, employees participate in quality improvement activities. | N/A | 1  2  3  4  5  6  7  8  9  10 |
| 13. This company has tools to assure the correctness of this information. | N/A | 1  2  3  4  5  6  7  8  9  10 |
| 14. This company provides software for aggregating, manipulating and summarizing this information. | N/A | 1  2  3  4  5  6  7  8  9  10 |
| 15. This company is developing a data dictionary to standardize data definitions across different computers or divisions. | N/A | 1  2  3  4  5  6  7  8  9  10 |
| 16. In this company, employees are able to take actions to improve the quality of information. | N/A | 1  2  3  4  5  6  7  8  9  10 |
| 17. This company has recently moved this information to a different hardware or software system. | N/A | 1  2  3  4  5  6  7  8  9  10 |
| 18. In this company, ensuring the quality of this information is the responsibility of those who use the information. | N/A | 1  2  3  4  5  6  7  8  9  10 |
| 19. This company has new (database) software for managing and storing this information. | N/A | 1  2  3  4  5  6  7  8  9  10 |
| 20. In this company, it is relatively easy to improve information as needed. | N/A | 1  2  3  4  5  6  7  8  9  10 |

Thank you very much!

## References

[1]  Codd, E. F., "A Relational Model of Data for Large Shared Data Banks," *Communications of the ACM,* 13(6), 1970, pp. 377–387.

[2]  Codd, E. F., *The Relational Model for Database Management: Version 2.* Addison-Wesley, Reading, MA, 1990.

[3]  CRG, *Information Quality Assessment Survey: Administrator's Guide.* Cambridge Research Group, Cambridge, MA, 1997.

[4]  CRG, *Integrity Analyzer: A Software Tool for TDQM.* Cambridge Research Group, Cambridge, MA, 1997.

[5]  Lee, Y. W., "Why 'Know Why' Knowledge is Useful for Solving Information Quality Problems." In *Proceedings of Americas Conference on Information Systems*, Phoenix, AZ, 1996, pp. 200–202.

[6]  Lee, Y. W., D. M. Strong, L. Pipino, and R. Y. Wang, *A Methodology-based Software Tool for Data Quality Management* (No. TDQM-97-02). MIT TDQM Research Program, Cambridge, MA, 1997.

[7]  Maier, D., *The Theory of Relational Databases.* 1st ed. Computer Science Press, Rockville, MD, 1983.

[8]  Pipino, L., Y. W. Lee, and R. Y. Wang, *Measuring Information Quality* (No. TDQM-97-04). MIT Sloan School of Management, Cambridge, MA, 1998.

[9]  Wang, R. Y., "A Product Perspective on Total Data Quality Management," *Communications of the ACM,* 41(2), 1998, pp. 58–65.

[10] Wang, R. Y., Y. L. Lee, L. Pipino, and D. M. Strong, "Manage Your Information as a Product," *Sloan Management Review,* 39(4), 1998, pp. 95–105.

[11] Wang, R. Y., and D. M. Strong, "Beyond Accuracy: What Data Quality Means to Data Consumers," *Journal of Management Information Systems (JMIS),* 12(4), 1996, pp. 5–34.

# Create Organizational Knowledge

*H*ow can an organization know and act? What does it mean to be a knowledgeable organization? Do some organizations know better than others? What does it take for a company to be continuously knowledgeable regardless of employee turnover? How does a firm learn to create, retain, and reuse organizational knowledge? Above all, why does organizational knowledge matter to companies? Consider Mr. Smith's story.

---

TWO TALES OF CUSTOMER SATISFACTION

SPORTSWEAR COMPANY

*Mr. Smith orders his daughter's snow boots from Sportswear Company. He is not sure about the size. The salesperson on the phone somehow knows his daughter's shoe size and recommends that he order two sizes bigger for the particular pair of boots. Mr. Smith is happy, as is his daughter when the boots are delivered and tried on.*

EYEWEAR COMPANY

*Mr. Smith visits Eyewear Company to order his eyeglasses. He is well prepared with the optometrist's exact prescription for his new eyeglasses. On receipt of the eyeglasses, Mr. Smith has to return them for a rework of the lenses.*

---

In these two scenarios, what is the likelihood that Mr. Smith will call Sportswear Company again for other items or a second pair of boots for his daughter? What is the likelihood that he will return to Eyewear Company for his next pair of eyeglasses? The answer is obvious. Eyewear is losing Mr. Smith as its customer, whereas Sportswear has increased its opportunity for future business with Mr. Smith.

# ORGANIZATIONAL ALZHEIMER'S DISEASE

Success or failure in customer service, such as Mr. Smith's case, is often attributed to one particular salesperson. There is no question that one salesperson makes a difference and indeed good customer service starts with one particular person. Good customer service, however, requires much more than one good salesperson. A company's customer service reveals the competence of this company as a whole. Mr. Smith's story is about how knowledgeable a company is about its product, business process, and customers. Does the company know and remember its customers? Simply put, Mr. Smith's story is a litmus test of organizational Alzheimer's disease. Sportswear passed the test, but Eyewear did not.

Does the salesperson at Sportswear know Mr. Smith? Does the salesperson remember the previous purchases made by Mr. Smith? Does the salesperson remember Mr. Smith's daughter's shoe size? No, not personally. The Sportswear case is a clear example of using well-managed organizational knowledge. The company collects information about customers' purchasing behavior, such as items and sizes for purchases and returns. The company then rearranges, integrates, and reformulates the transactional information with a clear idea of how and why the information can be useful for the company's future business and particularly for the company's internal consumers, salespersons.

Developing a sensibly integrated customer information database from various transactions and making it accessible for the company's internal customers is a clear example of making the organizational memory explicit and accessible for future reuse. This rearranged and readily accessible information is transformed into the company's organizational knowledge when it is shared and reused by salespersons in their specific business context.

When a salesperson answers a customer's call, the organizational knowledge about the customer's purchasing behavior patterns becomes this salesperson's knowledge during the sale. The salesperson understands the procedures and purposes of using this information and asks questions nonintrusively and answers informatively. The salesperson connects the business process with the information so that they work together to serve the external customer in a specific context of a sale. The salesperson is instantly empowered by the company's knowledge about utilizing the customer's purchasing history and patterns. Thus, this knowledge is distributed to the company's internal knowledge consumer, the salesperson who then uses the knowledge to deliver individualized service to the external customer, Mr. Smith [13].

# INFORMATION AND EXPERIENCE ARE KNOWLEDGE SOURCES

Mr. Smith's story illustrates how information and experience attained by various individuals working for different units of an organization can be collected, recorded, and reformulated to create useful and reuseable organizational knowledge that more members can share. To create organizational knowledge, it is important for organizations to recognize that information and experience are the sources. On the one hand, we must uncover the knowledge used and captured in information. On the other hand, we must produce new knowledge based on the information collected and experiences accumulated. Information collected across functions and everyday work experiences accumulated by individuals are a reservoir for tapping organizational knowledge.

## Information Contains Knowledge

Since information is socially constructed, information is not guaranteed to be neutral or objective [21]. Likewise, the information required for organizations may not necessarily be objective. The information that companies collect and use reflects the knowledge employed to produce the information, and the context that created the purpose of and the settings for the knowledge. Companies uncover the knowledge embedded in the information and they develop new knowledge based on the information. This is why firms need to pay closer attention to producing quality information and the entire information manufacturing process. Once the context of information and knowledge used to produce information is divorced from the information, particularly transferred to another database or location, it becomes difficult to identify and reproduce the inherent knowledge from the information.

For example, a hospital's information system contains information that reveals the hospital's clinical procedures. This clinical procedure information is designed to serve mainly the medical reimbursement process. Traditionally, the hospital's database was organized based on fees for medical procedures and Diagnosis Related Groups (DRGs). Naturally, the principles for data collection and storage processes were designed for meeting the specific requirements for insurance reimbursement. The reimbursement was calculated based on medical procedures. Thus, the input data were bundled based on medical procedures, not on patients. A case in point is a major hospital which reorganized its database system [25]. This hampered the hospital's ability to know how much the hospital spent on each patient. This knowledge was required under a new medical reimbursement system. The reorganization of the information structure, collection, and storage processes in the new context helped the hospital to capture the hospital's cost per patient. Without a plan for collection, storage, and reuse, information is lost or available but cannot be retrieved for integration and access for companywide purposes.

## Experience Manifests Knowledge

Experience contains knowledge as knowledge manifests previous experiences. The working experiences of individuals, such as marketing experiences gained from direct interactions and observations of customers, are valuable because they offer an opportunity for analysis and planning for future marketing. The outcome of this analysis is valuable input for revising organizational knowledge. Utilizing such experiences enables a company to transform these experiences into more structured knowledge through analysis and feedback. Organized efforts to analyze a company's business experiences is a critical step toward capturing and creating organizational knowledge.

Bankers Trust's *Corporate Gameware* [11] exemplifies how companies use collective experiences of old-timers to train new employees. The standard bank operations and the common mistakes made by previous employees are captured and reproduced in a new context. With colorful graphics and sound, Bankers Trust's Corporate Gameware is aimed at the generation that grew up on Nintendo. It combines training simulations and learning exercises. Says one managing director, "When you think of computer games, there's lots of engagement but little content. Business has lots of content, but no engagement. Put the two together and you have a way to learn the business through computers that makes sense for this generation."

Corporate Gameware's innovations include game templates that can be modified according to the lessons to be learned or the information to be transmitted. The Battle of the Brains, for example, is a question-and-answer game based on a popular U.S. television game show. It is a "day in the life of a banker" game that simulates difficult decisions a banker must make. The Bankers Trust's business process and approach are to transform experiences captured in the example games so that the company's organizational knowledge about typical procedures are kept and reused by newcomers [11].

# WHAT IS ORGANIZATIONAL KNOWLEDGE?

Organizational knowledge, in the context of business, refers to companywide collective knowledge of its products, services, processes, markets, and customers. Organizational knowledge is created, stored, disseminated, and reused throughout the organization. It is embedded in the company's products, services, and its business processes [14].

Organizational knowledge is not merely a collection of each individual's knowledge in an organization. While knowing something starts with one particular individual, this individual's knowledge may not necessarily represent organizational knowledge. When individual knowledge is not registered, used, or shared with others, it ends at the individual level [3]. Because the nature of organizational knowledge is intangible, a part of it is stored somewhere, such as in a book, product, database, tape, video, or a person. The entirety of a company's organizational knowledge about one area can be observed when the knowledge is used and enacted by an employer. This is why we recommend that not only the knowledge as a final product, but also the processes of production and use of the knowledge in context need to be understood and recorded for reuse by other members.

The critical area is the link between the individual and organizational level, and the functional or departmental and the organizational levels. Short-term purpose versus long-term purpose also needs to be considered for organizational knowledge. Companies must focus on progressing from the individual level to the group, and to the organizational level. To effectively develop organizational knowledge from individual knowledge, companies use network technologies such as Lotus Notes and Internet/intranet technologies. The recent resurgence of interest in organizational knowledge focuses on diffusion of knowledge. Organizational knowledge creation, however, is a key factor for continuous innovation [8, 19], meaningful organizational learning, and developing core competency and intellectual capital [23].

## Organizational Knowledge in Three Modes

Knowledge in an organization is a prerequisite for and a product of organizational learning [2, 3, 5, 27]. Knowledge is applied to, gained from, and accumulated through organizational experiences. This is why it is pertinent to recognize explicitly the different roles individuals play in an organization. Understanding different modes of knowledge helps to reconcile and integrate different views and information about the same product and service.

We identify three modes of knowledge that are pertinent for shaping organizational capabilities [15]:

*Know-what* pertains to factual knowledge.

*Know-how* pertains to procedural knowledge.

*Know-why* pertains to axiomatic knowledge. This aspect explicitly includes knowledge of the reasons and axiomatic assumptions underlying work practices in organizations.

When a firm examines organizational knowledge, it is important to anchor its organizational knowledge in a specific area. Otherwise, the discussion on organizational knowledge loses scope and the direction of the discussion becomes ambiguous. For example, in the area of information quality, organizational knowledge of each mode is gained from experience and the understanding of the objectives and causal relationships underlying the activities involved in collecting, storing, and utilizing information. To capture these three modes of knowledge, companies must identify a target domain knowledge area. We illustrate this for Information Quality (IQ) as follows:

> IQ-related know-what knowledge is the accumulated understanding of the activities and procedures involved in producing, storing, and utilizing information.

> IQ-related know-how knowledge is the accumulated skills for applying routine procedures to known IQ problems.

> IQ-related know-why knowledge is the ability to analyze and discover previously unknown IQ problems or solutions.

## Assess Organizational Knowledge

Based on the three modes of organizational knowledge, we have developed an assessment tool. The graph shown in Figure 5.1, summarizes the assessment of organizational knowledge about IQ in a financial company [14]. The IQ knowledge assessment tool described in Chapter 4 was used to obtain the data [6]. The assessment tool is shown in the Figure 5.1 and the questionnaire is attached in the appendix of this chapter.

A problematic area for this company is information collection. This company has wide gaps of knowledge about IQ among the groups who perform different roles in the information manufacturing system. For example, the information providers have high-level factual and procedural knowledge, but they lack the axiomatic knowledge that is necessary to understand the context and reasons for collecting the information. The information consumers exhibit a relatively high level of knowledge about all aspects of knowledge on information collection. Specifically, information consumers hold a high level of knowledge about what information to collect. Not surprisingly, information custodians (IS professionals in their IS department) have the highest (among the surveyed groups) level of know-what knowledge about information storage and maintenance. Their know-why knowledge about information collection, however, is lower than their knowledge in other areas.

This knowledge assessment can be conducted for different functional areas, databases, locations, and times to gain further insights and to answer questions such as; Which areas need more training? Which groups have both breath and depth of knowledge in specific areas? Which area exhibits the widest gap among different groups? Answers to these questions provide the basis for establishing the directions and methods to improve organizational knowledge across different roles and groups.

With knowledge of the assessment results, the financial company streamlined its information collection formats and restructured its procedures for establishing new customer accounts. The company had an opportunity to resolve information collection problems and develop respective solutions. The company plans to conduct repeated surveys to measure and assess the results of their improvement efforts.

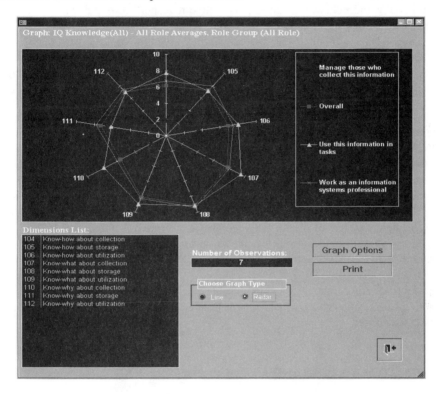

Figure 5.1: Assessment of Organizational Knowledge about Information Quality

(Source: *Cambridge Research Group* [14])

## WHY CREATE ORGANIZATIONAL KNOWLEDGE?

As firms evolve from competition based on cost to value to core competency, knowledge is increasingly recognized as the most valuable asset of the firm [1, 2, 4, 7, 9, 10, 16-19, 22, 23]. Creating organizational knowledge is a prerequisite for any firm to gain competitive advantage. The time it takes for competitors to learn comparable knowledge is an advantage to the firm. Creating and sharing organizational knowledge benefits critical areas such as decision making and companywide learning.

Because organizational knowledge is readily available and accessible, it can speed up decision making and enhance its quality. Effective management of knowledge facilitates companywide learning because solutions found by one employee can be disseminated and used by many others. In turn, the disseminated knowledge can stimulate collaboration among the global workforce which can improve existing solutions — a positive feedback phenomenon. The above benefits translate directly into improved customer satisfaction, cost reduction, and revenue generation. The result is improvements to the company's bottom line.

Customers demand and deserve high-quality products and services. Typically, customer satisfaction is verified by competent salespersons or agents working at the final stage of the value chain of the company's business process. Delivering customer satisfaction requires transforming the company's organizational knowledge into action. It takes the company's strategy, process, technical, and organizational infrastructures to create and share organization knowledge [13]. Cost reduction is achieved by an informed workforce making intelligent decisions and performing mindfully with minimal errors [26]. More importantly, knowledgeable organizations do not reinvent what is invented; they reuse it or enhance the status quo. As a result, innovation is accelerated and cost and time for product development are reduced. All the above factors combine to strengthen market dominance and revenue streams.

In short, creating organizational knowledge is a key factor for innovation, cost reduction, and customer satisfaction, which in turn, generate increased revenue and a competitive position in the market.

## How to Create Organizational Knowledge

Becoming a knowledgeable organization means creating organizational knowledge across all levels and functions of the organization. It means establishing an explicit policy of transforming a company's information and experiences into a company's knowledge for sharing and reuse.

We identify three key processes for creating organizational knowledge. First, information must be of high quality to be transformed into organizational knowledge. Second, the experiences and tacit knowledge of employees must be made explicit. Third, know-what, know-how, and know-why knowledge must be obtained and shared (arrows 1-3 in Figure 5.2).

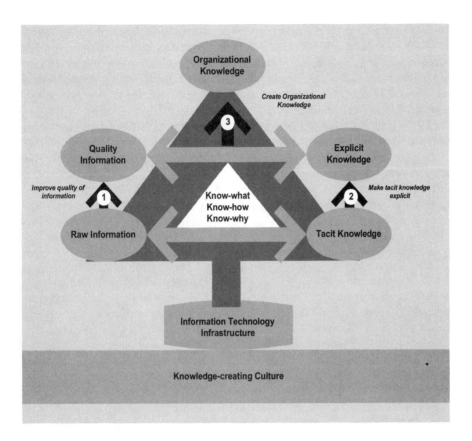

Figure 5.2: Creating Organizational Knowledge

(Source: *Cambridge Research Group* [14])

**Improve IQ**  (Figure 5.2, arrow 1) Companies must improve the quality of their information. Information quality includes the quality dimensions that define fitness-for-use by the information consumers. Improving information quality requires an understanding that information is a product. Companies need to understand the changing information needs of consumers, manage the information production process, and manage the information as a product with a life cycle (see Chapters 2–4 for details).

**Transform tacit knowledge into explicit knowledge** (arrow 2). Companies need to transform tacit knowledge into explicit knowledge. Tacit knowledge is difficult to share [12, 19, 20, 24] when isolated from its source context and the assumptions that hold the meaning of the tacit knowledge. When distributed to members of a company who do not share the context, the tacit knowledge can easily be misinterpreted. This results in an adverse effect on the quality of their decision making and, eventually, the quality of the company's overall performance. Nonaka and Takeuchi [19] describe a good example that explains in detail the tacit knowledge held by a baker. This tacit knowledge represented the baker's life-long baking experiences. These had to be explicitly recorded to build an electromechanical bread maker. Several rounds of experiments with the baker were needed in order to make the baker's tacit knowledge explicit.

    <u>**Obtain and share all modes of knowledge**</u> (arrow 3). Companies must obtain and share know-what, know-how, and know-why knowledge. For organizational knowledge to be explicit, companies must strive to elicit knowledge that encompasses all three aspects. Incomplete knowledge transferred to other departments can hamper the quality of the firm's information, processes, and products. This eventually causes customer dissatisfaction. We illustrate this with the following Eyewear Company case.

# EYEWEAR COMPANY REVISITED

Eyewear Company exemplifies the importance of understanding and obtaining complete organizational knowledge and embedding this knowledge into everyday work practice. As shown in Figure 5.3, know-what knowledge about lens grinding parameters held by the grinders is critical for shaping know-why knowledge needed for opticians. Opticians need to know the reasons for suggesting appropriate lens and frame types for customers. The opticians must be able to easily recognize a complicated lens order so that they can send orders to the special lab that specifically grinds complicated lens. What constitutes a special grinding is well understood by the grinders; the company designated a special lab for this purpose. The opticians, however, did not have the knowledge of the basic parameters for special grinding, and thus, the criteria for processing orders for special grinding were neither well established nor practiced. In sum, the opticians' lack of know-why knowledge about lens order service produced the repeated rework on the complicated lenses, and further dissatisfied the customers.

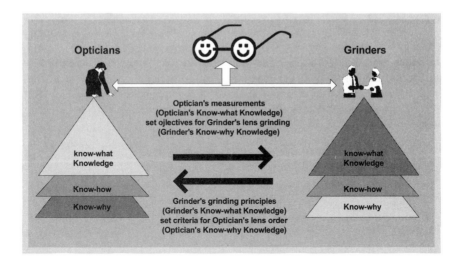

Figure 5.3: Complete Knowledge Creates Quality Products and Service

(Source: *Cambridge Research Group* [14])

The problem occurred in the process that transfers the measurement information from the optician to the lens order that is forwarded to the grinders. The complicated prescriptions and measurements fall into a special-order category. The company designates this job for their special laboratories: the lenses must be ground perfectly for vision, yet remain within the manufacturing safety rules of thickness. The skillful grinders at the special lab are trained to know all the parameters to produce perfect and safe lenses. Among the opticians at the store, only a few old-timers are knowledgeable about the constraints of lens grinding. These experienced opticians know *why* they need to give a complete set of measurement information and consider the effect of the complicated grinding operation on the lenses and frame. This knowledge was tacit and was not explicitly documented. New opticians entered orders through the computerized order systems. The knowledge, particularly know-why knowledge, necessary for opticians was not available, and incomplete at best. The result amounted to regrinding 3 percent of the lens orders.

The company is undergoing a project for recording all knowledge (know-what, know-how, and know-why knowledge) for all processes. This will be used to revise the training materials and the computerized order system at the stores. For a long-term solution, the company is formulating a strategic plan to include knowledge and information quality as its backbone of operation and management: creating "perfect knowledge for perfect vision."

## CONCLUSION

In this chapter we introduced the concept of organizational knowledge and linked the need for quality information to the development of organizational knowledge. We also presented a process to create organizational knowledge. In the next chapter, we will address the management of organizational knowledge, or what is commonly referred to as knowledge management.

# APPENDIX: IQK SURVEY

Information Quality Knowledge Study

(Continued from the IQA Survey)

This study is being conducted in cooperation with your company and MIT's Total Data Quality Management (TDQM) Research Program. We ask you to assess the quality of your organization's information along many dimensions of quality. These quality dimensions all relate in some way to whether the information is "fit for use" in organizational tasks and decision making. We also ask you to characterize your company in terms of its quality activities.

Before filling out this questionnaire, you will be told which information to respond to. This set of information was selected because its quality is important to your company.

Your participation in this study is voluntary. If you object to any questions, you may choose not to respond. However, your cooperation is strongly desired and appreciated. This study can only be successful if you carefully and honestly answer the questions.

©Wang, Strong, and Lee, 1996 - 1997

Please do not duplicate or distribute the questionnaire without explicit consent of the authors.

---

*Section 4: Background Information (This section is for research purposes only)*

---

1.      Briefly explain the ways in which this information is important to your company.

2.      Your background:

| How long have you worked for this company? | How long have you held your current job? | How many years of work experience do you have? |
|---|---|---|
| ____Less than 1 year | ____Less than 1 year | ____Less than 1 year |
| ____1 to 5 years | ____1 to 5 years | ____1 to 5 years |
| ____6 to 10 years | ____6 to 10 years | ____6 to 10 years |
| ____Greater than 10 years | ____Greater than 10 years | ____Greater than 10 years |

| Gender? | Highest educational level or degree? |
|---|---|
| ____Female | ____High school |
| ____Male | ____Associate's degree |
| | ____College degree |
| | ____Graduate degree |

| Section 5 Information Collection | | | |
|---|---|---|---|
| | Very Small | Average | Very large |
| | Disagree | | Strongly Agree |

| | |
|---|---|
| 1.   I know which group collects this information. | 1  2  3  4  5  6  7  8  9  10 |
| 2.   I know how to fix routine problems with collecting this information. | 1  2  3  4  5  6  7  8  9  10 |
| 3.   I know the sources of this information. | 1  2  3  4  5  6  7  8  9  10 |
| 4.   I understand the information collection procedures well enough to recognize why this information is collected incorrectly. | 1  2  3  4  5  6  7  8  9  10 |
| 5.   I know the usual solutions for problems with collecting this information. | 1  2  3  4  5  6  7  8  9  10 |
| 6.   I know the problems encountered in collecting this information. | 1  2  3  4  5  6  7  8  9  10 |
| 7.   I cannot find the causes of new problems in collecting this information. | 1  2  3  4  5  6  7  8  9  10 |
| 8.   I do not know the sources of this information. | 1  2  3  4  5  6  7  8  9  10 |
| 9.   I know why it is difficult to collect all this information. | 1  2  3  4  5  6  7  8  9  10 |
| 10.  I know the standard procedures for correcting deficiencies in information when collecting it. | 1  2  3  4  5  6  7  8  9  10 |
| 11.  I know who creates this information. | 1  2  3  4  5  6  7  8  9  10 |
| 12.  I can detect sources of new problems in collecting this information. | 1  2  3  4  5  6  7  8  9  10 |
| 13.  I know the steps taken to gather this information. | 1  2  3  4  5  6  7  8  9  10 |
| 14.  When typical problems arise with collecting this information, I know how we handle them. | 1  2  3  4  5  6  7  8  9  10 |
| 15.  I cannot diagnose why this collected information is deficient. | 1  2  3  4  5  6  7  8  9  10 |
| 16.  I do not know the usual solutions for problems with collecting this information. | 1  2  3  4  5  6  7  8  9  10 |
| 17.  I can recognize new problems as they arise in collecting this information. | 1  2  3  4  5  6  7  8  9  10 |
| 18.  I do not know which group collects this information. | 1  2  3  4  5  6  7  8  9  10 |
| 19.  I know how to fix recurring problems with collecting this information. | 1  2  3  4  5  6  7  8  9  10 |
| 20.  I know the procedures by which this information is collected. | 1  2  3  4  5  6  7  8  9  10 |
| 21.  I do not know how to fix routine problems with collecting this information. | 1  2  3  4  5  6  7  8  9  10 |

| *Section 6: Information Storage* | Disagree                Strongly Agree |
|---|---|
| 1.  I know the steps taken to store and maintain this information in our computers. | 1  2  3  4  5  6  7  8  9  10 |
| 2.  I know some of the problems in storing this information appropriately in our computers. | 1  2  3  4  5  6  7  8  9  10 |
| 3.  I know how to fix recurring problems with storing this information in our computers. | 1  2  3  4  5  6  7  8  9  10 |
| 4.  I know which group maintains this information in our computers. | 1  2  3  4  5  6  7  8  9  10 |
| 5.  I can recognize new problems as they arise in storing and maintaining this information in our computers. | 1  2  3  4  5  6  7  8  9  10 |
| 6.  When typical problems arise with storing this information in our computers, I know how we handle them. | 1  2  3  4  5  6  7  8  9  10 |
| 7.  I know which software is used for storing this information in our computers. | 1  2  3  4  5  6  7  8  9  10 |
| 8.  I do not know how to fix routine problems with storing this information in our computers. | 1  2  3  4  5  6  7  8  9  10 |
| 9.  I know the procedures used to store this information in our computers. | 1  2  3  4  5  6  7  8  9  10 |
| 10. I know why people have difficulty with computer access procedures for this information. | 1  2  3  4  5  6  7  8  9  10 |
| 11. I understand our computing environment well enough to analyze why this information is stored inadequately. | 1  2  3  4  5  6  7  8  9  10 |
| 12. I know why it is difficult to store all this information in our computers. | 1  2  3  4  5  6  7  8  9  10 |
| 13. I know how to fix routine problems with storing this information in our computers. | 1  2  3  4  5  6  7  8  9  10 |
| 14. I know who maintains this information in our computers. | 1  2  3  4  5  6  7  8  9  10 |
| 15. I know the usual solutions for problems with storing this information in our computers. | 1  2  3  4  5  6  7  8  9  10 |
| 16. I know why it is difficult to store this information in our computers in an easy-to-interpret manner. | 1  2  3  4  5  6  7  8  9  10 |
| 17. I do not know how to fix recurring problems with storing this information in our computers. | 1  2  3  4  5  6  7  8  9  10 |
| 18. I do not know which group maintains this information in our computers. | 1  2  3  4  5  6  7  8  9  10 |
| 19. I know our standard procedures for correcting deficiencies in information when storing it in our computers. | 1  2  3  4  5  6  7  8  9  10 |
| 20. I know which of our computers stores this information. | 1  2  3  4  5  6  7  8  9  10 |
| 21. I know why this information is displayed in this form in our computers. | 1  2  3  4  5  6  7  8  9  10 |

| Section 7: Information Use | Disagree          Strongly Agree |
|---|---|
| 1.  I know which group uses this information. | 1  2  3  4  5  6  7  8  9  10 |
| 2.  I know the usual solutions for problems with using this information. | 1  2  3  4  5  6  7  8  9  10 |
| 3.  I know the steps taken when using this information. | 1  2  3  4  5  6  7  8  9  10 |
| 4.  I do not know how to fix routine problems with using this information. | 1  2  3  4  5  6  7  8  9  10 |
| 5.  I can recognize new problems as they arise in using this information in a new task. | 1  2  3  4  5  6  7  8  9  10 |
| 6.  I can diagnose problems in using this information. | 1  2  3  4  5  6  7  8  9  10 |
| 7.  I know the tasks which require the use of this information. | 1  2  3  4  5  6  7  8  9  10 |
| 8.  I do not know our standard procedures for correcting deficiencies in information when using it. | 1  2  3  4  5  6  7  8  9  10 |
| 9.  I cannot find the causes of new problems in the use of this information. | 1  2  3  4  5  6  7  8  9  10 |
| 10. I know the computer access procedures for obtaining this information. | 1  2  3  4  5  6  7  8  9  10 |
| 11. I know some of the problems in ensuring that this information is used appropriately. | 1  2  3  4  5  6  7  8  9  10 |
| 12. I know who (individual or group) uses this information. | 1  2  3  4  5  6  7  8  9  10 |
| 13. When typical problems, such as interpretation or access, arise with using this information, I know how we handle them. | 1  2  3  4  5  6  7  8  9  10 |
| 14. I cannot recognize when new problems arise in using this information in a new task. | 1  2  3  4  5  6  7  8  9  10 |
| 15. I do not know how to fix recurring problems with using this information. | 1  2  3  4  5  6  7  8  9  10 |
| 16. I know how to fix routine problems with using this information. | 1  2  3  4  5  6  7  8  9  10 |
| 17. I know the procedures in which this information is used. | 1  2  3  4  5  6  7  8  9  10 |
| 18. I do not know which group uses this information. | 1  2  3  4  5  6  7  8  9  10 |
| 19. I can detect sources of new problems in using this information. | 1  2  3  4  5  6  7  8  9  10 |
| 20. I know our standard procedures for correcting deficiencies in information when using it. | 1  2  3  4  5  6  7  8  9  10 |

Additional Comments or Suggestions about this Study:

Thank you very much!

## References

[1] Adler, P. S., "When Knowledge is the Critical Resource, Knowledge Management is the Critical Task," *IEEE Transactions on Engineering Management,* 6(30), 1989, pp. 997–1015.

[2] Argyris, C., *Knowledge for Action: A Guide to Overcoming Barriers to Organizational Change.* Jossey-Bass, San Francisco, CA, 1993.

[3] Argyris, C. and D. A. Schön, *Organizational Learning: A Theory of Action Perspective.* Addison-Wesley Publishing Co., Reading, MA, 1978.

[4] Beers, M. C., T. H. Davenport and S. L. Jarvenpaa, "Improving Knowledge Work Processes," *Sloan Management Review,* Summer), 1996, pp. 53–65.

[5] Cohen, M. D. and P. Bacdayan, "Organizational Routines are Stored as Procedural Memory: Evidence from a Laboratory Study," *Org. Sci.,* 5(4 (November)), 1994, pp. 554–568.

[6] CRG, *Information Quality Assessment Survey: Administrator's Guide.* Cambridge Research Group, Cambridge, MA, 1997.

[7] Davenport, T. and L. Prusak, *Working Knowledge.* Harvard Business School Press, Boston, MA, 1997.

[8] Dougherty, D. and C. Hardy, "Sustained Product Innovation in Large, Mature Organizations: Overcoming Innovation-to-Organization Problems," *Academy of Management Journal,* 39(5), 1996, pp. 1120–1153.

[9] Drucker, P. F., *Post Capitalist Society.* Butterworth Heineman, Oxford, 1993.

[10] Henderson, R. M., Technological Change and the Management of Architectural Knowledge, in *Transforming Education,* T. A. Kochan and M. Useem, Editors. 1992, Sloan School of Management, Boston, MA, 1992.

[11] IBM, *The Learning Organizations: Managing Knowledge for Business Success.* IBM Consulting Group, North Tarrytown, NY, 1996.

[12] Kogut, B. Z., U., "What Firms Do? Coordination, Identity, and Learning," *Organization Science,* 7(5), 1996, pp. 502–518.

[13] Lee, Y., *Collective Knowledge: An Institutional Learning Perspective.* Cambridge Research Group, Cambridge, MA, 1997.

[14] Lee, Y., *Quality Information, Organizational Knowledge, and Core Competency.* Cambridge Research Group, Cambridge, MA, 1997.

[15] Lee, Y. W. Why "Know Why" Knowledge is Useful for Solving Information Quality Problems. in *Proceedings of Americas Conference on Information Systems.* Phoenix, AZ, pp. 200–202, 1996.

[16] Leonard-Barton, D., *Wellsprings of Knowledge: Building and Sustaining the Sources of Innovation*. Harvard Business School Press, Boston, MA, 1995.

[17] Newell, A., "The Knowledge Level," *AI Magazine,* 1981.

[18] Nonaka, I., "The Knowledge-Creating Company," *Harvard Business Review,* 69(6), 1991, pp. 96–104.

[19] Nonaka, I. and H. Takeuchi, *The Knowledge-Creating Company: How Japanese Companies Create the Dynamics of Innovation*. Oxford University Press, New York, NY, 1995.

[20] Polanyi, M., *The Tacit Dimension*. Doubleday, Garden City, NY, 1966.

[21] Popper, K. P., *Objective Knowledge*. Clarendon Press, Oxford, 1972.

[22] Quinn, J. B., *Intellegence Enterprise*. The Free Press, New York, 1992.

[23] Quinn, J. B., P. Anderson and S. Finkelstein, "Managing Professional Intellect: Making the Most of the Best," *Harvard Business Review,* 2(74), 1996, pp. 71–80.

[24] Spender, J. C., "Making Knowledge the Basis of a Dynamic Theory of the Firm," *Strategic Management Journal,* 17(Winter Issue), 1996, pp. 45–62.

[25] Strong, D. M., Y. W. Lee and R. Y. Wang, "Data Quality in Context," *Communications of the ACM,* 40(5), 1997, pp. 103–110.

[26] Weick, K. E., "Collective Mind in Organizations: Heedful Interrelating on Flight Decks," *Administative Science Quarterly,* 3(38), 1993, pp. 357–381.

[27] Weiss, A. R. and P. Birnbaum, "Technological Infrastructure and the Implementation of Technological Strategies," 35(8), 1989, pp. 1014–1026.

# Manage Knowledge as Assets

$K$nowledge management is becoming an idea in good currency. Companies are grappling with creating and reusing organizational knowledge, in part, due to the need to work and compete in the global marketplace. This trend is further accelerated by the presence of an enabling technological infrastructure. In particular, advanced network technology has expanded the capacity and the boundaries of systems applications. Web-based and Internet-, intranet-, and extranet-based applications such as groupware, play an active role in pushing knowledge reuse to a broader and deeper level in its scope and contents.

To some organizations, knowledge management is a shorthand for e-mail, data mining, or file-sharing projects. To others, it means transforming the entire organization into a knowledge creating and sharing entity. Regardless of the disparities in practice, we witness commonalities among these organizations. Knowledge management efforts are aimed at creating and sharing collective knowledge across traditional boundaries.

## POWER OF COLLECTIVE KNOWLEDGE

"You lost, Man," stated the *Boston Herald* on chess master Garry Kasparov's defeat in a seven-game series against IBM's Deep Blue supercomputer (Figure 6.1).

We have witnessed the power of collective knowledge through this well-known event. The chess match between IBM's chess playing computer Deep Blue and chess master Kasparov marks a new beginning of knowledge production and reuse. Deep Blue defeated Kasparov in 1997. The match may appear to have been a contest between a human and the computer. It is not. In fact, the game was a contest between individual effort and collective effort. Deep Blue's decisions and actions during the game represent collective knowledge which has been reproduced. This knowledge has been recorded, programmed, and constructed by humans, collectively, and is based on historical information. Kasparov's decisions and actions at the game represent his individual intuition, emotion, skills, experience, and his individual knowledge.

What lessons can we learn from this match? Deep Blue clearly marks a renewed perspective on collective knowledge. It demonstrates that knowledge originated by multiple individuals at different times can be captured and reused effectively by one entity, Deep Blue. Kasparov's emotion, commitment, and spontaneous judgment make Kasparov's chess moves holistic but hard to predict. The embodiment of Deep Blue clearly departs from the traditional perspective on knowledge. Deep Blue was not an artificially intelligent machine, but rather a number-crunching dynamo that was able to calculate more than 200 million potential chess moves each second, and then tap into a vast knowledge bank of how past chess games were played to evaluate and choose the most promising option. It demonstrated the power of applying today's advanced information technology to assist in collaborative efforts and knowledge sharing to generate winning results. Deep Blue, however, performs intelligently up to the limits of its recorded data bank of chess moves and strategies. Deep Blue's performance symbolizes the power of a firm's collective knowledge. Just imagine Kasparov's chess-playing capability aided by Deep Blue! Kasparov represents an empowered knowledge worker [12].

In short, firms must capture and record their previous experiences and lessons learned so that all individuals who work as agents of the firm can readily use the firm's reproduced knowledge for their business engagements at different times, in different locations, and with different media.

Figure 6.1: Deep Blue vs. Kasparov

(Source: *International Business Machines* [11])

# WHAT IS KNOWLEDGE MANAGEMENT?

Everyone has a notion of knowledge management but it is hard to pinpoint what we mean by knowledge management in practice. One simple but useful exercise IBM consultants have conducted is simply asking the following question: If you had five minutes to rescue key assets of your business from fire, which would you choose? Experience has shown that the answers of typical executives have their basis in critical organizational knowledge [7].

We define knowledge management as organizing and structuring institutional processes, mechanisms, and infrastructures to create, store, and reuse organizational knowledge. Because managing collective knowledge in a firm is interconnected with various areas of organizational performance, knowledge management needs leadership from the top, leadership that transcends functional and hierarchical boundaries.

Despite the increasing attention as a critical area, knowledge management is not sufficiently recognized as a core discipline that affects the bottom line. Management usually focuses on profits and has a narrow view of knowledge assets. Some firms define knowledge-related assets as royalties and patents [1]. These are point-in-time knowledge artifacts. They do not represent a dynamic process of identifying, storing, accessing, learning, sharing, and reusing knowledge across the organization and extended enterprise. Unlike equipment, buildings, or accounts receivable, management of knowledge assets does not appear on the company's financial and accounting ledgers. A few companies, such as Skandia of Sweden, present exceptions to this rule [4].

## Why Knowledge Management?

As in any other area of management, organizational knowledge must be managed using a well-established methodology. A firm's knowledge is hard to replace or replicate. It is an asset. It is the essence of the firm's core competency. Companies exploit knowledge management for business reasons. Managing a firm's knowledge assets increases the speed in the delivery of products and services because knowledge is reused instead of reinvented. Consequently, costs are reduced and profits increased.

Productive firms compete based on their knowledge. Businesses evolve from competing on cost, to competing on value, to competing on knowledge. A cost-oriented firm does not pay attention to knowledge management. A value-oriented firm is customer driven. As such, it is more likely to adopt a knowledge management philosophy. A knowledge-oriented firm takes knowledge management seriously. It incorporates principles and methods of knowledge management into all aspects of its business strategies and processes [6].

## How to Manage Knowledge Assets

Organizational knowledge can be managed with a top-down or bottom-up approach. A firm that follows a top-down approach first initiates an assessment of the firm's core knowledge, which is fundamental to the business. Once the assessment is completed, the core knowledge asset is identified. Next, the firm develops a strategy and establishes technical infrastructures, organizational mechanisms, and business processes necessary for managing the core knowledge as an asset. Finally, the firm makes decisions on how to embed knowledge management in everyday business processes. It also ensures that the appropriate mindset becomes part of the firm's culture.

In the bottom-up approach, a firm follows the path of knowledge creation and reuse, which is a knowledge "harvesting" process. Knowledge hunting, harvesting, and hardening are the terms used by firms such as IBM [9]. Knowledge hunting refers to the process of collecting knowledge, harvesting the process of filtering, and hardening the process of structuring tacit, useful knowledge into explicit, reuseable knowledge. Once the knowledge is created, the firm undertakes the "hardening" process. The process of knowledge hardening begins with applying harvested organizational knowledge to specific business contexts.

The application of organizational knowledge to a particular business context produces best practices (arrow 4, Figure 6.2). Once the firm has developed its best practices in the critical business areas, the knowledge that generalizes beyond the original context is identified and retained as a core competency.

Core competency is the end product of harvesting and hardening organizational knowledge. It can be transferred and reused efficiently and effectively across functional areas (arrow 5).

Firms practice knowledge management using a top-down approach, bottom-up approach, or a combination of the two. The top-down approach focuses on managing the hardening process of organizational knowledge (arrows 4-5). The bottom-up approach focuses on harvesting organizational knowledge (arrows 1-3).

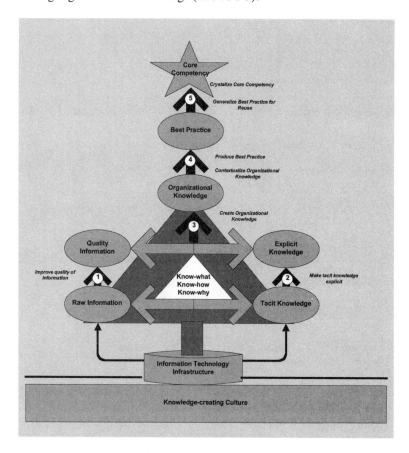

Figure 6.2: From Organizational Knowledge to Core Competency

(Source: *Cambridge Research Group* [13])

## Platform for Knowledge Management

Knowledge management requires addressing both organizational and technological issues. The way in which knowledge is transferred is different from that of physical goods. Knowledge is transferred by distribution, propagation, and interaction. Knowledge can be transferred without the original owner's authorization or awareness. The value of the knowledge output created by the knowledge receivers can be far greater than the original producer and is dependent on the individual mental process and application context. For example, at IBM they identify four major platforms (Figure 6.3) that are used to direct knowledge sharing and collaboration. Its vision is to embed knowledge management into the fabric of their business operations. The platform includes four drivers:

> making knowledge visible,
>
> building knowledge intensity,
>
> building knowledge infrastructure and deployment, and
>
> developing a knowledge culture.

Increasing knowledge intensity and addressing cultural change remain the most challenging issues.

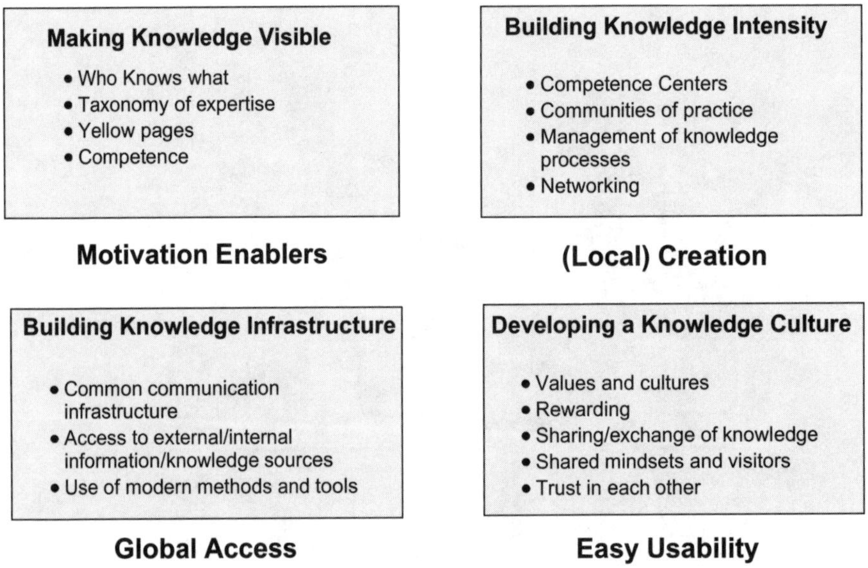

| **Making Knowledge Visible**<br><br>• Who Knows what<br>• Taxonomy of expertise<br>• Yellow pages<br>• Competence | **Building Knowledge Intensity**<br><br>• Competence Centers<br>• Communities of practice<br>• Management of knowledge processes<br>• Networking |
|---|---|
| **Motivation Enablers** | **(Local) Creation** |
| **Building Knowledge Infrastructure**<br><br>• Common communication infrastructure<br>• Access to external/internal information/knowledge sources<br>• Use of modern methods and tools | **Developing a Knowledge Culture**<br><br>• Values and cultures<br>• Rewarding<br>• Sharing/exchange of knowledge<br>• Shared mindsets and visitors<br>• Trust in each other |
| **Global Access** | **Easy Usability** |

Figure 6.3: Knowledge Management Platform

(Source: *International Business Machines* [9])

# Ten Strategies for Knowledge Management

Firms develop and implement pragmatic strategies for knowledge Management [3, 9, 14-16]. We describe ten strategies that have been successfully employed by the early adopters of knowledge management. Each strategy focuses on a different aspect of knowledge management, yet the ten strategies are related.

## 1. Establish a Knowledge Management Methodology

Managing the knowledge assets of a firm requires a common process and a common language. The roles and responsibilities involved in knowledge management must be well understood by all participants. As part of creating and sharing a common language in knowledge management, IBM has developed the Intellectual Capital Management (ICM) methodology, as shown in Figure 6.4. The ICM methodology incorporates the following key components [8, 9]:

A *vision* that values sharing and reusing knowledge

*Processes* for efficiently gathering, evaluating, structuring, and distributing intellectual capital

A *competency community* consisting of knowledge workers in a core competency area

*Technologies* that enable companywide knowledge sharing

*Incentives* to encourage intellectual capital contribution and reuse

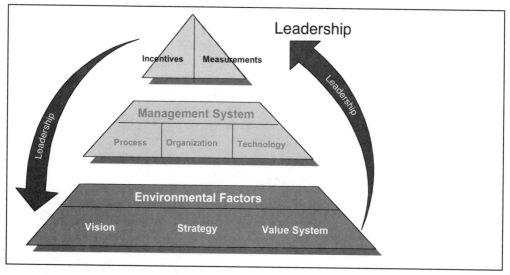

Figure 6.4: IBM's Intellectual Capital Management Methodology
(Source: *International Business Machines* [9])

This methodology is developed at IBM to feed the knowledge obtained from a project back to its competency community. This reduces the cycle time in transferring knowledge gained from specific projects. Because of the temporal nature of projects such as consulting engagements, it is critical that the knowledge gained from these projects be harvested, hardened, and reused.

Since 1994, the IBM Global Services has employed ICM methodology to support intellectual capital and asset reuse for their engagement teams. The purpose of using ICM is to institutionalize the knowledge management process throughout IBM Global Services and Global Industries [9].

## 2. Designate a Pointperson

Many early adopters of knowledge management have created a focal point for accountability. The most common focal point is the Chief Knowledge Officer (CKO), whose responsibility is to oversee knowledge management for the firm. Regardless of the aliases used for CKO, firms need a person to be in charge of promoting and managing the activities of knowledge management in the firm. Appointing a CKO clearly signals that the company is committed to knowledge management. The CKO is responsible for overseeing the harvesting and hardening of organizational knowledge from knowledge workers representing different disciplinary areas, project teams, and geographic locations. The CKO is an administrator, a planner, and a marketer of the firm's knowledge assets. As an administrator, the CKO seeks to maximize the value of the company's knowledge assets. As a planner, the CKO provides the key leadership in designing and implementing knowledge management strategies to guide the process of managing the knowledge assets. As a marketer, the CKO directs the campaign to market knowledge assets internally and externally.

In large organizations, the CKO often delegates the management responsibilities to local department managers who are responsible for domain-specific knowledge. As re-engineering of the organization progresses and the organizational structure becomes more process oriented, as opposed to domain specific, the CKO assigns the process managers the responsibility for knowledge management of a specific process. The CKO then oversees the firm's knowledge assets across domains and processes.

## 3. Empower Knowledge Workers

Knowledge workers are the source of knowledge and its derivatives. A key to successful knowledge management is to empower and leverage knowledge workers by making them an essential component of a knowledge management system. Empowering the workforce must be a firm's fundamental commitment instead of merely a line in the mission statement. A better trained workforce strengthens the firm's core competency. Management must understand that the empowerment of the knowledge worker establishes communities of competent agents for the firm

There are other reasons to institute empowerment policies in firms. The effects of disintermediation and globalization are increasingly being experienced by firms. This changing environment demands increased decision making at the lower levels of the firm. It requires that more organizational knowledge be available. All levels of decision makers, therefore, need to acquire new competencies necessary to operate in the market. In addition, an increasing trend toward group work and virtual teaming demands more management and technical support for knowledge exchange. The knowledge harvested and hardened in the knowledge management system should be made available to all members of an organization.

To create, share, and transfer organizational knowledge, all participants must play their roles in identifying their tacit and explicit knowledge. To achieve this end, the management team, the organizational culture, and the incentive structure must create a conducive environment. Management must carefully identify and eliminate inhibitors that prevent the creation and sharing of knowledge within and across departments. A company's value, incentive, and reward system must work coherently with its empowerment policy.

To implement an empowerment policy, two levels of programs must be launched. The first level involves skill management programs based on the domain knowledge of knowledge workers. For example, Rover in Britain and Levi in the United States engage in education and training policies as a critical part of empowering their knowledge workers [10]. The second level involves integrating the knowledge of the workforce with the business processes and information systems.

# 4. Manage Customer-Centric Knowledge

Customer-centric knowledge management is a management approach that focuses on knowledge about the customer. Externally, it aims at improving customer satisfaction, which in turn, strengthens the firm's competitive position in its market. Internally, it aims at transforming the firm's operation into an agile operation based on the knowledge of and the feedback from customers, which in turn, strengthens the firm's internal performance. Practicing agile operation means rapidly reconfiguring business operations and delivering products and services that fit the changing needs of customers. It requires the firm to transform the information collected on customer behaviors into knowledge that can be reused to gain market share.

To achieve customer-centric knowledge management, firms must improve two key areas. First, firms must streamline the business processes based on information and knowledge gained from customers. Second, firms must restructure their information. They need to adopt the view that information flows from customers to the firms, not the other way around. *Customer-centric systems* capture this view of customer information flow. To restructure customer information, firms must follow the following five steps:

Define their customers,

Understand their customers' changing needs over time,

Identify the knowledge that can be used to differentiate customers,

Integrate information across product/service lines producing a common customer database, and

Link all customer-related activities to the common customer database.

Within the knowledge management process, firms require a model that specifically structures how information collected from customers will be used in business operations for customer care management. Figure 6.5 illustrates the framework used at a leading Japanese office product manufacturer for its customer knowledge management.

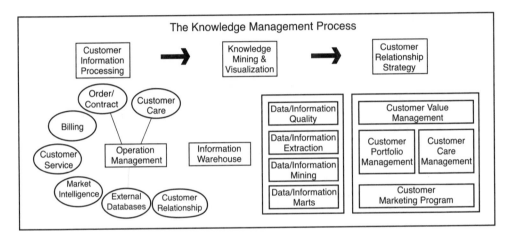

Figure 6.5: A Framework for Customer-centric Knowledge Management

(Source: *International Business Machines* [5])

Using the bottom-up approach to knowledge management, this framework begins with customer information collected from various business operations and stored in an information warehouse. This information is further improved, extracted, and analyzed. The results are harvested and hardened knowledge that is reused in developing customer relationship strategies encompassing customer value management, customer portfolio management, customer care management, and customer marketing programs.

Projects such as data mining and data warehousing represent common responses to retrieving and restructuring customer-centric knowledge. Companies also streamline their business processes to improve the relationship with their customers. The following example reported by the *Wall Street Journal* illustrates how BMW moved their distribution channel closer to customers.

---

**DESIGN YOUR OWN CAR: CUSTOMIZED ORDER AT BMW**

BMW's new retailing program has been rolled out at 5 of its 350 U.S. dealerships. Instead of the usual sales team of three (salesperson, manager, and finance officer), a single "customer counselor" is assigned to every car being sold. The counselor deals directly with the customer, overseeing everything from customizing and purchasing of the vehicle to maintenance.

The BMW counselors will use a new multimedia ordering system to place, track, and display on-line orders for customized vehicles. BMW wants to put more emphasis on selling cars customized to order rather than from inventory. One of the criticisms of traditional auto retailing is that salespeople are under tremendous pressure to unload vehicles in stock rather than trying to meet a customer's individual wants.

As of May 1997, BMW had increased its share of the U.S. market to 0.8 percent from 0.6 percent a year earlier. For all 1996, BMW's share of the U.S. market amounted to 0.7 percent. The new program is expected to cut average BMW inventory levels to about a 10-day supply of vehicles from the present 30. That is already about half of what most U.S. automakers currently consider adequate to ensure sufficient customer choice.

---

## 5. Manage Core Competencies

Managing knowledge concerns management of the domains of knowledge that customers value. To successfully compete in the future a company must be capable of enlarging its opportunity horizon. This requires top management to view the company as a portfolio of core competencies rather than a portfolio of individual business units. Business units are typically defined in terms of a specific product-market focus, whereas core competencies connote a broad class of customer benefits such as "user friendliness" at Apple, "pocketability" at Sony, and "untethered communications" at Motorola.

Managing knowledge assets is necessary for producing a firm's core competencies. A core competency is the end product of combining human capital, processes, intellectual and intangible assets, and technologies to enable a company to provide a unique benefit to customers (Figure 6.6). It represents the sum of learning in the areas across individuals, business units, and product/services.

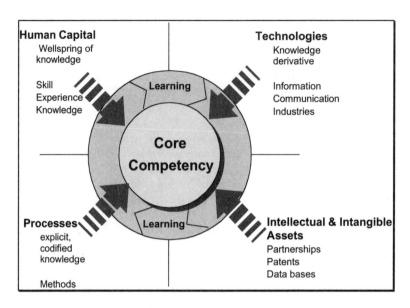

Figure 6.6: Manage Core Competency


(Source: *International Business Machines* [6])

   A core competency is not easily replicated by other firms because it is an organizational capability (not individual) that has been created by combining knowledge assets, business processes, and supporting technology. This strategy is often used in knowledge-intensive firms, such as professional service firms. Firms considered leading edge in other industries also use their competencies effectively. Examples of core competencies in various companies are shown in Figure 6.7.

| Companies | Market Dynamics | Product Facilities | Vendor Relationships | Competency |
|---|---|---|---|---|
| **Nike** | Rapid Change | None | Suppliers | Research, designing and marketing high-tech, athletic footwear |
| **Reebok** | Rapid Change | None | Suppliers | Designing and marketing women's fitness footwear |
| **Charles Schwab** | Rapid Change | None | Partners | High-value, low-cost service provider in financial service industry |
| **Dell** | Rapid Change | Assemble | Suppliers | Modular component electronics |
| **Honda** | Fundamental Shift | Key Engine Components Only | Suppliers | Small engine technology |
| **Canon** | Growth | Assemble | Suppliers | Opto-electronics & imaging |
| **Sony** | Dynamic | Assemble | Suppliers | Miniaturization; Psycho-graphics |
| **Ikea** | Mature with unmet need | Limited | Suppliers with idle production capacities | Designing and packaging modular goods |

Figure 6.7: Examples of Core Competency-based Business

(Source: *International Business Machines* [6])

   Firms must manage knowledge assets and the derivatives of applying knowledge. Examples of knowledge assets include methodologies, tools, techniques, analytics, intellectual property, priced knowledge derivatives, packaged solutions, and customer knowledge. In particular, the firm's knowledge assets that are part of the core competency must be identified, recorded, shared, and protected. The power of competencies becomes clear when corporate architectures are identified and reconfigured dynamically according to business change. An example of competency reconfiguration is shown in Figure 6.8.

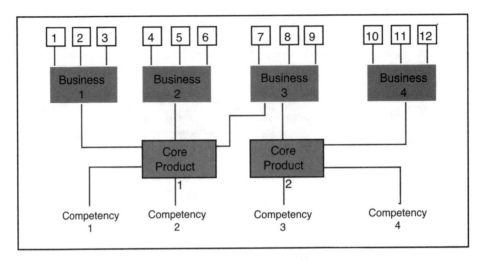

Figure 6.8: Configuration of Competencies for Business Solutions

(Source: *International Business Machines* [6])

To effectively manage competency, three major processes are needed: (1) develop and identify competency, (2) formalize and deploy competency, and (3) protect, extend, and reconfigure competency. To further maximize asset reuse, the processes used by the firm must be mapped out. Figure 6.9 illustrates IBM's approach of competency networks mapped into industry-domain solutions. The resulting structure provides a foundation for a consistent, knowledge-based approach for sharing intellectual capital. It maximizes reuse of common structures and implementations. It also improves the process of customizing, delivering, and enhancing solutions. The intellectual assets reflect experiences and best practices in customer solutions. They encompass intellectual capital such as business architecture, business models, technical architectures, methods, and tools.

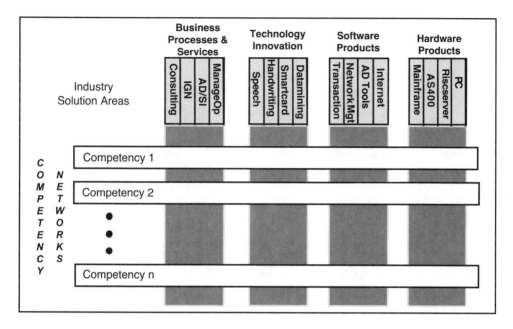

Figure 6.9: IBM's Approach to Competency across Industries

(Source: *International Business Machines* [6])

# 6. Foster Collaboration and Innovation

Continuous innovation must be at the center of knowledge management, for the optimum value of knowledge is realized when ideas are turned into innovative solutions. Companies are constantly searching for ways to effectively manage people and processes without the bureaucracy that stifles creativity and innovation. Accelerating the speed of innovation depends on how well the organization fosters collaboration. A 1996 study [10], conducted by IBM in cooperation with the Economist Intelligence Unit, indicates that organizational values are responsible for ineffective cross-functional communications. The study uncovered the four key points to foster collaboration and cooperation.

Emphasize the value of teamwork, learning, sharing, trust, and flexibility.

Seek the leadership who focuses on team building that integrates performance and learning, shares visions and ideas, and fosters collaboration in diverse configurations.

Utilize the partnerships within the organization.

Maintain close alliances with suppliers, customers and even competitors to form a collaborative community to maximize growth and opportunities.

Leaders who foster collaboration are mentors, moderators, and miners. They should have the ability to guide the policy, to facilitate the collaborative process, and to build knowledge and solutions. As mentors, they guide the process of interaction and communication, promote shared vision, inspire and support learning and innovation, and direct and lead the planning and implementation of collaborative policies and strategies. As moderators, they facilitate the collaborative process, provide an open, interactive environment, assist the team process of ongoing dialogue and decision making, coordinate cross-business, cross-functional collaboration, reconcile conflicts, provide alternative solutions, and nurture interpersonal relationships and interdependency. As miners, they cultivate and develop the learning and collaborative environment, identify and reward innovative individuals and teams, promote and enhance system thinking and scenario planning, create expectation and amplify collaborative powers, and design and create the process of capturing emerging knowledge and delivering innovative solutions.

The IBM study [10] exemplifies an insurance company working as a virtual global team. The insurance company linked every salesperson to everyone else in the business. Collaboration technologies enabled the company to effectively engage in sales and technical support of customers. Although their technology ranking is "medium" compared with other high-tech companies, their laptop office technology ranked high for a collaborative computing environment. They exploited the e-mail, database, and forum environment for collaboration.

Providing information infrastructure further facilitates collaboration. Figure 6.10 depicts one such infrastructure that IBM provides. Another example is Buckman Laboratory that employs the knowledge network, K'Netix, to provide e-mail and seven forums. Each forum includes a message board, a library, and a virtual conference room [10].

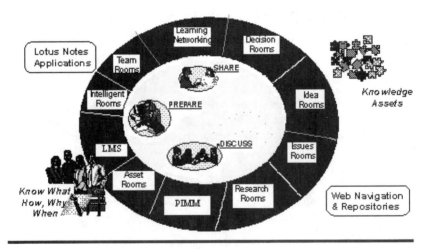

Figure 6.10: Information Infrastructure for Collaboration
(Source: *International Business Machines* [6])

Innovation starts with an individual or a group of individuals. Strategy for innovation must center on cultivating human capabilities. How to cultivate and unlock the creative potential of all is one of the major tasks of knowledge management. Innovation must be embedded in every phase of the knowledge management plans. These plans should cover the areas of business strategy, value creation, and technology. They must promote the principles and practice of innovation, identify innovative teams, offer support structure, and provide incentives for innovation efforts. Although the innovation process may be long and unpredictable, the policy of explicitly encouraging and supporting innovative activities is the only way to foster the creative solutions necessary for the organization to survive in this dynamic business environment.

Successful innovation can be the key to prosperity. It may also be the ultimate source of survival. Of the 500 companies that make up the *Fortune* index, 50 to 60 percent of them disappear every ten years. To adapt and excel in the global knowledge-based economy, companies must create organizational infrastructure where innovation is cultivated and promoted. Companies may also need to preserve high degrees of uncertainty, diversity, and turbulence within the organization to maintain the environment of creativity and long-term viability. The company of the future is not only a "learning organization," or an "intelligent organization," but also an "innovative organization." Innovative organizations create and share organizational knowledge.

## 7. Learn from Best Practices

Successful firms learn from best practices that are produced either internally or externally. Best practices can come from other industries as well. Companies must provide a networked environment for recording and sharing best practices.

IBM has structured their knowledge assets based on business processes. It provides an extensive Lotus Notes network. The company has developed a best-practices database to record and share project solutions. Their business strategy is fundamentally a knowledge creation and reuse strategy since they are in the business of transferring knowledge to their clients.

A global semiconductor company focuses on sharing best practices as a way of knowledge transfer and innovation. They have established the office of best practices. The best-practice office provides a facilitator network in the form of a professional help desk and coordinates the recording and reuse of best practices. Their key message is, "Don't reinvent what has already been discovered."

Firms also learn from best practices developed by other firms. Conferences and consortia provide a forum for learning about best practices.

## 8. Extend Knowledge Sourcing

Knowledge sourcing refers to a method of retrieving information from multiple sources and delivering value-added knowledge for customers to solve business problems. The media for retrieval and delivery of the knowledge product include intranets, the Internet, and extranets. Knowledge sourcing is provided in the context of a domain of knowledge, a business discipline, or a competency of a firm. This is the electronic equivalent of conducting a library search or requesting a research study to gain knowledge and solve business problems. Competitive analysis, market research, and financial analysis are the product examples. Information collected, integrated, and analyzed is posted on an Internet site as "yellow pages," the knowledge products. This is one way in which information retrieved from multiple sources is packaged into a knowledge product. As technology advances rapidly and accessibility improves, knowledge sourcing will become a more important mechanism for entrepreneurial firms to efficiently provide business solutions electronically to consumers.

The Internet and extranets create a new dimension and opportunity for "information-related products." These products include corporate image, marketing messages, customer support, news, entertainment, business knowledge, and market intelligence. Both Gartner Group and BPR strategic analysis reports indicate that the essential role of IS in organizations will expand over the next five years from transaction processing to the enabling of information and knowledge management. Therefore, information and knowledge management will become the dominant driver of IS organizations. IS will be required to cover the extended enterprise, which includes customers, manufacturing and development divisions, geographic marketing units, trading partners, and vendors.

For internal yellow pages, firms must identify what the contents are (subjects of the contents), where the original information comes from (sources of the contents), and who developed the contents (entity of knowledge developer). Before developing their yellow pages, firms must also consider what the total cost of development is, who pays for the cost, how the cost is measured, and how the policy on liability, privacy, and ethical issues must be established.

## 9. Interconnect Communities of Expertise

Firms interconnect internal and external communities of expertise [2]. The internal experts have the primary responsibility for problem solving. The external experts constitute the network of experts who are loosely connected to the senior management of the firm. Firms interconnect their internal communities of experts by using electronic libraries, often called "knowledge banks" or "white pages." They establish electronic corporate white pages to share documents and information. The following is a semiconductor company's system.

---

**CORPORATE WHITE PAGES CONNECT COMMUNITIES OF EXPERTISE**

A computer company utilizes its Corporate White Pages (CWP) to network subject-matter experts. Their "professional profiles" are recorded and maintained. They also implemented a corporate skills repository in the human resources department. This repository is integrated into, and accessible from, the corporate yellow pages. Electronic mail and newsgroup functions are provided using the same underlying technology suite as CWP uses; news groups are accessible through the browser's built-in news-reading capability and e-mail discussions on shared aliases are treated as "documents" by CWP and archived for future reference by interested consumers [10].

---

External experts do not participate in daily operations. They participate as experts in a specific area. A pool of networked experts serve as sounding boards and advisors. They consult on specific issues in question and test and discuss new ideas. Consulting companies, among others, are using these communities of experts extensively. Firms need to integrate the knowledge gained from the external experts with their internal knowledge management efforts. Both internal and external communities of experts function as a competency network, which is the engine for creating, sharing, and reusing knowledge assets in firms.

### Competency Networks

IBM has addressed these aims through the implementation of competency networks —informal networks of practitioners—supported by common processes, tools, and other drivers that enable IBM professionals to create, identify, store, and efficiently reuse intellectual capital. They have implemented asset management processes which identify, harvest, and harden structured assets that have high potential in customer solutions. Moreover, they have established a program to drive community participation. Ultimately, the efforts of the ICM team have culminated in the creation of the ICM AssetWeb, a dynamic Lotus Notes-based collaboration system that gives practitioners in IBM the power to leverage intellectual capital.

## 10. Report the Measured Value of Knowledge Asset

A clear measure that quantifies how knowledge management contributes to the business is needed. Skandia, a Stockholm-based insurance company has established a methodology for recording knowledge assets in their financial report [4]. Skandia links the value of intellectual capital to their balance sheet. It supplements its annual financial report with an emphasis on qualitative and quantitative value of their intellectual capital. Extensions of traditional measures for customers, processes, and "competence" are some of the ways Skandia reports to its shareholders. Skandia believes that the real return on its business expense is human resource training. Some may interpret this as dollars spent on education and training. Skandia interprets it as a knowledge asset. They believe that the difference between market capitalization and assets is the value of the business's intellectual capital.

Skandia [4] differentiates two kinds of capital: human capital and structural capital. Human capital refers to the knowledge, skill, and capability of individual employees to provide solutions to customer problems. Structural capital is the items that remain within the firm when employees go home, such as customer files, software codes, and trademarks.

They use the management tool Navigator to supplement traditional accounting so that they can generate a report that combines financial and nonfinancial indicators of the company's assets.

The basis for reporting the measured value of a knowledge asset is the knowledge-based business plan. This business plan sets the guidelines for the management and use of knowledge assets. It seeks to create a healthy asset-based business. The business plan provides the guidelines and directions for managing the organizational knowledge. It shows when, why, where, and to what extent the organization must invest in or exploit knowledge. It is the basic blueprint for managing organization knowledge. The business plan should cover

Description of the asset

Opportunity and competitive analysis

Forecasts and marketing and sales strategies

Knowledge development plan

Support plan

Financial projections

The plan describes the who, what, where, when, why, and how that keep the knowledge development concept foremost in the minds of the organization's executives and managers. The plan's structure allows the asset manager to make critical business decisions, understand the financial aspects of asset management, anticipate and avoid obstacles, and exploit and reevaluate knowledge assets' applications. The business plan sets specific goals and measurements. Business plans can be tailored to individual assets or a group of assets to form the subplans.

## CONCLUSION

Knowledge management fundamentally changes how a firm conducts business. Knowledge management is a new way of leveraging the value derived from the collective knowledge of customers, expertise, processes, and products and services. Companies are leveraging their knowledge capital for competitive advantage in the market. Effectively managing knowledge as a strategic asset will enable companies to adapt to new ways of thinking, to respond to change quickly and easily, and to adopt a broader view when defining products and services.

A successful knowledge management effort requires leadership with vision, commitment, and an organizational culture that facilitates collaboration. The process of managing knowledge involves designing and implementing policies and procedures that utilize technology, measure performance, and provide rewards for collaboration and innovation. As companies continue to explore ways to strengthen their competitive advantage, they need to manage their intellectual assets prudently. In this age of information explosion, knowledge will be the most valuable asset of the company and the "innovative organization" is the way of the future.

In this chapter, we introduced the concept of knowledge management and described ten strategies for knowledge management. In the next chapter, we present an approach for creating customizable solutions from the carefully managed organizational knowledge.

## References

[1]   Brooking, A., *Intellectual Capital: Core Asset for the Third Millennium Enterprise*. International Thomson Business Press, London, 1996.

[2]   Brown, J. S. and P. Duguid, "Organizational Learning and Communities-of-Practice; Toward a Unified View of Working, Learning and Innovation," *Organization Science*, 2(1), 1991, pp. 40–57.

[3]   Davenport, T. and L. Prusak, *Working Knowledge*. Harvard Business School Press, Boston, MA, 1997.

[4]   Edvinsson, L. and M. Malone, *Intellectual Capital: Realizing Your Company's True Value by Finding Its Hidden Brain Power*. Harper Business, New York, NY, 1997.

[5]   Hu, J., K. T. Huang, K. Kuse, G. Su and K. Wang, "Customer Information Quality and Knowledge Management: A Case Study Using Knowledge Cockpit," *Journal of Knowledge Management*, 1(3), 1998, pp. 225–236.

[6]   Huang, K. T. "Creating and Exploiting Organizational Knowledge to Speed up Business Growth," in IBM Internal Report, North Tarrytown, NY: IBM, 1996.

[7]   Huang, K. T., "Capitalizing, Collective Knowledge for Winning, Execution, and Teamwork," *Journal of Knowledge Management*, 1(2), 1997, pp. 149–156.

[8]   Huang, K. T. "Knowledge Is Power: So Use It or Lose It," in http://www.ibm.com/services/articles/inttelcapsum.html: IBM, 1998.

[9]   Huang, K. T., "Capitalizing on Intellectual Assets, not Infrastructure," *IBM Systems Journal*, Forthcoming.

[10]  IBM, *The Learning Organizations: Managing Knowledge for Business Success*. IBM Consulting Group, North Tarrytown, NY, 1996.

[11]  IBM "Kasparov beats Deep Blue 4-2," in http://www.chess.ibm.park.org/, 1997.

[12]  Lee, Y., *Collective Knowledge: An Institutional Learning Perspective*. Cambridge Research Group, Cambridge, MA, 1997.

[13]  Lee, Y., *Quality Information, Organizational Knowledge, and Core Competency*. Cambridge Research Group, Cambridge, MA, 1997.

[14]  Nonaka, I. and H. Takeuchi, *The Knowledge-Creating Company: How Japanese Companies Create the Dynamics of Innovation*. Oxford University Press, New York, NY, 1995.

15]  Quinn, J. B., P. Anderson and S. Finkelstein, "Managing Professional Intellect: Making the Most of the Best," *Harvard Business Review,* 2(74), 1996, pp. 71–80.

[16] Quinn, J. B., J. J. Baruch and K. A. Zien, *Innovation Explosion: Using Intellect and Software to Revolutionize Growth Strategies*. The Free Press, New York, NY, 1997.

# Create Customized Solutions

*H*ow does a company keep creating customized solutions when customers, their environment, and technology keep changing? It resembles the challenge of hitting a moving target. In fact, at a higher, logical level, firms confront challenges that are not necessarily new. One such example is to deliver products and services fit for customers' needs. We revisit Deep Blue, the chess-playing system [5]. In the previous chapter, we uncovered the power of collective knowledge embedded in Deep Blue. Deep Blue offers a new way of analyzing strategies and finding solutions for each chess move. The debut and the victory of Deep Blue also mark a new way of enlarging the pool of possible solutions for reuse. By structuring and enlarging the pool of solutions, Deep Blue can efficiently tailor the solutions to specific problems each chess move presents. Because of the expanded pool of reuseable solutions, the possible match between the type of problem and the solution becomes more precise and diverse. One such example is customer feedback, which expands the pool and can be transformed into new customized solutions [6].

Companies continue to confront business challenges ranging from transforming existing legacy business to creating new product lines to developing information infrastructure for innovative solutions. Regardless of the variety of challenges, the winning business solutions are always the ones that fit the customer's needs best. Mass customization is one such strategy [7] to combine efficiency of mass production with effectiveness of customization. In order to meet these challenges, companies must adopt a new organizational process and culture that explicitly structure and reuse various solutions and collective knowledge. They must institutionalize a process to collect, store, and reuse solutions [6]. Firms can reuse this collective knowledge to create yet new and innovative solutions more effectively and efficiently at different times, in different locations, through different media. Structured, collective knowledge is accessible by members of the knowledge base. They benefit from the knowledge base and, in turn, further improve the knowledge base collectively and continuously.

Creating customizable solutions entails creating solutions from reusable solutions and assets. First, firms must establish a *knowledge reuse process* and an *enterprise knowledge structure*. The reuse process streamlines the contribution and reuse of knowledge assets for creating solutions. The knowledge structure formally identifies the architecture, components, and the layers of the contents of reuseable knowledge assets. Second, companies must also carefully manage the life cycle of its intellectual assets. Finally, firms must provide tools and establish processes for data mining and knowledge search. This chapter begins by defining terms that are often used interchangeably.

## DEFINING INTELLECTUAL CAPITAL, INTELLECTUAL ASSET, AND SOLUTION

### Intellectual Capital

Intellectual capital encompasses both the inventory of knowledge-based assets as well as the capacity to acquire and assimilate new learning rapidly. It is often invisible, intangible, or difficult to detect and quantify. In fact, many companies view intellectual capital as a spectrum, ranging from ideas, thoughts, the "stuff" in people's heads (implicit knowledge) to "concrete" intellectual assets, like software code, with true measurable value that can be tracked and managed. By this definition, it includes the organization's intellectual property —its legally protected and exploitable intangible assets. Intellectual capital is, however, much more than merely intellectual property. At its roots, it is used in the skills that people hold. It encompasses the intellectual and learned abilities of the workforce—its skills, knowledge, abilities, and behaviors. It is a compilation of the individual, group, and corporate knowledge brought to the table in solving complex business problems. It consists of information, experience, and ideas that are linked to the organization's mission or principle purpose, and which will ultimately add value to the consumer of that organization's output. Intellectual capital represents the resources that produce inventiveness and competitiveness, through the generation and dissemination of ideas, approaches, and solutions.

Three types of intellectual capital are identified: human capital, structural capital, and customer capital. Human capital is composed of the skill, knowledge, and expertise of the employee base. It is a resource for a company's collective capability to create the best solutions for customers. Human capital resides in the individuals who walk in and out of the office everyday.

Structural capital represents a firm's organizational capabilities to meet market requirements. It is the knowledge that has been captured and institutionalized within the structure, processes, and culture of an organization. It includes patents, copyrights, proprietary software, trademarks, trade secrets, and general organizational know how. It can be stored in the form of documented procedures, databases, expert systems, decision-support software, and knowledge management systems. Structural capital is everything left at he office when the employees go home and can clearly be regarded as company property. This is the reason it is important to capture human knowledge as structured capital. Unlike human capital, structural capital can be owned and thereby traded.

Customer capital refers to the organization's network of satisfied clients and their loyalty to the company. The value of an organization's intellectual capital should be measured in terms of the quantity and quality of the client relationships that have been built up over time. It is the clients' confidence in the products and services provided that has value. Customer capital is increasingly recognized as a critical resource. More systems are designed to capture and reuse customer-centric knowledge.

In sum, intellectual capital entails much more than intellect. It also represents a degree of intellectual action. Intellectual capital, therefore, is not a static, intangible asset, but an ideological process—a means to an end. While critically important, the collective knowledge, skills, and behaviors of the organization can only really be deemed a "capital" asset if they support the strategic direction of the organization.

## Intellectual Asset and Solution

An *intellectual asset* is a group of structured knowledge items that are reuseable and that have added value to an organization. In practice, we use the word intellectual asset, knowledge asset, and intellectual capital interchangeably, unless specified otherwise.

A *solution* is an integration and packaging of assets, products, and services for delivery to solve a specific or general business problem. In general, intellectual assets are managed as components of a solution and are not used separately.

In solving a business problem, intellectual assets are bundled with products and services, resulting in a customized solution. Thus, a solution contains reuseable assets. Through projects, acquisitions, and in-house development, firms accumulate intellectual assets that will be the key to increased profitability as a result of delivering customizable solutions to clients through asset reuse. Since intellectual assets vary greatly, from documents containing competitive analysis to system development artifacts, the skills needed to perform the tasks of evaluation and capturing assets also vary greatly. It is best to use highly skilled individuals who understand the context in which an asset will be reused and are experienced in the development of similar assets. Thus, the assets are managed with the spirit of continuous improvement.

## HARVESTING AND HARDENING ASSETS FOR REUSE

Reuse of intellectual assets does occur, but in an ad hoc manner. In order to have a systematic approach to create and reuse an intellectual asset, a clear process model is needed. Some might argue that assets can simply be harvested from projects and reused with little additional effort. Unfortunately, the "painful" experience from many companies has shown that assets collected in an ad hoc manner without systematic supporting processes are difficult to leverage. The assets are difficult to find and understand. Assets from different sources do not work together effectively. Intellectual property rights are not protected. Poor quality and lack of documentation and support damage the reputation of the asset base and turn it into a "junkyard" that soon disappoints users. Overcoming these problems is a function of effectively managing people, processes, and the large quantities of reuseable assets.

Reuse is the process of taking the work of one project and using it on subsequent projects with the objective of reducing the overall effort required for the new projects. To be successful in sharing and reusing intellectual assets, it is essential that a company adopt an integrated approach across functional areas. In particular, one must

- ensure the understanding of the fundamental principles of intellectual asset reuse, and how it affects innovation;
- decide how to measure the results of intellectual asset reuse;
- understand what is involved in implementing intellectual asset reuse throughout the company;
- create and implement a vision of how a company can become a mature intellectual asset reuse company.

## KNOWLEDGE ASSET REUSE PROCESS

Knowledge is created and used in the act of applying information to problem solving. The more times information can be applied to specific problem-solving contexts, the more likely this knowledge can be structured into a reuseable intellectual asset. The knowledge creation and reuse processes are cyclical and innovations are most likely to come from continuous improvement. Figure 7.1 depicts the knowledge reuse process used at IBM's Global Services. This process identifies and converts solution information into structured knowledge. Once structured, the knowledge can be easily shared and further improved by members of a knowledge base.

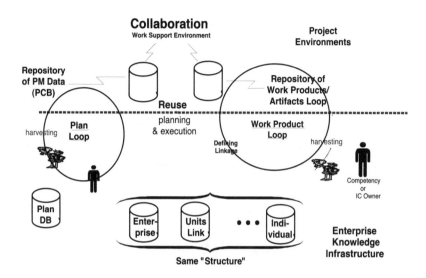

Figure 7.1: Intellectual Capital from Engagement Projects

(Source: *International Business Machines* [4])

## Intellectual Capital from Project Information

Reuse of intellectual capital is one of the most effective ways of improving the speed of creating customized solutions. In reuse, a context-sensitive linkage between the project management environment and intellectual capital management is critical. In a project environment, one needs to have a collaborative work support environment to capture dialog and work products. The knowledge cycle is the process for knowledge creation, use, and reuse with continuous improvements. The scope of the knowledge cycle is the context boundary of the users. In a business context, it is linked to the evolving marketplace. Figure 7.1 shows two examples of intellectual capital generated from engagement projects at IBM: Work Products/Artifacts and Project Control Books (PCB). The flow of the cycle (Figure 7.1) is shown by the loops going from the project environment to the enterprise knowledge infrastructure of multiple kinds of Intellectual Capital (IC) to the engagement or solution development context and back. Numerous kinds of IC must be brought to bear (or created) in the project context including proposals, methods, project control books, workproduct descriptions, workproduct examples, and best-practice materials of all types.

Typically, the IC must be situated and adapted in the new context with the possible changes needed as determined by intensive discussion and decision making on the project as it evolves. A large volume of project-specific information and knowledge will be generated (adapted or new) and must be managed. As a project progresses, and certainly at its conclusion, the return part of the cycle must occur where project knowledge is "harvested" back into the longer-term IC repository. Both Product Management (PM) and Intellectual Capital Management (ICM) occur within the encompassing business environment of an enterprise which generates its own operational and financial information, knowledge types, and management requirements.

This view of the knowledge cycle shows the need for supporting the complex interlinking of information and knowledge from the project level to the enterprise knowledge infrastructure. It is also part of the business processes for operations and interactions. There are other nested cycles of communication and collaboration that must occur among people in a wide variety of roles and levels in conjunction with the development, delivery, documentation, hand-off, harvesting, generalizing, storing, retrieving, and so on, of the essential knowledge flow within the business.

## Customized Solutions from Customer Knowledge

As more firms engage in knowledge reuse, expedience is increasingly important. The Internet shortens the distance between customers, suppliers, and business partners; it also reduces the time to inform for all participants in the marketplace. It provides a convenient medium for customer self-services and reduces the level of intermediation in the marketplace. Conversely, the Internet can proliferate virtual intermediaries. Businesses therefore need to renovate their customer services and seek to achieve customer loyalty and retention. Early adopters are undergoing customer-driven realignment of their demand and supply value chains. Companies need to have a mechanism in place to capture and communicate with customers. They need to have systems to quickly transform feedback from customers into products and services to bring back to customers. Speed and the efficiency in transforming customer knowledge into deliverable solutions are the differentiators for today's product and service organizations.

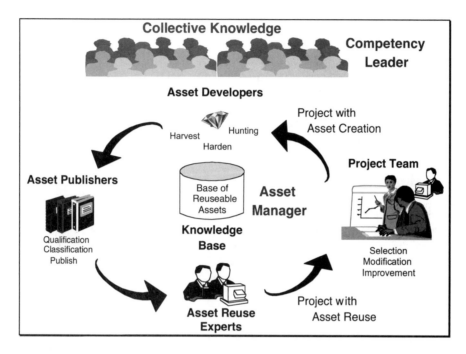

Figure 7.2: Knowledge Asset Development Process

(Source: *International Business Machines* [3])


# KNOWLEDGE ASSET DEVELOPMENT PROCESS


Collaboration is the process of shared creation. Shared creation is at the heart of the generation, and reuse of knowledge assets. Issue-based resolution can help to facilitate and capture
the dialogue and decision making that must always take place when situating and adapting a
piece of knowledge asset in a new project context.

As shown in Figure 7.2, a set of roles is associated with the knowledge development
process. Among the roles, establishing competency leaders and asset (knowledge) managers
is most critical. They help to organize the source of intellectual capital, teaming the different
subject experts and determining ownership of the assets. An asset without an owner will
likely "die on the vine." This owner will be identified as the asset manager. We summarize
the roles and responsibilities required for each role in the following text.

## Competency Leader

Competency leaders organize a community of subject experts and practitioners on competency topics. They facilitate and energize community building and teamwork. They identify the intellectual-asset requirements of business strategies and project teams. They lead activities to structure and value intellectual capital from collective knowledge. They also energize the community of experts and practitioners to continue improvement and contribute to intellectual asset creation.

## Asset Manager

Asset managers are responsible for coordinating reuse activities across an organization. They are leaders for organizational reuse. They manage reuse processes in an organization and ensure that reuse skills are available. They identify support needs. They also coordinate with solution domain architects, business managers, and project managers.

## Knowledge Architect

Knowledge architects develop a specification for the domain knowledge. They are responsible for the design of solutions and knowledge assets. They have detailed knowledge of the business, the technical architectures, and the business models. They also define requirements for creation and evolution of knowledge assets.

## Asset Publisher

Asset publishers encourage and support project managers to register projects and provide updates during the project life cycle. They encourage and support project managers to provide experience reports. They support domain experts to provide and maintain high-quality solutions and asset information. They assist with the collection of asset packages and storage in the designated library system connected to knowledge bases. They also announce availability of assets and solutions.

## Asset Broker

Asset brokers understand the contents of the solutions and assets within a domain. They also assist project teams in understanding solutions and assets. They assist project teams and architects in understanding solutions or assets. Asset brokers assist project teams in configuring and designing solutions. They network with other brokers across different business units.

## ENTERPRISE KNOWLEDGE STRUCTURE

The knowledge development process presented in the previous section identifies the roles of the players in the process and their relationships. Parallel to the process is a knowledge structure that also needs to be developed. Benefits of an enterprise knowledge structure are the following:

Provides a clear, consistent approach for reuse across business units.
Creates and drives intra- and interorganizational standards.

Optimizes investment funding and resources for reuseable intellectual capital.

Optimizes development and delivery capabilities.

Increases product innovation, and improved time to market at lower cost with less risk.

Creates reuseable assets, including architectures, models, tools, and reuses them
for problem solving and new product design.

The objective of defining an enterprise knowledge structure is to improve the representation of the tacit knowledge in a structured format so knowledge workers of the competency network have access to this structured knowledge asset. Figure 7.3 depicts a knowledge structure from the perspectives of *problem solving* and *knowledge architecture*. It specifies the relationships that exist between these two perspectives.

Each perspective relates to the type of reuse analysis that needs to be performed when developing reuseable solutions. The problem-solving perspective relates to the creation of solutions based on the requirements and the delivery of reuseable *solutions* that encompass *products, knowledge assets,* and *services. Solutions* are customized in order to be *customer specific.* The knowledge architecture of these *solutions* can be minimal or extensive.

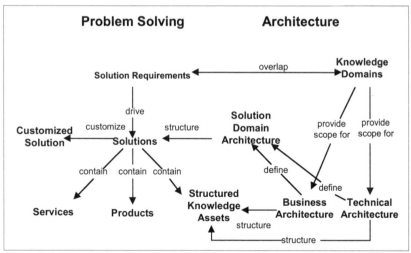

Figure 7.3: An Enterprise Knowledge Structure
(Source: *International Business Machines* [2])

## Requirements for Asset Identification

The requirements for intellectual assets are generated from various sources in the firm, most frequently from groups that are responsible for business strategies such as those in the marketing area. A business strategy describes plans and priorities of the firm's needed assets to justify the efforts of acquisition, maintenance, support, and reuse. The business plan sets the context for the harvesting activities. It should include cost benefit analysis that considers the costs of creating and maintaining the asset as well as the anticipated benefits derived from this asset. The asset's anticipated lifetime must be used for both cost and benefit calculations. Two critical issues need to be addressed when performing this analysis:

Ongoing costs to support an asset over its lifetime.

Risk of business or technical obsolescence.

Once the requirements have been identified, the tasks for asset hunting, harvesting, and hardening ensue. Before any hunting tasks begin, the selection criteria for potential assets are determined.

## Selection Criteria for Asset Hunting

The criteria to determine a candidate asset's suitability must be established before the asset hunting task is performed. Different types of assets require different types of criteria. General criteria include the asset's functionality, targeted architecture, platform, resources required, schedule and costs, accessibility, complexity, available support, and ownership. Additional criteria for intellectual assets can be timeliness of information, subject areas, and context where the asset was created. Additional criteria for system development assets include methodology, techniques, standards used, and implementation language. The following sections define six high-level criteria for assets.

### 1. Business Value

When selecting and measuring asset potential, the asset hunter must consider what is reuseable vs. reuseful (ease vs. value). Just because an asset is reuseable doesn't mean that additional resources should be expended to make it available if the value that the asset offers is not significant or a priority. Also, the legal rights to an asset must be considered for both the immediate and future needs.

### 2. Functionality

Functionality is an obvious factor to consider in asset hunting. If the potential asset doesn't provide the targeted functionality, then it will not add value to the firm. However, an asset that provides a significant portion of a desired functionality should be considered if the costs to remedy the deficiencies are less than the costs to build.

## 3. Complexity

The asset's complexity as a function of size and the number of relationships within the asset's implementation are very significant factors in understanding an asset and eventually reusing an asset.

## 4. Reuseability

In evaluating reuseability of assets, knowledge architectures form the basis for consideration or acceptance of potential assets. Assets with architectures that are not adaptable to the firm's standard business or technical architectures should not be seriously considered. To reach higher levels of reuse, firms must develop assets based upon common/consistent technical and business architectures. They must manage asset reuse at the firm level with a master asset development plan.

For example, a company wishes to expand their technical capability into a related area and they are considering acquiring the technology through a purchase. To get maximum value, the assets should fit into the existing business and technical architectures. When the assets do not meet current architectural standards or frameworks, then the risks to reuse the assets increase.

One must consider the asset's commonalities and variances along with the asset's suitability to business needs. To determine commonalities, the candidate asset is compared to the ideal state where the domain model, platform characteristics, and architecture models converge. The variances from the ideal state must be noted because they represent areas where resources will be required to make an asset reuseable in a specific business context. These areas represent asset improvement opportunities for members of a solution development team or a competency network.

## 5. Documentation and Support

One must consider the completeness of the asset's documentation because it can reduce the complexity of understanding. Without clear and accurate documentation, the reuser can expend considerable resources just trying to determine suitability to business needs. If the documentation lacks clarity, avoid the asset unless it is believed to be of critical value. One must consider the support material that is available for the asset and the availability of people with skills related to the asset.

## 6. Business and Technology Risk

Selection and measurement should also include an understanding of the asset's potential target areas. Target areas that have low risks should be given stronger consideration than high-risk areas. Technology risks are those for which the underlying technology will rapidly change and the asset's shelf life will be too short to recover the costs. Business risks are those for which the business needs are changing so rapidly that the asset is again subject to a short shelf life.

One must consider whether marketing and sales can adequately reduce these risks. While the costs of a "yet to be found" potential asset are unknown initially, the costs to create an asset that satisfies the needs can be roughly estimated. This estimation helps to establish criteria because if an asset is discovered to cost more to retrofit than to create, it should be cataloged but not be pursued. This general rule changes when other factors intervene, such as time to market considerations and partnering strategies. The output from the asset hunting task is a collection of unstructured knowledge, which needs to be filtered and structured for reuse.

## LIFE CYCLE MANAGEMENT

### Quality of Intellectual Capital

The Internet can be considered a gold mine of information by some people, and at the same time a junkyard by others. It depends on the content quality of the information you find and how the information is presented. The *Wall Street Journal* [8] reported that thousands of Web sites are simply not updated for lengthy periods of time, resulting in the devaluation of their information content. This condition provides a clear picture of how information can become useless if not managed through its quality life cycle [9]. Maintaining high-quality content and frequently refreshing it with new information are critical for Web sites to attract visitors. Likewise, companies need to manage both tacit and explicit information and knowledge as dynamically as possible to make them valuable to their internal and external customers.

### Levels of Life Cycle

There are different levels of reuse that an organization may want to achieve depending on its particular goals and constraints. This section discusses three levels of reuse in the management of intellectual assets. As shown in Figure 7.4, these levels refer to both the management of the reuseable entities and to the characteristics of the reuseable entities themselves.

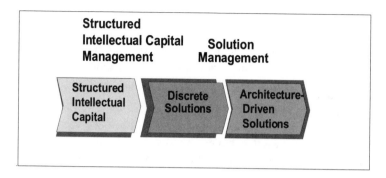

Figure 7.4: Levels of Intellectual Asset Life Cycle

(Source: *International Business Machines* [2])

The first level for reuse is *Structured Intellectual Capital*. It is characterized by the creation and use of assets (mostly documents) outside the context of a solution. The assets are structured and reuseable but cannot be combined to create other solutions automatically.

The second and third levels are *Discrete Solutions* and *Architecture-driven Solutions*. They focus on creating reuseable solutions. Discrete solutions refer to solutions created from the marketing perspective. These solutions are integrated into an overall solution-domain architecture that describes common assets that *are* reused across multiple solutions within a defined scope.

As an example of developing and reusing discrete solutions as opposed to architecture-driven solutions, consider the "Visual Banker" solution. The Visual Banker solution from Footprint/IBM is the result of an architecture-driven solution approach. The solutions in both the sales and services (product sales and teller services) segments are integrated into one overall architecture that uses common assets across those solutions.

Choosing which level on which to focus requires circumscribing the business problem, which we refer to as the scope. If Visual Banker is taken into the larger scope of finance, it will be seen as a discrete solution that would be the result of following processes in a discrete solution level corresponding to the retail banking market segment. The assets and solutions within Visual Banker are not part of a larger finance architecture and are not designed to be reused in this larger scope.

Efforts to achieve the reuse of Visual Banker or its assets in the scope of finance will require adapting the processes used at Footprint to be an architecture-driven solution. Efforts to use solutions and assets outside the scope for which they were intended is a good indication of a need to move to the next level and its processes. As a comparison, evolution of a solution or asset inside its intended scope would refer to increasing the segments across which it is reuseable. Trying to combine solutions is an indication of moving from the Discrete Solutions level to the Architecture-driven Solutions level. An overall architecture that defines how the solutions work together and, in particular, that identifies common assets across the solutions would be more advantageous.

Solutions and assets have a life cycle of creation, evolution, and retirement or migration. Assets can be created on projects or by an organization tasked to develop and maintain assets. When assets are created on projects, they must be harvested (removed from the context of the customer's solution) and then hardened (have their reuseability improved through increasing the generalization, the documentation, and the quality). Assets are then reused in projects, typically as part of a solution.

As the assets are used, lessons on how to improve them within the intended context are learned. New uses emerge which can lead to new asset requirements. The application of the resultant modifications is called asset evolution. An asset evolves until the economics of the domain lead to a decision to migrate it to the laboratory so that it can be developed into a new asset. Alternatively, the asset may become obsolete because technology changes or other assets replace it. An asset should not be retired until all users have completed their migrations to a new asset. Elements of retired solutions may become part of new solutions.

## FROM DATA TO KNOWLEDGE

The lowest level of known facts is data. Data can be stored in a structured relational database system or unstructured document management system. Data includes nontext data, such as voice and image. Data are collected, sorted, grouped, analyzed, and interpreted. When data are processed in this manner, they become information. Information contains substance and purpose. "Knowledge" is generated when information is combined with context and experience.

In practice, the terms data, information, and knowledge are often used interchangeably. First, the differentiation is generally difficult because the differentiation lies in where data are located in terms of the information manufacturing system. Data are collected, processed, used, and further aggregated, and collected again. Moreover, data are never consumed until they are off the shelf by deleting. Until the end of the life cycle of the data, data move on to various processes of data manufacturing systems. Second, users interpret data when they use them. Users' contexts and the information manufacturing process make it difficult for users to determine precisely whether the piece is data, information, or even knowledge. Although it might take a decade just to define all three words, we all agree that the transformation of data for clearer and more meaningful information to users is important. Structuring and managing knowledge assets in an organization are also critical for all organizations. Therefore, the words data, information, and knowledge are used somewhat interchangeably in this book, unless specified otherwise.

Everyday, large amounts of data are poured into a business—sales transactions, inventory figures, billing information, marketing campaign responses and much more. More data, in fact, than anyone can be expected to review, which is why the average business uses only a limited amount of the data it collects. But data mining is changing all that. As increasing amounts of data are captured and digitized, companies need the ability to combine and correlate their data to create useful and reuseable knowledge from them. The knowledge available will create enormous advantages in many areas. Examples include mass customization for marketing and sales, dynamic team building for disaster response, and underwriting profitability analysis for insurers. Technologies to support the knowledge discovery are described next: data and knowledge mining, data warehouses, and network agents.

## Data and Knowledge Mining

Data Mining is the process of extracting valid, previously unknown, and comprehensible information from large databases and using it to make crucial business decisions. It is quickly being recognized as an essential business intelligence tool to discover the information necessary to improve a company's market presence and differentiate their products and services in today's global marketplace. Using a set of end-user tools makes data mining accessible to everyone — not just data analysts but also marketing managers and salespeople. This process changes the way businesses make decisions and capitalizes on their investment in data as never before.

Knowledge mining, similar to data mining, is a process for abstracting valid, previously unknown, ultimately comprehensible knowledge from a variety of information sources. Knowledge mining dramatically enhances the power of information searching by expanding the diversity of information sources. Timely and comprehensive knowledge discovery is made possible with the integration of current events and transaction data into the sources. Information that was excluded from relational databases can now be harvested.

The knowledge mining techniques utilize traditional data mining techniques such as clustering, classification, value prediction, association discovery, sequential pattern discovery, and similar time sequence discovery. It also incorporates new technologies, such as compilation, tokenization, keyword abstraction, semantic analysis, and concept/feature recognition, as well as metadata analysis techniques such as context and semantics analysis.

A typical knowledge mining application incorporates four steps: (1) information collection to harvest and filter information, (2) feature recognition to generate features/metadata, (3) metadata analysis to abstract knowledge, and (4) visualization to present knowledge to users.

The need to automate the generation of knowledge in order to control the workload of human labor has intensified as we enter the information age. With the proliferation of new products and services, the knowledge intensity of products and services (especially the IT industry) increasingly results in high costs of knowledge work per product. Furthermore, the knowledge required by business processes changes rapidly. The life cycle of knowledge continues to be shortened. In addition, the time span in which to make decisions is shorter and the decision makers are increasingly mobile and dispersed.

Business executives make on-the-fly data queries from huge data warehouses hundreds of miles away using a laptop computer. Data analysts tap into huge external databases on the Internet that, combined with their company's data warehouse, reveal their customers' buying patterns in rich detail. Salespersons plug into their department's data mart, recognize that they have overstocked, and then make a decision to sell—all on the customer's sales floor.

## Knowledge Cockpit

Knowledge Cockpit is a framework (Figure 7.5) used at IBM for knowledge mining [1]. By giving individuals the power to mine the information world, Knowledge Cockpit helps revolutionize the way people work:

Business-related information and knowledge are just a query away.

Hundreds of mobile agents can collect relevant information throughout the Internet.

Intellectual capital and asset management is integrated into everyday tasks and business operations.

Knowledge Cockpit "captures" information from a wide range of sources and "funnels" the information to one location. Time and money are saved by not searching through vast numbers of individual databases trying to locate the information needed. Knowledge Cockpit utilizes advanced knowledge mining techniques to process, discover, and synthesize knowledge. Knowledge Cockpit transforms information from these different sources into a consistent network of knowledge. Decision support components utilize the produced network of knowledge to assess the retrieved information's quality and to translate the knowledge into a compact, comprehensible format. The following are high-level examples of how Knowledge Cockpit might be used by a supermarket chain.

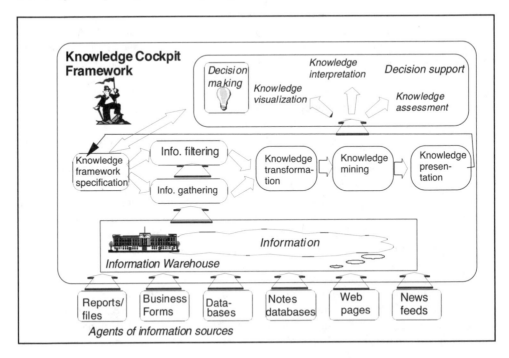

Figure 7.5: Knowledge Cockpit Framework for Knowledge Mining
(Source: *International Business Machines* [1])

### Customer Information

A supermarket offers a price saving card to its customers. Each time the customer makes a purchase, this card is presented to the cashier and a record of the customer's transactions is captured in the store's database. Knowledge Cockpit utilizes this information to provide the supermarket with the purchase history of all its regular customers and specific knowledge on an individual's shopping habits, such as shopping frequency, brand preferences, money spent, utilization of in-store services and promotions, and coupons redeemed. Using Knowledge Cockpit to analyze this information, the supermarket can provide discount coupons to its best customers and incentives to other customers to shop more frequently.

### Market Information

A supermarket chain needs access to up-do-date information on all of its competitors. If one competitor suddenly begins to offer larger than normal discounts to its shoppers, it may be because the competitor is trying to capture more of the market share or these price cuts may be linked to other reasons. Knowledge Cockpit gathers and provides analysis information on competitors from all available sources (trade journals, Internet/intranet, financial and news services). The results may indicate that the rival is having financial problems because it opened too many new stores and now must cut back by closing the poor performers and liquidating the stock in each. Now, the supermarket utilizing this information is able to anticipate and rationalize the lower pricing of its competitor, rather than rushing to match the lower prices and thereby cutting its own profits.

### Business Experiences

Information on internal experiences might include lessons learned from different types of store floor plans, aisle layout, and item location; identifying what specialized departments the supermarket should include, such as a bakery, deli, prime meats or fresh fish counter, and so on. This information is sometimes gained through trial and error. Capturing and storing information on how you do your business is a valuable source of intellectual capital that can be applied and reused in other situations.

## Data Warehouses

Data warehouses serve as the primary information sources for companies in which information is made available by agents that actively collect, filter, store, and update information. Information sources include documents, files, news, logs, transactions, and various kinds of databases. A data warehouse generally contains relational databases and management tools, analytical tools, and information retrieval tools. It enables its users to readily gain access to information that provides insights into trends and patterns of business performance and customer activities. The data warehouse serves as a repository for the collection and integration of data from multiple sources and structures it into a form suitable to use in solving business problems.

Tools currently available can build informational databases that contain read-only data that have been reconciled or derived from multiple sources. These databases contain the source information for decision support applications. These applications, in turn, further analyze and present the data in formats requested by knowledge workers. The results of multiple sources in a multitude of formats dictate the need to focus on the information management process. A standardized process for managing information requirements and determining what data are appropriate for subsequent use must be provided.

The infrastructure of the data warehouse facilitates creation of the following deliverables to knowledge workers:

What information is available and how end users can access it

Interfaces to structured and nonstructured information

Heterogeneous data/information access

Periodic data extraction from operational sources

Data enhancement and refreshment (creation of reconciled and derived information)

Distribution and replication of information to multiple locations

Supporting infrastructure for integration and administration

## Network Agents as Knowledge Intermediaries

The explosion of new information poses a significant challenge to both individuals and organizations. The rate of new information created has been estimated to have doubled every 20 years in the last century and will be accelerating at a rate approaching doubling every 10 years. The majority of the information is carried in the form of documents. Interestingly, the biggest problem people encounter in finding information on the Internet or even an intranet is not that they are unable to find the information they are looking for, but that they are unable to digest the overabundance of data/information that they uncover. This is due to the lack of quality measurements for information to evaluate and filter out noise and abstract critical data into comprehensible knowledge. This problem impinges on the quality of information and may even deter users from utilizing information warehouses.

Recently, network agents have emerged as one way to effectively customize searches in order to filter out unrelated data and extract useful knowledge for Web users. A network agent is a piece of software that helps an end user gather and process information from multiple content sites. A software agent commonly used includes the ability to customize an informational search, the ability to be proactive to complete its task independent of the user's activities, and the ability to be adaptive by learning from its past actions and from its environment.

A network agent is a software agent with mobility through the network. Network agents, or network objects, are objects that have code (behavior), data, execution state, and an itinerary. These are logically bundled together and can move as a single unit. This is in contrast to stationary objects that have code (behavior) and data. In both cases, the behavior is represented by interfaces. However, for stationary objects, since they do not move, the code and data can be platform dependent. Network agents, on the other hand, can move and, therefore, their code, data, execution state, and itinerary must all be portable, or at least convertible from and into portable forms. Examples of network agents include repetitive searching of information, shopping for the best buy, and orchestrating events like ordering flowers or communicating messages.

Network agents can be applied to retail shopping with intelligence to help buyers compare products across suppliers' Web sites by comparing price as well as product features. They can also save a buyer's decision time. They can also be applied to financial services companies to detect possible fraudulent usage of credit cards by examining deviations in credit card usage patterns of customers. They can also help retailers forecast changes in customer buying patterns and keep abreast of comparisons of purchases to determine which products are most frequently sold in conjunction with other products, and thus stock these items accordingly to maximize sales opportunities. They can also help an insurance company perform customer segmentation data to create target marketing campaigns, or cross-sell services among existing customers. They can also help medical researchers identify common patterns of symptoms that lead to particular illnesses.

# Network Agents in Electronic Commerce

Network agents are becoming more sophisticated and pervasive and are expected to play a larger role as intermediaries in electronic commerce. The following sections describe two types of network agents that are applied to electronic commerce: a verification-driven agent and a discovery-driven agent.

## Verification-Driven Agent

A verification-driven agent requires a user to provide his hypothesis to the agent. The agent will transform the hypothesis into queries and use the queries against the collected information. This may invoke the network agent to collect information for the query. The verification-driven agent then consolidates the finding brought back from the network agent. The user will examine the finding of the query looking for affirmation or negation of the hypothesis. In a simple case, the work of the agent is completed; in a more complicated case, a new query is reformulated and the agent performs the task iteratively until the finding either verifies the hypothesis or the user decides that the hypothesis is not valid for the knowledge. There are three major functions performed by the verification-driven agent:

### Query and Reporting

The major purpose of this function is to validate a hypothesis expressed by the user. For example, sales of airline tickets increase during the summer. To validate a hypothesis, the following steps are needed. The six steps are: (1) create a query; (2) pose the query to the databases or other information repositories; (3) collect findings; (4) analyze findings; (5) generate a report if the results support the hypothesis, or reformulate new queries if the results refute the hypothesis; and (6) visualize the report in graphical, tabular, and textual form.

### Multidimensional Analysis

When traditional query and reporting are inadequate, in some domains, a complex query with a temporal dimension is needed. For example, the regional manager of a fast- food chain may ask the following question. Show me sales by week during the first quarter of this year for Asia region stores broken down by location. Multidimensional databases, often implemented as multidimensional arrays, organize data along predefined dimensions, for example; time, location, and product.

### Statistical Analysis

Statistical analysis is usually performed with the above two functions. Statistical operations are used in conjunction with data visualization tools for more complex hypotheses.

## Discovery-Driven Agent

A discovery-driven agent requires a user to express his interest to the agent. The agent will transform the interest into queries and use the queries against the collected information. This may invoke the agent to collect information for the query by performing the functions discussed in the following sections. The discovery-driven agent then consolidates the findings for users to analyze. There are four major functions performed by the discovery-driven agent: predictive modeling, link analysis, database segmentation, and deviation detection.

### Predictive modeling

The purpose of this function is to generate a model for predicting the future from historical data in databases. For example, a car loan manager may be interested in predicting the likelihood that a customer will apply for a loan. In this way, he can provide a promotion or incentive program to attract the customer. Predictive modeling can also be used in real estate.

### Link Analysis

The major goal of link analysis is to build linkages or relationships between the data in a database. For example, a department manager must determine what departments should be put together, that is, the children's department adjacent to the women's department, so when women go shopping for their own clothes, they will also shop for children's clothes.

### Database Segmentation

The goal of database segmentation is to divide the database into different segments and summarize the data in each segment. The functions discussed above can be applied to individual data segments. For example, by segmenting bank loan data, one can create segments that contain transactions from specific seasons, for example, summer, Christmas.

### Deviation Detection

The goal of this function is to identify data that cannot be associated with any segment. For example, by segmenting a department store's sales data, a point that falls outside the normal segment can be detected. By examining the point more carefully, users can determine the contributing factors. For example, sales dropped during the Christmas season because there was a big snowstorm in a region.

# Text Mining

If we suffer from information overload, much of the blame rests on text-based documents. Articles, opinions, letters, and other forms of free text constitute 80 percent of the world's stored information. How do we sort through these documents to get the information we need, without getting information overload?

Text mining solutions are designed to cut through mountains of text-based data and discover the hidden nuggets of information that one needs. Applying text mining techniques to customer complaint letters, for example, can uncover the major reasons for customer complaints and present them to users in a quick, intelligible manner. By searching and mining business news wire documents that mention a company, text mining can reveal a corporate image of the company in vivid detail.

### Information Filtering

Numerous information filtering methods are being developed to help users take full advantage of the on-line information explosion. Ideally these systems single out the few relevant nuggets while removing the noisy majority. Most information filtering systems include a notion-of-user profile, an important characteristic of agents.

### Collaborative Filtering

Collaborative filtering, an information filtering technique, uses statistical methods to make predictions based on patterns in people's preferences. These predictions are used to make recommendations to an individual user based on the correlation between their own personal profile and the profiles of other users who have similar preferences. A filtering agent with the knowledge of many users can often make more accurate predictions than traditional methods, such as group averages.

# CONCLUSION

In this chapter, we presented what is needed to create customized and customizable solutions from two general sources: one from the internal collective knowledge by structuring and the other from networked sources by data and knowledge mining. Although potential assets are plentiful in most organizations, attaining the full value of these assets requires careful planning, adequate funding, and effective execution. In the next chapter, we present an approach for developing a networked knowledge infrastructure.

## References

[1] Hu, J., K. T. Huang, K. Kuse, G. Su and K. Wang, "Customer Information Quality and Knowledge Management: A Case Study Using Knowledge Cockpit," *Journal of Knowledge Management,* 1(3), 1998, pp. 225–236.

[2] Huang, K. T. "Industry Guide to Management of Asset Based Solutions," in IBM Internal Report Tarrytown, N.Y, IBM, 1996.

[3] Huang, K. T., "Capitalizing, Collective Knowledge for Winning, Execution, and Teamwork," *Journal of Knowledge Management,* 1(2), 1997, pp. 149–156.

[4] Huang, K. T., "Capitalizing on Intellectual Assets, not Infrastructure," *IBM Systems Journal,* Forthcoming.

[5] IBM "Kasparov beats Deep Blue 4-2," in http://www.chess.ibm.park.org/, 1997.

[6] Lee, Y., *Collective Knowledge: An Institutional Learning Perspective.* Cambridge Research Group, Cambridge, MA, 1997.

[7] Pine, B. J. I., *Mass Customization: the New Frontier in Business Competition.* Harvard Business School Press, Boston, MA, 1993.

[8] Sandberg, J. . "At Thousands of Web Sites, Time Stands Still: Many Web Sites Need Updating," *The Wall Street Journal,* March 11, 1997 p. B1.

[9] Wang, R. Y., Y. L. Lee, L. Pipino and D. M. Strong, "Manage Your Information as a Product," *Sloan Management Review,* 39(4), 1998, pp. 95–105.

# Network Knowledge Infrastructure

$A$n effective operation of knowledge management depends on a networked knowledge infrastructure. In this chapter, we present technologies that can be deployed to create the corporate knowledge infrastructure necessary for knowledge management. To a large extent, we use an early adopter's case, IBM, to illustrate how they accomplished the networked knowledge infrastructure for managing their intellectual assets. Specifically, IBM's ICM AssetWeb and networking and collaboration technologies are described as an example. We first describe corporate knowledge technology infrastructure in terms of its components and key design issues. We then discuss functionality and implications of using the Internet, intranets, and extranets for collaboration and innovation. Finally, issues related to security in the corporate knowledge infrastructure are discussed.

## CORPORATE KNOWLEDGE INFRASTRUCTURE

Applying technologies to the process of knowledge management is accomplished with specific goals established. Among these goals are

> to make knowledge widely, rapidly, and easily accessible
>
> to facilitate the creation, cataloging, and retrieval of knowledge
>
> to provide security control

At a higher level, it is important to provide compatibility across the entire organization, to facilitate skills and competence development and to enable collaboration and innovation.

Although a more advanced technology for knowledge management is yet to be developed, existing and appropriate technologies, when properly integrated, can provide necessary functionality and flexibility for achieving most goals of knowledge management. In seeking technologies for managing knowledge, the emphasis must be placed on the stability and interoperability of the technology rather than complexity and "newness." Given the limitation of time and resources, most firms do not have the luxury of developing in-house, customized technology for managing organizational knowledge. They seek innovative ways for exploiting existing technologies.

Technologies available for knowledge management include knowledge representation, document management, decision support, data mining, expert systems, groupware (collaborative-ware), the Internet, intranets, network computing, e-mail, and multimedia. In general, existing organizational information systems can be extended for managing the explicit knowledge in an organization. At the same time, a referral (mapping) system can be developed to manage the tacit knowledge that is not easily describable using existing media.

One of the main objectives of using technology for knowledge management is to provide access to critical business information as quickly as possible. Network computing, the Internet, intranets, and e-mail play key roles in making knowledge easily accessible. Hypertext and multimedia provide user interfaces that make accessing the information in the knowledge system both entertaining and easy to use.

## KNOWLEDGE ARCHITECTURE FOR THE EXTENDED ENTERPRISE

In the past, most corporate IT architectures and infrastructures were primarily host centric. The standard platforms and common applications were proprietary in nature. Electronic commerce has changed the way companies serve customers, perform work, and collaborate with and leverage business partners. To exploit the new market realities, many corporations have gone through a profound business transformation. Their current and future business needs require a more flexible, responsive architecture, one that enables business units to rapidly respond to the dynamics of the various segments of their marketplace.

Moreover, the technology must facilitate information exchange across what has become an ***extended enterprise*** consisting of customers, manufacturing and development divisions, geographic marketing units, trading partners, and vendors. To enable communication across the extended enterprise and to streamline business processes, a knowledge infrastructure needs to be established. This infrastructure can facilitate interunit communicability and provide flexibility and security control. The extended enterprise is a challenging and complex business environment. It is the environment that may revolutionize many aspects of information systems, the organization, and the role of the CIO. A vision of a knowledge infrastructure in this environment is critically needed.

The goal of the corporate knowledge infrastructure is to accelerate the firm's success by creating competitive advantage through the best information infrastructure for knowledge sharing, collaboration, and teamwork. It consists of multiple component layers, depicted in Figure 8.1.

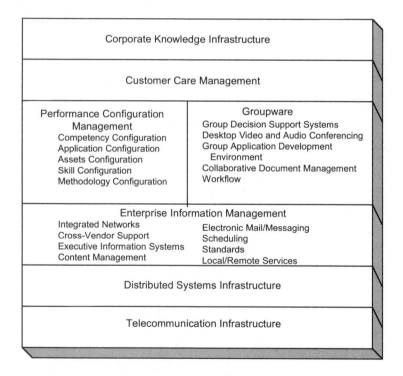

Figure 8.1: Layers of Infrastructure for Corporate Knowledge Management

(Source: Adapted from *International Business Machines* [2])

The corporate knowledge infrastructure is the hardware, software, network, and services that facilitate and support information and knowledge management. It provides a common network computing platform for the collection, analysis and publication of information and knowledge. It serves as a flexible mechanism to keep knowledge workers informed of new developments on key topics and issues. For the knowledge worker, it supports a set of navigation tools to organize, share, store, and retrieve knowledge and a set of communication tools, beyond e-mail, to collaborate and discuss projects.

## DESIGN REQUIREMENTS

The key design issue for knowledge applications is to allow knowledge workers to create knowledge with their own customizations by putting information in context from timely, relevant, and reliable information and knowledge sources. To enable corporate business units to satisfy their unique needs, to best leverage their global information assets, and to attain a competitive advantage, they need to have a consistent yet flexible information and knowledge architecture and computing infrastructure. The IT architecture needs to operate within an open systems environment while maintaining interunit communicability and interoperability. IT organizations must work within the environment to provide streamlined, cost-effective, responsive solutions. To best support the company's business units and to facilitate the delivery of flexible, responsive business solutions, firms need to develop a computing model that

> permits a rapid response to business requirements,
>
> facilitates interunit information exchange,
>
> enables collaborative distributed computing,
>
> supports multiplatform/multiproduct solutions,
>
> facilitates reuse of services and/or applications, and
>
> permits any-to-any access, where needed.

There are different hardware and software platforms used across the extended enterprise. Also, quite often standard industry solutions are available. It is far more cost-effective and certainly more responsive to acquire these solutions rather than build them. The new technical architecture must be flexible enough to quickly integrate these purchased solutions into a chosen platform. Information and, in many cases, business processes must also be shared across the extended enterprise. Thus, the interoperability of solutions on various platforms and interunit communicability are fundamental requirements of an IT architecture framework if the enterprise is ready to collaborate internally, to partner externally, and to interact with customers in the market.

# THE INTERNET, INTRANETS, AND EXTRANETS

The Internet began in the 1960s as a project of the Advanced Research Projects Agency (ARPA) to create a network that would provide the safe transmittal of data between military computers at different sites by using redundant communication routes. In 1991, the National Science Foundation eased restrictions and allowed commercial usage of Internet access. Subsequently, the growth of users and traffic has been phenomenal. Initially, there was the public Internet, then private intranets. Now the concept of an extranet is a reality for many corporations.

The **Internet** is the public, global network of networks which is based on the Internet protocol and related standards. It was designed to provide a standard means of interconnecting networks so that any system could communicate with any other system and offer universal accessibility. An **intranet** is a private application of the same Internet technology, software, and applications within a private network for use within an enterprise. It is constructed for such internal uses as improving employee productivity, sharing information and knowledge, and updating human resources information. It may be entirely disconnected from the public Internet, but it is usually linked to it and protected from unauthorized access by security firewall systems. Intranets can help guide different business units such as sales, manufacturing, and IS teams, in a common direction.

Along with many internal needs satisfied by intranets, there is an urgent need to find better ways to communicate with external customers and suppliers. **Extranets** meet these needs. They can alleviate the burden of sales, marketing, customer service, and supplier relations by allowing these groups to access extranet Web sites for needed information.

The distinction between an intranet and an extranet is that the extranet network extends beyond a single company to multiple organizations that must collaborate, communicate, and exchange information in order to achieve joint business objectives. Applications on extranets are built for external business interactions that enable collaboration and transaction with business partners, vendors, and customers. These new networks take a company's existing intranets and extend them beyond the enterprise to reach out to people who may physically work outside the firewall but who are an important part of the business strategy, product-delivery system, or customer-support apparatus. Many corporate CIOs or IS professionals are working on building their company's extranet applications such as database marketing, logistics, and supply chain management. Extranets can create a synergy that helps firms increase productivity and align themselves more closely with the needs of their customers and business partners. Table 8.1 illustrates the differences among the Internet, intranets, and extranets.

**Table 8.1: A comparison of the Internet, extranets, and intranets**

|  | Internet | Extranet | Intranet |
|---|---|---|---|
| Service Community | Public | Semi-Private Semi-Public | Private |
| Users | Anyone | Selected business partners | Company employees |

| | | All potential customers | |
|---|---|---|---|
| Connection | Public-Accessible servers worldwide | Public-Accessible servers with link to servers inside firewall | Servers inside the firewall within a company |
| Purpose | Communication, collaboration, and exchange | Communication, collaboration, exchange, transaction, and services | Communication, collaboration, exchange, transaction, and services |
| Content | All areas | Business specific<br>Public & proprietary | Proprietary<br>Closely held |

## Intranets for Knowledge Sharing and Collaboration

A corporate intranet is a flexible environment to keep knowledge workers informed of new developments on key topics and issues. It is a common electronic platform for the collection, analysis, and publication of information and knowledge. It contains a customized collection of current, relevant, and reliable data sources and flexible navigation tools designed to create knowledge by putting information into context for key decisions. The intranet supports a set of management functions to organize, share, store, and retrieve knowledge. Because information comes from both external and internal sources, corporate intranets need to support security features to restrict who can read, modify, send, or copy the information at individual or group levels. Advanced and flexible multilevel security is needed to ensure information delivery, analysis, and published results are accessible to only selected users.

In the intranet environment, individuals have great freedom to convey and conceal information. When powerful encryption systems are readily available, it becomes easy for people to render the contents of the information they are storing or transmitting inaccessible to third parties.

## ICM ASSETWEB

### IBM's INTELLECTUAL CAPITAL MANAGEMENT SYSTEM: ICM ASSETWEB

IBM recognized that its business is intellectual-capital intensive. The firm decided to develop knowledge management as one of its core competencies. As a part of its reengineering projects, IBM developed and deployed the Intellectual Capital Management (ICM) system with management processes and intranet tools to empower its professionals. As Lou Gerstner, chairman of IBM, states, "We have to win through brilliant execution that can only be done with teamwork." IBM has leveraged its network computing solutions to help the firm stay ahead of competition [4].

   IBM's intranet application, ICM AssetWeb, is a dynamic Lotus Domino-based collaboration system that gives practitioners in IBM Global Services and Global Industries the power to leverage intellectual capital. The application is designed to fulfill a variety of needs, such as to provide convenient Web access, easy navigation, enhancement capabilities, and a structured framework for issue-based discussions. From almost anywhere in the world, IBM professionals can navigate through the ICM system to access the intellectual capital they need. They can quickly scan a summary page to see if it includes what they are looking for. They can access the item, work with it, provide feedback, enhance it, team with others who have used it, and submit newly created items. Several comprehensive tools are built into the ICM AssetWeb such as version management, automatic multidatabase searching, yellow pages, and user preference configurators.

   The ICM AssetWeb also includes an automatic tracking tool that allows management to continually monitor the knowledge activity and intensity of the competency networks. This helps to identify reuse patterns and the most useful intellectual capital (Figure 8.2).

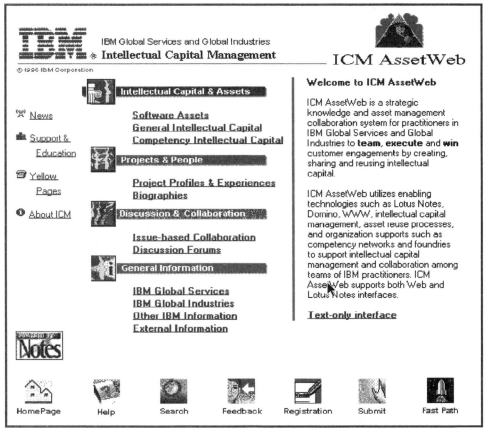

Figure 8.2: IBM's Intellectual Capital Management AssetWeb
(Source: *International Business Machines* [Huang, Forthcoming #1629])

ICM AssetWeb provides the infrastructure for IBM's knowledge management solutions. It is a strategic knowledge and asset management collaboration system used by IBM Global Services and Global Industries to team, execute, and win customer engagements by creating, sharing, and reusing intellectual capital. Intellectual capital consists of information, know-how, experiences, ideas, objects, code, models, and technical architectures that are structured to enable sharing for reuse to deliver value to customers and shareholders. ICM AssetWeb supports a vast number of features, including organizational support centering on competencies, asset management support, and structured collaboration support. ICM AssetWeb delivers the collective knowledge of IBM professionals from around the world to the fingertips of its users. ICM AssetWeb won the Gold Medal of the 1998 Giga Excellence Award on Knowledge Management, a prestigious industry award, for its implementation excellence and innovation [5, 9].

With the evolution of technology, content improvements, application upgrades, and end-user feedback, the ICM AssetWeb is being improved continuously.

## Competency Networks

Competency Networks are an integral part of IBM's intellectual capital management program for identifying and reusing intellectual capital. A competency network of a particular core competency is a community of subject knowledge experts within the company which represents a core competency. It generally consists of a core team and an extended team. A major responsibility of the competency networks is to enable the effective and efficient collection and sharing of intellectual capital pertaining to the competency, and to make it available to practitioners throughout IBM. Each competency network is responsible for creating, evaluating, and structuring the intellectual capital that goes into its own database and then sharing with interested practitioners. By increasing the breadth and depth of competencies and sharing intellectual capital created by these competencies, companies are able to provide greater value to their customers and better-quality delivery.

Each competency network creates an intellectual capital database containing the most current thinking, research, best-client examples, techniques, education, and marketing materials related to that competency's sphere of expertise. These databases are available to consulting, solution, and services practitioners. Anyone may submit material to a competency database at any time. The competency network database supports advanced features such as issue-based structured collaboration, forums, group configuration, different levels of security control, reconfigurable categories and subcategories, and document repository.

## Best Practice

Asset management support in ICM AssetWeb is designed to enable the development of the best practices for asset-based services businesses through understanding gained from the experiences of practicing consultant and solution groups. Support in asset management includes the support of the competency networks in solution areas to facilitate the transformation of IBM and its services and solution organizations into asset-based businesses. This is accomplished by developing a worldwide community of practitioners who are aware of, and execute, the best practices of asset-based services. They facilitate codification of methods, techniques, and processes for asset-based services into a methodology, software reuse libraries that manage the software-related assets, and collaboration utilities to connect the distributed community into a global net. The software reuse library provides a set of functions that support reasoning-driven workflow support for submission, requesting, and distributing the software re-lated assets. Optionally, the owner of an asset can choose to have an encrypted string of the requester's information and reason stored into the asset for future tracking. The security control of the assets is at the individual asset level for flexibility and security.

## Navigator

Using ICM AssetWeb's Navigator, users can easily maneuver through a vast web of infor-mation. This view and each one thereafter provides clear, intuitive pathways to every item in the system. In a few clicks, the powerful search feature helps users find the information they need and the people who can help.

## Idea Generation and Team Collaboration

Innovation is key to the success of a business [6, 7]. The culture of creativity and idea gen-eration needs to be linked to the daily activities of employees as a mindspring. Recognizing the importance of this undertaking, the ICM AssetWeb provides discussion forums as well as an issue-based tool for structured collaboration.

## Issue-Based Structured Collaboration

The issue-based structured collaboration is a model of discussion that has been around in theory for years but has not been utilized in major applications. By linking the structured collaboration to the competency network and asset management process, IBM created a flexible, easy-to-use, and robust discussion forum that enables practitioners to focus on the resolution of the issues and displays the process of collaboration and resolution in a struc-tured view. The tool enforces the discussion discipline but provides an easy-to-use interface and dynamic group configuration coupled with security control. The action items created in the collaboration are tracked to ensure that the issues get to closure.

One can think of forums as informal meeting places where ideas, comments, and thoughts are shared. All users are welcome to use the forums available on the ICM AssetWeb. The histories of discussion threads are preserved in an easy-to-follow main topic/response format. Users can browse through the topics that are open for discussion and review the re-sponses that others have contributed. They can also take a more active role in discussions by composing their own responses and proposing new main topics for discussion.

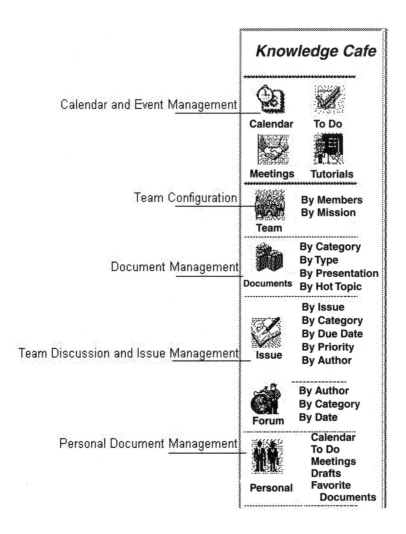

Figure 8.3: Knowledge Cafe for Team Collaboration

(Source: International Business Machines [3])

Knowledge Cafe (Figure 8.3) is a Lotus Notes application designed to support processes that help people work together. Knowledge Cafe facilitates the creation and ongoing development of processes and practices common to high-performance teams. Knowledge Cafe is a powerful tool for information sharing and collaboration on a business unit, team, project, or individual level. As a Lotus Notes application, Knowledge Cafe supports teams whose members are geographically distributed and sometimes unable to be connected to their computer network. Knowledge Cafe supports calendar and event functions, team configuration, issue-based structured collaboration, team discussion forums, and document management for individual team members.

Knowledge Cafe provides a way for practices and teams to customize intellectual capital or select a subset or path of the methodology to instantiate to fit their unique needs. Some of the benefits of using Knowledge Cafe are described below.

## Shared Central Repository

A shared central repository maintains information for users to access and retrieve information. It is more efficient to post information once to a team, rather than numerous times to specific individuals. Knowledge Cafe's configurable categories and subcategories make knowledge transfer more efficient and effective.

## Capture Team Dialog and Issue Resolution

Structured collaboration allows for a flexible, easy-to-use, and robust discussion forum that supports the user's ability to focus on the resolution of issues and displays the process of collaboration and resolution in a structured view. Knowledge Cafe enforces the discussion discipline but provides an easy-to-use interface and dynamic group configuration coupled with security control. The action items created in the collaborations are tracked to ensure the issues get to a closure or that follow-up actions need to be carried out.

## Managing Team's Knowledge

The team leader has total responsibility for structuring the team configuration. This responsibility corresponds to the role of helping to manage the goals and tasks of the team. The team leader facilitates managing both the structure of the team and the way team members use Knowledge Café, and highlights the importance of managing the knowledge of the team that is captured in Knowledge Cafe. Examples of activities made easier and more efficient with Knowledge Cafe include

raising and discussing issues and concerns,

creating (collaborative) products (memos, presentations, and other deliverables),

brainstorming,

preparing for meetings,

tracking meeting agendas and resulting action items, and

posting events and schedules using the calendar function.

Teams are more likely to do their best when they are committed to a common purpose with clear, specific goals, and have a well-defined plan as individuals and as a team on how to achieve these goals. Knowledge Cafe enables the team to define its mission, understand its goals, and manage the activities and tasks to "team, execute, and win" [4].

## Extranets for Customer Care Management

There is a strong demand to focus on customer knowledge management as business adapts to customer-centric operation. The issue is how to capture customer data from several sources, both internal and external, and utilize the critical data and information for areas such as distribution, field services, customer service, marketing, and management.

Extranets are extremely powerful for delivering customer care management. They can mirror, support, and streamline business processes across firms, thereby creating operational efficiencies for both internal and external constituents. Customer care demands efficient links and effective control between the internal and the external business processes. Extranets can control access to information and applications in real time, allowing participating organizations to restrict access to specific information throughout the on-line business cycle. These extranet applications can be used to solve problems and streamline processes in areas such as marketing, human resources, sales and distribution, finance, engineering, and customer service.

### Net Car Dealerships

Consider the impact of the information superhighway on car dealerships. The two appear to be an unlikely pairing. The growth of the networked economy, however, has led to an increasing amount of activity on the Web. Customers are now using Internet services to do their car browsing, studying, servicing, financing, and even purchasing. The big question now is: "How will this emerging networked economy enhance and affect all the members of the automotive industry team: the manufacturers, the dealers, the customers, and the newly established Net dealers?" Visitors to the extranet Web sites will find virtual showrooms, programs to build their own cars, dealer locaters, a narrative of the firm's history and future, news flashes of interest, and financial services.

A customer is no longer only someone who visits a dealership wanting to buy a car. With extranets, a wider variety of people can be reached, ranging from those who are planning on purchasing a car to those with an interest in purchasing to those surfing the Nets. The information on extranets makes everyone a potential customer. Studies show that 73 percent of the 37 million Internet users have searched on-line for information about a specific product or service. The Internet is influencing 14 percent of car purchases. What can a customer gain from surfing the information and knowledge on the Internet?

The entrance of Net dealerships into the automotive distribution channel has greatly changed the marketing model, especially from the customer's point of view. Customers no longer deal solely with dealers; they now have many other options. They can go to any of them for the information they need in making the purchase. As of 1998, there are 48 manufacturers on the Net, over 25,000 dealers on the Net, major car buying services on the Internet, and a large number of dealer Nets. It has been estimated that about 15 percent of all car purchases are attributable to the Net.

   Net dealers advise customers to "do your homework," "select your car," and obtain competing prices before submitting an offer. The dealers hope that only customers who are truly interested in purchasing or leasing a car use their services. The customer submits a price quote request to the Net dealer. The Net dealer goes to its network of dealers and finds the one with the best offer. This dealer then calls the customer with the price quote. The customer can then take a look at the car and decide to buy the car or look elsewhere. The customers can request price quotes for only one car. The following is the business model of this type of new Net dealers [8].

   Customers are allocating more time on the Internet. Manufacturers should make themselves as prominent as possible in the cyber community. With the growth of the automotive industry's exposure on the Internet, manufacturers have the opportunity to advertise and increase public awareness of their cars. By scanning the extranet content of car manufacturers, a company can obtain additional information on customer needs and make use of this information to provide targeted information about their car on their Web pages. Advertising on the Web is less expensive and perhaps more influential than classified advertising. A manufacturer can reach a broader base of customers at a lower cost.

---

| **EXTRANET DEALERSHIPS AT FORD** |
|---|

Ford Motor Company deploys its FocalPt extranet, a system that is designed to support sales and service. This network will provide over 15,000 Ford dealers worldwide with promotional, inventory, and financial information to facilitate closing a sale. In the past, information of this type resided only in printed form and was not readily accessible. The new system uses Web browsers to present sales and promotional literature, including video clips on financing to help prospective customers. It will allow dealers to keep track of repairs and customer preferences. Each dealership will receive a system from Ford running as a server in the FocalPt network connected through an extranet. Communications between the dealers and Ford will be through FordStar, a satellite-based TCP/IP network that already exists for transmitting business information between Ford and its dealers [8].

## Groupware for Collaboration

Collaboration and innovation are essential to knowledge management. Groupware is a system that supports work group computing by enabling communication, sharing, and coordination of information using computers and networks to link a group of users working on a common project (Figure 8.4). Such a system requires the support of high-performance computers, data storage media, and networks. Today's high performance PCs and advanced software have made such systems possible. Currently, Lotus Notes is one of the most widely adopted groupware. It not only manages documents and data, but also manages the flow of work among team members. For maximum effectiveness, groupware should be used to co-ordinate strategic business processes. With a groupware system, members share information and exchange opinions, while delegating the mechanical tasks, such as automatic notifica-tion and message passing, to the computer. In such a collaborative work environment, "tacit" knowledge can be exchanged through the system and new ideas can be generated rapidly. To safeguard the knowledge, Lotus Notes uses an encryption distributed system to provide four levels of security: authentication, access control, field-level privacy, and digital signatures. It protects business-critical information from sabotage and at the same time al-lows authorized end users to assign the proper levels of access to individual documents.

## The Internet and Intranets for Networked Communication

The explosion of Internet communication has provided a tremendous opportunity for com-panies to utilize this technology in knowledge management. Companies can use the Internet as a low-cost communication system to communicate and interchange knowledge internally or externally. From e-mail to file transfer to World Wide Web lookup, knowledge can be shared with millions of users on the Internet. The Internet creates a sharing and collaborating environment that provides one of the best and least expensive ways to learn and develop skills. It greatly reduces the lead time for information gathering and can often obtain valu-able feedback instantly from others.

An intranet is an organization's internal networks that utilizes Internet technologies. It has the added safeguard feature of restricting the access to certain information to authorized users only. The Internet and intranets are excellent media for knowledge sharing and skills development. Knowledge management can utilize the Internet and intranets to establish a virtual knowledge center that serves as a central referral site which provides links to local knowledge banks. The local knowledge banks can store information and knowledge pointers that provide the linkage to other knowledge sources. By keeping knowledge at its source, the bank avoids the redundant storage of knowledge and facilitates knowledge creation and dis-semination.

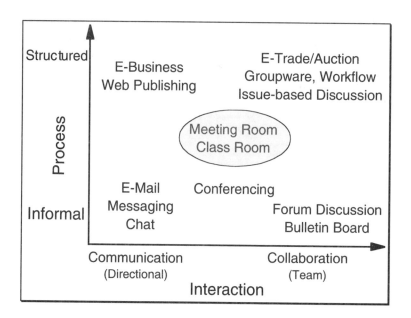

Figure 8.4: Technologies for Collaboration and Communication

(Source: *International Business Machines* [1])

## SECURITY

The growing dependence of organizations on the knowledge infrastructure requires special efforts to provide security protection. Electronic content is particularly sensitive and vulnerable in comparison to paper documents. Risks such as unauthorized access and use, misappropriation, alteration, and destruction all increase in an electronic environment. The firm must raise awareness of the risks and must establish processes and procedures to meet security challenges.

To secure the knowledge infrastructure requires the protection of availability, confidentiality, and integrity of the knowledge content. Availability refers to the infrastructure being accessible and useable on a timely basis in the required manner. Confidentiality means that the data and information are disclosed only to authorized persons, entities, and processes at authorized times and in the authorized manner. Integrity requires that the infrastructure be accurate and complete and that accuracy and completeness be presented over time. The relative priority and significance of availability, confidentiality, and integrity vary according to the information content.

A company must define a security strategy that provides end-to-end protection for applications and information across multiple hardware and software platforms and networks. The company also needs to define a security architecture that properly integrates security services, mechanisms, objects, and management functions across multiple hardware and software platforms and networks. The basic security architecture will include

security services,

security mechanisms,

security objects,

security management (including audit), and

system integrity.

The security strategy must specify a set of common security facilities that can provide protection to resources. ISO Security Standard 7498-2 identifies a set of services that include

identification and authentication (including single logon),

access control (including workstation security),

data confidentiality,

data integrity,

nonrepudiation, and

security management (including audit).

The ability to provide security is bounded by the system and the technology. The diversity of system users—employees, consultants, customers, competitors, or the general public—and their various levels of awareness, training, and interest compound the potential difficulties of providing security. Managing human awareness and institutionalizing a security culture that reflects the corporate value system can contribute significantly to the infrastructure's security. Proper security training with adequate follow-up is fundamental to the reduction of security problems.

## CONCLUSION

In this chapter, we introduced the concept of the corporate knowledge infrastructure. Intranets and extranets will be the main infrastructure to support the new corporate wealth of information and knowledge. Knowledge sharing and collaboration among customers, business partners, and vendors will be the major forces of growth for the communication infrastructure. Intranets and extranets (and their successors) will be the main information superhighways carrying these communications. Internet work communication and collaboration will become a common way to conduct business in the future. The continuous development of digital signature technology and encryption schemes will help ensure secure communications between authorized parties. The users' concern for data and transaction security will be reduced as systems become more secure and users gradually trust the system. The cost of storage capacity and processing power will continue to be reduced. Larger volumes of information will be supported adequately. Much higher speed networks will make it easier to handle the increasing traffic loads demanded by content-rich extranets. Companies that know how to leverage these wellsprings of information and knowledge in extranets will be the winners.

## References

[1] Huang, K. T. "Creating and Exploiting Organizational Knowledge to Speed up Business Growth," in IBM Internal Report, North Tarrytown, NY, IBM, 1996.

[2] Huang, K. T. "Industry Guide to Management of Asset Based Solutions," in IBM Internal Report Tarrytown, NY, IBM, 1996.

[3] Huang, K. T., "Capitalizing on Intellectual Assets, not Infrastructure," *IBM Systems Journal,* Forthcoming.

[4] IBM Annual Report. In http://www.ibm.com/AnnualReport/1997, IBM, 1997.

[5] "IBM Global Services Wins Top Honor For Its Knowledge Management Innovations," in http://www.ibm.com/services/pressrel/pr.889566539.html, IBM, 1998.

[6] Leonard-Barton, D., *Wellsprings of Knowledge: Building and Sustaining the Sources of Innovation.* Harvard Business School Press, Boston, MA, 1995.

[7] Quinn, J. B., J. J. Baruch and K. A. Zien, *Innovation Explosion: Using Intellect and Software to Revolutionize Growth Strategies.* The Free Press, New York, NY, 1997.

[8] Ren, S. and K. T. Huang, "The Automotive Industry and its Newest Recruit: the Net Dealerships," *IBM Intranet Webpage Report,* 1997.

[9] WARIA , *WARIA and Giga Information Group Announce the Finalists of 1998 Giga Excellence Awards for Excellence in Document /Knowledge Management and Workflow/Process Management in North America, http://www.waria.com/awards98.html.* 1998.

Knowledge
Auskunft Conocimient
Informazione
INDICIUM 지식 Savoir
Informative インフォーメーシオ
Nozione
Information ノウ Wissen
정보 SCIENTIA
Información

# Prosper in the Digital Economy

*N*apoleon Bonaparte (1769–1821) once said: "War is ninety percent information." In today's global environment, quality information and organizational knowledge are the firm's new competitive arsenal. Poor-quality information can do more harm than good because it can mislead the user into making wrong decisions. Organizations must collect information from both internal and external sources; manage the information effectively; and utilize it intelligently. Having access to quality information alone, however, does not help the outcome. A decision maker must also have the corresponding knowledge to make judgments based on the information. One who has information but does not hold the domain knowledge to leverage it could be worse off than another who does not have any information at all. Napoleon might have pondered when he was attempting to judge whether a situation was in favor of him for a victory or not. He must have realized that only with high-quality information and comprehensive knowledge of his own troops, his enemies, and how to wage warfare in the specific theater could he win the war.

The next century will witness warfare being waged in an emerging digital economy in which firms will be extinct or distinct because of their abilities to adapt to the digital environment. Firms will survive and prosper through their capabilities to make first moves to implement digital strategies. The implementation will be Web-enabled applications based on the arsenals that they have carefully developed in the forms of quality information and organizational knowledge.

The trend toward the emerging digital economy is clear. As the *Wall Street Journal* reports, "Radio and TV were available for 38 years and 13 years, respectively, before 50 million people tuned in. The Internet hit that benchmark within four years." The Commerce Department has estimated that Internet commerce could pass $300 million a year by 2002 because information technology, led by booming business on the Internet, is spurring growth and curbing inflation simultaneously.

While there is no shortage of Web-based applications, the issue lies in whether these Web-based applications will be fully utilized as mechanisms for changing the way companies conduct business. To compete in the digital economy, Web-based applications must serve the purpose of implementing the three major principles:

> helping customers to win
>
> empowering knowledge workers to execute
>
> configuring business partners to team

With these principles in mind, we present an approach, based on IBM's experience, for deploying Web-based applications. We substantiate how these Web applications, when based on quality information and organizational knowledge, can be efficiently implemented and effectively deployed to increase business in the booming digital economy. We conclude this chapter and book with a prognosis of life in the future.

## KNOWLEDGE-BASED ECONOMY

As we approach the digital economy, the business environment is experiencing a tremendous change. Globalization, technological innovations, and competition are forcing companies to shift the fundamentals of how business is conducted. Increasingly, companies are moving rapidly from labor-based businesses to knowledge-based businesses. Companies are seeking to leverage vast stores of their information and expertise to capitalize in this emerging knowledge-based global economy while embracing the ideas of "knowledge management" to further define and facilitate this new knowledge revolution [1, 3]. They realize that the benefits of institutionalized knowledge management are broad in scope. People from different disciplines, teams, and locations are working together to share and improve the knowledge created to implement the internal processes so that this knowledge can be leveraged worldwide in a repeatable and sustainable manner, thereby extending the reach of their differentiating values. Companies are working to leverage their own competencies to focus on sharing a wide variety of intellectual capital among units, ranging from processes, business patterns, design solutions, to lessons learned. They are learning the importance of embedding technology into effective business designs so that markedly different patterns of sustained value growth can be achieved. The advent of high-capability intranet technologies is enabling the collaboration that is critical to the ability of rapidly transforming customer needs into deliverable value [5]. These new capabilities can strip away the boundaries within corporations that have traditionally inhibited the ability to tap the wellspring of knowledge that often exists in isolated pockets throughout a company [6]. To survive and excel in this rapidly changing global economy, a new emphasis on innovation, competency, and collaboration is needed [4, 7, 10]. The goal of managing knowledge as a strategic asset is not only to seek the short-term returns, but to maximize the long-term advantage over competitors. The ability to learn, collaborate, and innovate faster than your competitors becomes the only sustainable source of competitive advantage in the coming knowledge-based economy. To stay competitive, companies need to capitalize on their intellectual assets [5].

In the late 1980s, Peter Drucker predicted that "the factory of tomorrow will be organized around information rather than automation" [2]. Today his insight is becoming a reality. Developments in business such as networking in the economy and extending enterprises are compelling corporations to manage their knowledge as an asset. Yesterday's economies rewarded firms for maintaining strong organizational hierarchies and strict work rules. Therefore, as the economy of tomorrow emerges, a company's prosperity is becoming increasingly dependent on the intellectual capacity of its workers and their ability to change in a dynamic business environment. Consequently, finding and applying methodologies to generate and reuse knowledge faster and more effectively are becoming the most promising and valuable new management practices [1, 5, 7, 10].

## COMPETITIVE DRIVERS

The world in which we live is changing in a fundamental way. Markets are increasingly international, tariff barriers have disappeared, and the economy is becoming more information based [11]. To succeed, an enterprise must meet the challenge of global competition for markets. These are the four change drivers that most of today's Chief Executives Officers (CEOs) focus on: innovation, responsiveness, productivity, and competency. While they present a challenge to today's enterprises, they also open the door to a wealth of opportunities.

The solutions and methodologies that enable information and knowledge management have been available. Today, however, trends in the marketplace and new technology are redefining the way many of them can be used which make them more critical than ever before to intellectually intensive companies. The knowledge management program needs to focus on addressing these four key drivers.

## Innovation

In today's business, one of the critical success factors for enterprises is the ability to innovate. That is, to quickly develop products, processes, and services which are desired by customers at a competitive price; to find new solutions to old problems; be able to adapt solutions to changing circumstances; and apply the lessons of experience, and technologic solutions to the new challenges presented in a changing world. More importantly, no enterprise is self-sufficient — even a company as large as IBM. The most important shift is that the innovation process now extends outside the enterprise. In many industry sectors, individual companies are really part of a broader business system. One example is in automobile production, with its networks of designers, material suppliers, parts manufacturers, assemblers, and dealers. The computer industry is another, involving chip designers, component manufacturers, assemblers, system software manufacturers, application software manufacturers, and distributors of all kinds ranging from mail order to superstores.

Many experienced CEOs would agree that business performance is ultimately limited by the external environment. An enterprise's ability to compete depends on interactions with suppliers, customers, banks, shareholders, the educational system, and government regulators. The more effective a company's interactions with these external players, the better it will perform. An enterprise needs to extend the management of its knowledge sharing network beyond its own knowledge workers to its customers, business partners, and suppliers.

## Responsiveness

Hockey player Wayne Gretzky once said that his success was due to his ability to skate "not to where the puck is but where it will be." An enterprise needs to have the same instincts to provide customer services. In today's world of open information architectures, customers have many choices, and enterprises have to move quickly and efficiently, so they cannot only react to, but also anticipate, customer needs. In this fast-moving world, product availability is essential. Enterprises have to ensure customers can get the products they want, with the features they're looking for, at the places where they want to buy. The key measure of cycle time — how long it takes to get from customer purchase order to ready to use — is a major yardstick of measuring responsiveness.

Speed of implementation has always been a major determinant in the success of companies. The integration of electronic commerce and other technologies in the business mainstream has made this factor even more consequential. Today, neither a company nor its clients can afford to wait long for the implementation of global solutions. Therefore, the processes for developing them must make optimal use of available knowledge resources. In order to streamline these processes, it is imperative to establish a means for eliminating the costs associated with reinvention and to alleviate the frustrations endured by practitioners when they cannot benefit from lessons learned by others.

Today's workforce with its sophisticated technology is more mobile than ever before. In the past, when a new employee came on board, he or she would simply ask, "Where is my office? Which PC do I get?" Today, workers want to know what kind of network facilities are available that they can dial up and work from globally. They constantly need access to information and knowledge assets from various locations. This requires truly interactive, transaction-intensive, on-line support to enable them to accomplish real work — to reshape the way products are designed, the way customers are supported, and the way decisions are made [5].

## Productivity

Robert Reich [11] describes in *The Work of Nations* three emerging categories of work and competitive positions: routine production services, in-person services, and symbolic-analytic services. Routine production work can be performed anywhere in the world. Most in-person service workers receive the minimum wage, which has been declining in real terms in the United States. The symbolic-analytic services, which are essentially performed by the knowledge workers, are the key competitive advantage for the new economy. They are those who solve and identify problems by manipulating symbols. The intellectual capital-intensive business is the opportunity for growth.

Globalization, privatization, and alliances are progressively changing the face of the competitive market landscape. While these trends reveal an abundance of new opportunities for companies to take advantage of, they also pose the question of how to manage global businesses effectively and efficiently. Today, globalization is less about where you go. It is more about how you can provide services from there. Companies need to generate practices that can be tailored to accommodate the regional differences of where they are located, which involves creating a framework and culture for global collaboration.

Continuous improvement in operation efficiency and productivity is essential to long-term earnings growth and is a key vital determinant of an enterprise's competitiveness. Generally, all costs are ultimately controllable, even items such as depreciation. With this in mind, the emphasis for an enterprise is not simply on cost reduction, but also on maximizing global resource productivity in the context of long-term growth and profitable operations. Intellectual capital plays a key role in the increase of productivity. Effective measurement of the increase of productivity and new business opportunity by leveraging intellectual capital is the key.

## Competency

Companies need to establish their core competencies. A competency is a logical grouping of productive resources that represent a leading edge and differentiated capability that is valued in the marketplace. A core competency is not easily replicated by other firms because it is an organizational capability (not individual) that has been created by combining knowledge assets, business processes, and supporting technology. Each company must have a unique competency that identifies it as different from its competitors. For example, Sony of Japan is known for its "pocketability." It has the competency of skills, resources, and know-how to manufacture portable high-quality consumer products. The competency represents rapid transfer of experience and ideas that can be applied in a consistent manner across organizational and geographic boundaries. A competency is a company's focused capability that does not claim to be all things to all people. It is designed to accumulate knowledge assets through reuse to shed irrelevancies. Because competencies are difficult to duplicate, it reinforces a company to be more competitive [9].

## COMPETING FOR INTELLECTUAL INFLUENCE

Firms must set up and leverage an information and knowledge management system about their customers that is organized toward their customers' business needs dynamically. This is the key for the firm to maintain industry leadership and move up to the next level of growth. The effort should focus on the three principles described below: helping customers to win, empowering knowledge workers to execute, and configuring business partners to team [5].

### Helping Customers to Win

Many industries are experiencing a highly competitive marketplace with rising customer demands. A new focus on customer relationship management is driving fundamental change at many leading companies to create customer loyalty and stability by distinguishing themselves in their customers' eyes. To continue to succeed in maintaining the ongoing win-win relationship with customers, a company needs to focus on customer insight and customer alignment. Customer insight requires a firm to have in-depth knowledge of their customers' industries, businesses, and issues, challenges, and competitive environments. Not all customers are created equal. Combining this knowledge about the customer with technological expertise results in solutions that address each customer's unique business requirements. Customer alignment requires a firm to put itself in the mind of the customer and see business from their point of view and align the organization's capability in order to deliver value to customers. Armed with this customer relationship strategy and combined with insight into customer values, companies are able to consistently deliver quick response by bringing all aspects of resources, including IT solutions, to bear on a customer's problem when the customer needs it.

By working together with customers at every level of the organization, it cultivates and develops strong, enduring relationships with customers. In turn, it leads to repeat business, referrals, lower direct costs through improved targeting, and increased revenue. Quality information and knowledge management plays an essential role in providing continuous creation and sharing of intellectual capital about customers and industries. It also provides a process to collect a wealth of information about the customers and enable knowledge discovery.

## Empowering Knowledge Workers to Execute

In today's business environment, corporate knowledge is an increasingly valuable asset. Corporations are competing among each other for intellectual influence. Knowledge workers will actively surf from one network to another, searching for information and solutions. They will also publish on networks, sharing information that they have found and information or works they have produced themselves. To meet this challenge, the business infrastructure needs to support two-way communication and mutual persuasion. The keys will be collaboration and teamwork. Teaming is an essential part of everyday business. Teams succeed only on the collective strength of their members' skills and professionalism. Companies need to organize knowledge about customers and processes, particularly for front-line knowledge workers. This is especially critical for the front-line operations where the process and the customer are connected. As customers' problems are getting more complex in an ever-changing and increasingly networked world, organizations need to bring a unique combination of business experience, technological expertise, and intellectual assets to the customer at the right time and in the right place. Teams need to act with a sense of urgency and decisiveness, and leverage multidisciplinary teaming and knowledge sharing to create a faster and more effective way of getting the job done. Knowledge reuse must be everyday practice. Furthermore, teaming knowledge workers generates knowledge intensity from diverse viewpoints and opinions.

The world of information technology is growing and changing with unprecedented speed toward services — creating solutions for customers across geographic and functional boundaries. Organizations need to empower knowledge workers so that they are constantly encouraged to seek improvements, engage in innovative thinking, take necessary risks, and focus on creating solutions for customers. Functional departments and geographic divisions fragment and isolate the various activities and information about customers and how a company serves customers. This information is rarely brought together and shared. Companies need to establish a corporate knowledge infrastructure and develop global competency networks to team the best practice "subject expertise" to nurture the creation of best practice. The knowledge base can then be shared across all parts of the company, enabling the entire organization to work toward the same objective. Through intranet technology, they can be accessed anyplace, anytime. As the workplace changes, knowledge workers are becoming more flexible and mobile. They are more accountable, both individually and as teams. Furthermore, some of this effort can also be easily recustomized to share with customers. Intranets provide the base for increasing businesses, and extranets provides a mechanism to partner with customers.

## Configuring Business Partners to Team

In the electronic business marketplace, there is a shifting focus from value chains to value networks. Value networks allow for new value creation by focusing competency configuration to enable new capability. A strategic networked alliance is a powerful, systematic process that can configure different competencies to form a business alliance to deliver innovative solutions and dominate the market. It can significantly boost a firm's competitive position, react to market situations quickly, and minimize total risk and costs. Through strategic alliance, global corporations can create a competitive chasm between them and their competitors by redefining and restructuring relationships with their strength. Examples are the WinTel alliance between Microsoft and Intel on PC platforms, Visa, Mastercard, and IBM on the Security Electronic Transaction (SET) protocol. Strategic alliances provide a launching pad for greater innovation, faster time to market, and higher profitability. They can also be used to link suppliers and manufacturers on the supply and services network. Strategic networked alliances can also be applied to the globalized market, for example, Northwestern and KLM airlines. Many foreign companies have alliances with national local companies in Asian-Pacific countries to enter and dominate the telecommunication market.

The future marketplace will look and behave very differently from today's market. It will be much more dynamic and integrated. There will be rich opportunity to create strategic networked alliances. It will comprise powerful and demanding customers. The trend is for companies to work together toward common business goals. Individual companies are able to leverage their superior core business competency through the collective abilities of the team partners. Knowledge management is expected to expand beyond the intranet to extranet environment to support growing needs for strategic networked alliances. Extranets can link business partners and suppliers securely.

## A Web-Based Advisor

New business opportunities emerge based on new Web-based business capabilities. One such example is "e-business" at IBM. For example, a Web-based "e-advisor" would be a useful mechanism for customer care management in the health care industry. Consumers in the health care industry often seek independent third-party information and analysis. They need to know health care options, including coverage of a health care plan, medical treatments available, and options for financing their health insurance. The "e-advisor" would have access to all of the latest information from all relevant parties and be able to sort through a sea of information, compile useful information, conduct an analysis, and offer useful answers to consumers. It can include characteristics and performance ratings of the options, similar to those an independent financial advisor might offer. Prepackaged "e-advisors" similar to *Consumer Reports* or *Michelin Guides* to support various aspects of decision making would also be useful to consumers.

The set of capabilities gained by employing Web-based mechanisms will be critical to a company's competitive strategies, particularly for gaining consumer intimacy and loyalty. The Web-based business requires interactions with customers, links to partners, and networks of intraenterprise operations. Its successful implementation will also depend on secure, high-bandwidth, scalable networks operating under open standards that allow transmission of any type of digitized information such as data from laboratory to medical claims.

As we have seen in other industries, the Internet will allow companies in the health care industry to establish "value webs" with other players for mutual benefit. For example, the health care industry can generate information to support health care standardization, provide education and support to patients and families to increase compliance, and ultimately

establish comprehensive disease management programs that integrate care service into information service on-line.

To gain consumers' loyalty, companies must maintain strategic flexibility while moving rapidly to establish core competency. The winners are likely to be the ones that establish
new business models that exploit the new technologies and excel at customer intimacy and
loyalty, building strong nonsubstitutable relationships.

## TRANSFORMING THE FUTURE OF LIFE

Networks have begun to generate a profound impact on many aspects of everyday life in
society. As more people have access to networked communication, the information technology service market is getting even bigger than before. We identify changes in three key areas that are already occurring and that we expect to transform society and greatly impact the
business culture. First, people are networked; second, knowledge is shared, mined, and discovered; and third, teams and companies are virtual entities instead of physical entities.

### Networked Life

The *New York Times* reported on new aspects of the family vacation [8]. The wife, who is a
sales clerk and also moderator of an on-line discussion group, had insisted on packing the
portable computer. She checked her e-mail from the resort hotel and sneaked in a round of
her favorite on-line game, Slingo.

More than a quarter of American households own pagers, double the number a year
ago. More than one-third use cellular phones, and seven million people regularly check their
business E-mail from outside the office, according to an IDC report. Many business travelers
insist on booking their flights on the aisle seat so they can turn their tray table into a mobile
office. A lawyer, who sometimes spends hours at his weekend home on the phone and computer, said the technology had radically changed clients' demands of him on vacation. While
he used to be available by phone and documents could be faxed or delivered overnight, he
can now receive them in minutes by e-mail.

The network-connected world has changed our life and the way we do business and
perform our work. New opportunities are created from doing business anywhere, anytime.
Armed with an extranet connection to intellectual capital, the possibilities are only limited
by one's imagination!

### Knowledge Sharing and Mining

Knowledge is largely derived from information in context. Network computing technology
allows corporations to capture information, perform actions, and transfer information and
knowledge among everyone globally. The IS department is able to transfer information and
knowledge derived from the transaction processing systems and other sources to anyone

who can use it through corporate intranets. Internet technology gives us easy, instantaneous access to an electronic dynamic library with a gigantic wealth of information at our finger-tips. Some say, to a certain extent the Internet is a huge junk yard. Others say the Internet is a big gold mine. Both viewpoints are correct. The capability to access a flood of information sources has created the phenomenon of anxiety, mainly driven by the inability to deal with the overwhelming glut of information.

Many corporate senior executives need to read more than 20 different types of maga-zines in order to keep up to date with what is happening to their customers and the industry. This is only one of their extra jobs in addition to regular meetings, travel, office paper work, decision making, discussion forums and e-mails. They are fighting the "information gap" and do not have enough time to read and absorb all the information they have. This chal-lenge is true to all levels of today's business executives and knowledge workers who need to access both internal and external information resources as well as peers for consensus building and best practices.

What makes the difference in this new era of information revolution is being able to reach from the world of information processing to the world of communications, which until recently was based on analog technology. Governments in all parts of the world, including the United States, Europe, Japan, and other Asian countries, are strong advocates for the urgent need to construct the global information infrastructure or information superhighway. This effort creates new dimensions and opportunities for "information-related products" which include corporate image, marketing messages, customer support, news, entertainment, business knowledge, and intelligence. Both Gartner and BPR strategic analysis reports indi-cate that the basics of IS organizations will expand over the next five years from transaction processing to enabling information and knowledge sharing. Therefore, knowledge manage-ment will become the dominant driver of the IS organizations. This mission of corporate CIOs will have to address the new issues related to the knowledge infrastructure beyond the conventional transaction-processing view.

The National Information Infrastructure (NII) intends to enhance our national well-being by providing increased access to timely and reliable information with impact on edu-cation, life-long learning, government services, and entertainment and shopping. Likewise, the corporate knowledge infrastructure needs to use a wide range of technologies to provide a new way for employees and customers to learn, work, entertain, and interact with each other. The knowledge infrastructure must focus on capacity to share contents — organized data, information and knowledge for access, use, discussion, and continuous improvement and innovation. The knowledge infrastructure is built on top of two established information infrastructures. One is the telecommunication infrastructure which provides the high-bandwidth communication network for people to get connected and communicate. The other is the system infrastructure that integrated heterogeneous computers, information appliances, databases, and applications for information to flow freely through the network with appro-priate privacy and security protection. The knowledge infrastructure is a set of collaboration and knowledge discovery applications, such as e-mail, groupware, conferencing, and knowl-edge mining. Data mining is like a microscope which drills down to the details and allows us to dissect small things into even smaller pieces. Knowledge discovery is the opposite. It is like a telescope which can examine enormous objects and see the associations. Knowledge discovery capability differentiates a leader from the rest of the companies.

## Being Virtual Rather than Physical

Extranets provide an opportunity for systems to be as accessible as possible. Both large and small companies will have the same timely information and opportunity to best serve their clients. Any customers, whether they are large or small, are allowed to obtain the specific information they need, and are encouraged to think of other ways they can do business to their advantage. This presents an enormous opportunity for new business players. Size is no longer a dominant factor. Instead, services and customer care differentiate one company from the rest. Effective customer care can be a company's core competency for growth. Extranets can make a company that is in the information and knowledge-intensive business succeed. A company can sell "information products." It can provide essential information on key topics such as security, development tools, electronic commerce, outsourcing, knowledge management, customer care, and managing upgrades. It can be a virtual consultant and establish a brand name. It can also include referral directories of solution providers, plus an electronic community for peer-to-peer communication.

Video conferencing on the network is an inevitable next target. As a collaborative tool, it brings users together and fosters teamwork nearly as fast as it chews up bandwidth. A person on the North Slope can hold up a broken part to the camera and a technician in the Anchorage office can tell them how to fix it. An expert organ surgeon in Boston can instruct a doctor in Montana on how to perform a surgical operation while he views the scene on a video screen. With the increased availability of videoconferencing bandwidth, meetings can take place much more often without the participants being physically together. Teleconferencing is very popular in today's business environment. There are different levels of interactions preferred among knowledge workers. With video conferencing, the team dynamics among the conferencing participants can change. This can create both opportunity for interactions and new problems and resistance. It will change the aspect of employee-to-employee and employee-to-manager relationships dramatically. It also creates an unlimited environment for creativity and innovation for teamwork. In a more virtual than physical world, there will be unforeseen opportunities and problems for both individuals and businesses.

## CONCLUSION

We all need to have the right mix of knowledge and experience necessary to stay ahead in a fast-paced dynamic environment. Quality information and organizational knowledge are the critical foundations for excellence and dominance.

## References

[1]  Davenport, T. and L. Prusak, *Working Knowledge*. Harvard Business School Press, Boston, MA, 1997.

[2]  Drucker, P. F., "The Coming of the New Organization," *Harvard Business Review,* 66(1), 1988, pp. 45–53.

[3]  Drucker, P. F., *Post Capitalist Society*. Butterworth Heineman, Oxford, 1993.

[4]  Huang, K. T., "Knowledge Is Power: So Use It or Lose It," in http://www.ibm.com/services/articles/inttelcapsum.html: IBM, 1998.

[5]  Huang, K. T., "Capitalizing on Intellectual Assets, not Infrastructure," *IBM Systems Journal,* Forthcoming.

[6]  Leonard-Barton, D., *Wellsprings of Knowledge: Building and Sustaining the Sources of Innovation*. Harvard Business School Press, Boston, MA, 1995.

[7]  Nonaka, I. and H. Takeuchi, *The Knowledge-Creating Company: How Japanese Companies Create the Dynamics of Innovation*. Oxford University Press, New York, NY, 1995.

[8]  NYT , *http://www.nytimes.com/library/cyber/week/071397vacation.html*, 1997.

[9]  Porter, M. E., *Competitive Advantage*. Free Press, New York, 1985.

[10] Quinn, J. B., J. J. Baruch and K. A. Zien, *Innovation Explosion: Using Intellect and Software to Revolutionize Growth Strategies*. The Free Press, New York, NY, 1997.

[11] Reich, R., *The Work of Nations*. Alfred A. Knopf, New York, NY, 1991.

[1]     Bailey, R., *Human Error in Computer Systems*. Prentice Hall, Englewood Cliffs, 1983.

[2]     Ballou, D. and G. Tayi, "Managerial Issues in Data Quality," in *Proceedings of The 1996 Conference on Information Quality*. Cambridge, MA, pp. 186–206, 1996.

[3]     Ballou, D. P. and H. L. Pazer, "Modeling Data and Process Quality in Multi-input, Multi-output Information Systems," *Management Science, 31(2), 1985, pp. 150–162.

[4]     Ballou, D. P. and H. L. Pazer, "Cost/Quality Tradeoffs for Control Procedures in Information Systems," *International Journal of Management Science*, 15(6), 1987, pp. 509–521.

[5]     Ballou, D. P. and H. L. Pazer, "Designing Information Systems to Optimize the Accuracy-Timeliness Tradeoff," *Information Systems Research*, 6(1), 1995, pp. 51–72.

[6]     Ballou, D. P., R. Y. Wang, H. Pazer and G. K. Tayi, "Modeling Information Manufacturing Systems to Determine Information Product Quality," *Management Science*, 44(4), 1998, pp. 462–484.

[7]     Bowen, P. *Managing Data Quality in Accounting Information Systems: A Stochastic Clearing System Approach*. Unpublished Ph.D. dissertation, University of Tennessee, 1993.

[8]     Brodie, M. L., "Data Quality in Information Systems," *Information and Management*, (3), 1980, pp. 245–258.

[9]     Bruce, T. A., *Designing Quality Databases with IDEF1X Information Models*. Dorset House Publishing, New York, 1991.

[10]    Bulkeley, W., "Databases Are Plagued by Reign of Error," *Wall Street Journal*, May 26, 1992 p. B6.

[11] Chen, P. S., "The Entity-Relationship Approach," in <u>Information Technology in Action:</u> <u>Trends and Perspectives</u>, R. Y. Wang, Ed. 1993, Prentice Hall, Englewood Cliffs, NJ, 1993.

[12] Codd, E. F., "A Relational Model of Data for Large Shared Data Banks," *Communications of the ACM,* 13(6), 1970, pp. 377–387.

[13] Codd, E. F., "Extending the Relational Database Model to Capture More meaning," *ACM Transactions on Database Systems,* 4(4), 1979, pp. 397–434.

[14] Codd, E. F., *The Relational Model for Database Management: Version 2.* Addison-Wesley, Reading, MA, 1990.

[15] Corey, D. "Data Quality Improvement in the Military Health Services Systems and the U.S. Army Medical Department," in *Proceedings of the 1997 Conference on Information Quality.* Cambridge, MA, pp. 37–62, 1997.

[16] Corey, D., L. Cobler, K. Haynes and R. Walker, "Data Quality Assurance Activities in the Military Health Services System," in *Proceedings of the 1996 Conference on Information Quality.* Cambridge, MA, pp. 127–153, 1996.

[17] CRG, *Information Quality Assessment Survey: Administrator's Guide.* Cambridge Research Group, Cambridge, MA, 1997.

[18] CRG, *Integrity Analyzer: A Software Tool for TDQM.* Cambridge Research Group, Cambridge, MA, 1997.

[19] Cykana, P., A. Paul and M. Stern, "DoD Guidelines on Data Quality Management," in *Proceedings of The 1996 Conference on Information Quality.* Cambridge, MA, pp. 154–171, 1996.

[20] Deming, E., *Out of the Crisis.* Center for Advanced Engineering Study, MIT, Cambridge, MA, 1986.

[21] Deming, E., *Quality, Productivity, and Competitive Position.* MIT Center for Advanced Engineering Study, Cambridge, 1982.

[22] Denning, E. and P. J. Denning, "Data Security," *ACM Computing Surveys*, 11(3), 1979, pp. 227–250.

[23] Fellegi, I. P. and A. B. Sunter, "A Theory for Record Linkage," *Journal of the American Statistical Association,* 64(328), 1969, pp. 1183–1210.

[24] Firth, C. P. and R. Y. Wang, *Data Quality Systems: Evaluation and Implementation.* Cambridge Market Intelligence Ltd., London, 1996.

[25] Garvin, D. A., "Competing on the Eight Dimensions of Quality," *Harvard Business Review,* 65(6), 1987, pp. 101–109.

[26] Hansen, J. V., "Audit Considerations in Distributed Processing Systems," *Communications of the ACM,* 26(5), 1983, pp. 562–569.

[27]   Harvind, R., "Federal Express Wins in the Tough Services Category," in <u>Road to the Baldridge Award: The Quest for Total quality</u>. 1992, Butterworth-Heinenmann, Stoneham, 1992.

[28]   Hauser, J. R. and D. Clausing, "The House of Quality," *Harvard Business Review,* 66(3), 1988, pp. 63–73.

[29]   Huh, Y. U., F. R. Keller, T. C. Redman and A. R. Watkins, "Data Quality," *Information and Software Technology,* 32(8), 1990, pp. 559–565.

[30]   Jang, Y., A. T. Ishii and R. Y. Wang, "A Qualitative Approach to Automatic Data Quality Judgment," *Journal of Organizational Computing,* 5(2), 1995, pp. 101–121.

[31]   Jarke, M. and Y. Vassiliou, "Data Warehouse Quality: A Review of the DWQ Project," in *Proceedings of The 1997 Conference on Information Quality.* Cambridge, MA, pp. 299–313, 1997.

[32]   Kahn, B. K., D. M. Strong and R. Y. Wang, "Information Quality Benchmarks: Product and Service Performance," *Communications of the ACM,* Accepted for publication.

[33]   Knight, B. "The Data Pollution Problem," *Computerworld,* September 28, p. 81–82, 1992.

[34]   Kon, H. B., J. Lee and R. Y. Wang , *A Process View of Data Quality* (No. TDQM-93-01). Total Data Quality Management (TDQM) Research Program, MIT Sloan School of Management, Cambridge, MA, 1993.

[35]   Kwan, S. and D. Rotem. "Analysis and Tradeoff Between Data Accuracy and Performance of Databases," in *Proceedings of the Conference on Scientific and Statistical Database Management.* Germantown, 1992.

[36]   Lai, S. G. *"Data Quality Case Study - Optiserv Limited,"* Master Thesis, MIT Sloan School of Management, Cambridge, MA, 1993.

[37]   Laudon, K. C., "Data Quality and Due Process in Large Interorganizational Record Systems," *Communications of the ACM,* 29(1), 1986, pp. 4–11.

[38]   Lee, Y. W. "Learning by Solving DQ Problems: Managing DQ Knowledge," in *Proceedings of INFORMS,* Washington, D.C., 1996.

[39]   Lee, Y. W. Why "Know Why" Knowledge is Useful for Solving Information Quality Problems. in *Proceedings of Americas Conference on Information Systems.* Phoenix, AZ: pp. 200–202, 1996.

[40]   Lee, Y. W., D. M. Strong, L. Pipino and R. Y. Wang , *A Methodology-based Software Tool for Data Quality Management* (No. TDQM-97-02). MIT TDQM Research Program, Cambridge, MA, 1997.

[41]   LePage, N., "Data Quality Control at United States Fidelity and Guaranty Company," in <u>Data Quality Control: Theory and Pragmatics</u>, G. E. Liepens and V. R. R. Uppuluri, ed., Marcel Dekker, Inc., New York, 1990.

[42]   Levitin, A. and T. Redman, "Quality Dimensions of a Conceptual View," *Information Processing & Management,* 31(1), 1995, pp. 8.

[43]   Levitin, A. V. and T. Redman, "A Model of the Data (Life) Cycles with Application to Quality," *Information and Software Technology,* 35(4), 1995, pp. 7.

[44]   Liepins, G. E., "Sound Data Are a Sound Investment," *Quality Progress,* 22(9), 1989, pp. 61–64.

[45]   Liepins, G. E. and V. R. R. Uppuluri, ed. *Data Quality Control: Theory and Pragmatics.* D. B. Owen. Vol. 112. 1990, Marcel Dekker, Inc., New York. 360 pages.

[46]   Little, D. and S. Misra, "Auditing for Database Integrity (IS Management)," *Journal of Systems Management,* 45(8), 1994, pp. 6–11.

[47]   Little, R. J. A. and P. J. Smith, "Editing and Imputation for Quantitative Survey Data," 82(397), 1987, pp. 56–68.

[48]   Madnick, S. and R. Y. Wang. "Integrating Disparate Databases for Composite Answers," in *Proceedings of the Proceedings of the 21ˢᵗ Hawaii International Conference on System Sciences.* Hawaii, pp. 583–592, 1988.

[49]   Madnick, S. and R. Y. Wang, *Introduction to Total Data Quality Management (TDQM) Research Program* (No. TDQM-92-01). Total Data Quality Management (TDQM) Research Program, MIT Sloan School of Management, Cambridge, MA, 1992.

[50]   Madnick, S. E., ed. *The Strategic Use of Information Technology.* 1987, Oxford University Press, New York. 206 pages.

[51]   Madnick, S. E., "Integrating Information from Global Systems: Dealing With the "On- and Off-Ramps" of the Information Superhighway," *Journal of Organizational Computing,* 5(2), 1995, pp. 69–82.

[52]   Madnick, S. E., "Database in the Internet Age," *Database Programming and Design,* 1997, pp. 28–33.

[53]   Matsumura, A. and N. Shouraboura. "Competing with Quality Information," in *Proceedings of The 1996 Conference on Information Quality.* Cambridge, MA: pp. 72-86, 1996.

[54]   McGee, A. M., *Total Data Quality Management (TDQM): Zero Defect Data Capture* (No. TDQM-92-07). Total Data Quality Management (TDQM) Research Program, MIT Sloan School of Management, Cambridge, MA, 1992.

[55]   McGee, J. and L. Prusak, *Managing Information Strategically.* The Ernst & Young Information Management Series, John Wiley & Sons, Inc., New York, 1993.

[56]   Meyen, D. M. and M. J. Willshire. "A Data Quality Engineering Framework," in *Proceedings of The 1997 Conference on Information Quality.* Cambridge, MA, pp. 95–116, 1997.

[57]   Mollema, K. I. J., "Quality of Information and EDP Audit," *Informatie,* 33(7–8), 1991, pp. 482–485.

[58]   Myer, M. H. and M. H. Zack, "The Design and Development of Information Products," *Sloan Management Review,* (Spring), 1996, pp. 43–59.

[59]  Oman, R. C. and T. B. Ayers, "Improving Data Quality," *Journal of Systems Management,* 39(5), 1988, pp. 31–35.

[60]  O'Neill, E. T. and D. Vizine-Goetz, "Quality Control in Online Databases," in <u>Annual Review of Information, Science, and Technology</u>, M. E. Williams, ed.,  Elsevier Publishing Company, 1988.

[61]  O'Reilly, C. A. I., "Variations in Decision Makers' Use of Information Sources: the Impact of Quality and Accessibility of Information," *Academy of Management Journal,* 4(25), 1982, pp. 756–771.

[62]  Orr, K. "Data Quality and Systems Theory," in *Proceedings of the 1996 Conference on Information Quality.* Cambridge, MA, pp. 1–15, 1996.

[63]  Padman, R. and M. Tzourakis, "Quality Metrics for Healthcare Data: An Analytical Approach," in *Proceedings of the 1997 Conference on Information Quality.* Cambridge, MA, pp. 19–36, 1997.

[64]  Page, W. and P. Kaomea, "Using Quality Attributes to Produce Optimal Tactical Information," in *Proceedings of the Fourth Annual Workshop on Information Technologies and Systems (WITS).* Vancouver, British Columbia, Canada, pp. 145–154, 1994.

[65]  Paradice, D. B. and W. L. Fuerst, "An MIS Data Quality Methodology Based on Optimal Error Detection," *Journal of Information Systems,* 5(1), 1991, pp. 48–66.

[66]  Parasuraman, A., V. A. Zeithaml and L. L. Berry, "SERVQUAL: A Multiple-Item Scale for Measuring Consumer Perceptions of Service Quality," *Journal of Retailing,* 64(1), 1988, pp. 12–37.

[67]  Pautke, R. W. and T. C. Redman, "Techniques to Control and Improve Quality of Data in Large Databases," in *Proceedings of Statistics Canada Symposium 90.* Canada, pp. 319–333, 1990.

[68]  Percy, T. "My Data, Right or Wrong," *Datamation,* June 1, p. 123–128, 1986.

[69]  Pipino, L., Y. W. Lee and R. Y. Wang, *Measuirng Information Quality* (No. TDQM-97-04). MIT Sloan School of Management, Cambridge, MA, 1998.

[70]  Pipino, L. and R. Y. Wang, *Developing Measurement Scales for Data Quality Dimensions* (No. TDQM-96-04). MIT Sloan School of Management, Cambridge, MA, 1996.

[71]  Reddy, M. P. and R. Y. Wang. "Estimating Data Accuracy in a Federated Database Environment," in *Proceedings of 6th International Conference, CISMOD (Also in Lecture Notes in Computer Science).* Bombay, India, pp. 115–134, 1995.

[72]  Redman, T. C., *Data Quality: Management and Technology.* Bantam Books, New York, 1992.

[73]  Redman, T. C., *Data Quality for the Information Age.* Artech House, Boston, MA, 1996.

[74]  Ryan, J. F., "Data Quality with LIMS," *Quality,* May, 1988, pp. Q12–Q15.

[75]    Segev, A., "On Information Quality and the WWW Impact," in *Proceedings of the 1996 Conference on Information Quality*. Cambridge, MA, pp. 16–23, 1996.

[76]    Southern, G. and A. U. Murray, "Quality Information Management: The Way to a Better Company Culture," *Industrial Management & Data Systems*, 92(7), 1992, pp. 9-12.

[77]    Strong, D., Y. Lee and R. Y. Wang, "Ten Potholes in the Road to Information Quality," *IEEE Computer*, 30(8), 1997, pp. 38–46.

[78]    Strong, D. M. and B. K. Kahn, ed. *Proceedings of the 1997 Conference on Information Quality*. 1997, Cambridge, MA.  372 pages.

[79]    Strong, D. M., Y. W. Lee and R. Y. Wang, "Data Quality in Context," *Communications of the ACM*, 40(5), 1997, pp. 103–110.

[80]    Te'eni, D., "Behavioral Aspects of Data Production and Their Impact on Data Quality," *Journal of Database Management*, 4(2), 1993, pp. 30–38.

[81]    Wand, Y. and R. Y. Wang, "Anchoring Data Quality Dimensions in Ontological Foundations," *Communications of the ACM*, 39(11), 1996, pp. 86–95.

[82]    Wang, R. Y. and H. B. Kon, "Towards Total Data Quality Management (TDQM)," in Information Technology in Action: Trends and Perspectives, R. Y. Wang, ed., Prentice Hall, Englewood Cliffs, NJ, 1993.

[83]    Wang, R. Y., H. B. Kon and S. E. Madnick. "Data Quality Requirements Analysis and Modeling," in *Proceedings of the 9th International Conference on Data Engineering*. Vienna, 1993, pp. 670–677.

[84]    Wang, R. Y., Y. L. Lee, L. Pipino and D. M. Strong, "Manage Your Information as a Product," *Sloan Management Review*, 39(4), 1998, pp. 95–105.

[85]    Wang, R. Y., Y. W. Lee and D. Strong, "Can You Defend Your Information in Court?" in *Proceedings of The 1996 Conference on Information Quality*. Cambridge, MA, pp. 53–64, 1996.

[86]    Wang, R. Y., M. P. Reddy and A. Gupta, "An Object-Oriented Implementation of Quality Data Products," in *Proceedings of the Third Annual Workshop on Information Technologies and Systems (WITS)*. Orlando, Florida, pp. 48–56, 1993.

[87]    Wang, R. Y., V. C. Storey and C. P. Firth, "A Framework for Analysis of Data Quality Research," *IEEE Transactions on Knowledge and Data Engineering*, 7(4), 1995, pp. 623–640.

[88]    Wang, R. Y. and D. M. Strong, "Beyond Accuracy: What Data Quality Means to Data Consumers," *Journal of Management Information Systems (JMIS)*, 12(4), 1996, pp. 5–34.

[89]    Wang, Y. R. and S. E. Madnick. "A Source Tagging Theory for Heterogeneous Database Systems," in *Proceedings of International Conference on Information Systems*. Copenhagen, Denmark, pp. 243–256, 1990.

[90]    Weber, R., *EDP Auditing: Conceptual Foundations and Practices*. 2nd ed. McGraw-Hill Series in MIS, ed. G. B. Davis. McGraw-Hill Book Company, New York, 1988.

[91]    West, M. and R. Winkler, "Data Base Error Trapping and Prediction," *Journal of the American Statistical Association,* 86(416), 1990, pp. 987–996.

[92]    Zahedi, F., *Quality Information Systems.* Boyd & Fraser Publishing Company, Danvers, MA, 1995.

[1]     Adler, P. S., "When Knowledge is the Critical Resource, Knowledge Management Is the Critical Task," *IEEE Transactions on Engineering Management,* 6(30), 1989, pp. 997–1015.

[2]     Allee, V., *The Knowledge Evolution: Expanding Organizational Intelligence.* Butterworth Heinenmann, Boston, MA, 1997.

[3]     Alvesson, M., "Organizations as Rhetoric: Knowledge-Intensive Firms and the Struggle with Ambiguity," *Journal of Management Studies,* 30(6), 1993, pp. 997–1015.

[4]     Argyris, C., *Knowledge for Action: A Guide to Overcoming Barriers to Organizational Change.* Jossey-Bass, San Francisco, CA, 1993.

[5]     Argyris, C., and D. A. Schön, *Organizational Learning: A Theory of Action Perspective.* Addison-Wesley Publishing Co., Reading, MA, 1978.

[6]     Asker, D. A., "Managing Assets and Skills: The Key To a Sustainable Competitive Advantage," *California Management Review,* 2(31), 1989, pp. 91–106.

[7]     Attewell, P., "Technology Diffusion and Organizational Learning," *Organization Science,* 3(1), 1992, pp. 1–19.

[8]     Badaracco, J., "Knowledge Links," in <u>The Knowledge Link: How Firms Compete Through Strategic Alliances</u> 1991,  Harvard Business School Press, Boston, MA, 1991.

[9]     Barley, S. R., J. Freeman, and R. C. Hybels, "Strategic Alliances in Commercial Biotechnology," in <u>Networks and Organizations,</u> N. Nohria, ed.,  Harvard Business School Press, Boston, MA, 1992.

[10]    Black, J. B., "Understanding and Remembering Stories," in <u>Knowledge Structures,</u> J. A. Galambos, R. P. Abelson and J. B. Black, ed. 1986,  Lawrence Erlbaum, Hillsdale, NJ, 1986.

[11]    Blackler, F., "Knowledge and the Theory of Organizations: Oranizations as Activity Systems and the Reframing of Management," *Journal of Management Studies,* 4(6), 1993, pp. 350–372.

[12]    Brewer, M., J. P. Liebeskind, A. L. Oliver, and L. Zucker, "Social Networks, Learning, and Flexibility: Sourcing Scientific Knowledge in New Biotechnology Firms," *Organization Science,* 7(4), 1996, pp. 428–443.

[13]    Brodie, M., and J. Mylopoulos, *On Knowledge Base Management Systems.* Springer-Verlag, 1986.

[14]     Brooking, A., *Intellectual Capital: Core Asset for the Third Millennium Enterprise*. International Thomson Business Press, London, 1996.

[15]     Brown, J. S., and P. Duguid, "Organizational Learning and Communities-of-Practice; Toward a Unified View of Working, Learning and Innovation," *Organization Science,* 2(1), 1991, pp. 40–57.

[16]     Cohen, M. D., and P. Bacdayan, "Organizational Routines are Stored as Procedural Memory: Evidence from a Laboratory Study," *Organizational Science,* 5(4), 1994, pp. 554–568.

[17]     Collins, H. M., "Humans, Machines, and the Structure of Knowledge," in <u>Knowledge Management Tools</u>, R. L. Ruggles, ed., Butterworth-Heinenmann, Boston, MA, 1995.

[18]     Conner, K., and C. K. Prahalad, "A Resource-based Theory of the Firm: Knowledge Versus Opportunism," *Organization Science,* 7(5), 1996, pp. 477–501.

[19]     Constant, D., L. Sproull, and S. Kiesler, "The Kindness of Strangers: The Usefulness of Electronic Weak Ties for Technical Advice," *Organization Science,* 7(2), 1996, pp. 119–135.

[20]     CRG, *Information Quality Assessment Survey: Administrator's Guide*. Cambridge Research Group, Cambridge, MA, 1997.

[21]     Daft, R. L., R. L. Lengel, and L. K. Trevino, "Message Equivocality, Media Selection, and Manager Performance: Implications for Information Systems," *MIS Quarterly,* 11(3), 1987, pp. 355-366.

[22]     Davenport, T., and L. Prusak, *Information Ecology: Mastering the Information and Knowledge Environment*. Oxford University Press, New York, 1997.

[23]     Davenport, T., and L. Prusak, *Working Knowledge*. Harvard Business School Press, Boston, MA, 1997.

[24]     Davenport, T. H., "Saving IT's Soul: Human-Centered Information Management," *Harvard Business Review,* 72(2), 1994, pp. 119–131.

[25]     Davis, S., and J. Botkin, "The Intelligent Enterprise and New Paradigm," *Academy of Management Executive,* 4(6), 1992, pp. 48–63.

[26]     Dhar, V., and A. Tuzhilin, "Abstract-Driven Pattern Discovery in Databases," *IEEE Transactions on Knowledge and Data Engineering,* 5(6), 1993, pp. 926–938.

[27]     Dougherty, D., and C. Hardy, "Sustained Product Innovation in Large, Mature Organizations: Overcoming Innovation-to-Organization Problems," *Academy of Management Journal,* 39(5), 1996, pp. 1120–1153.

[28]     Drucker, P. F., "The Coming of the New Organization," *Harvard Business Review,* 66(1), 1988, pp. 45–53.

[29]     Drucker, P. F., *Post Capitalist Society*. Butterworth Heinenmann, Oxford, 1993.

[30]   Earl, M. J., "Knowledge as Strategy: Reflections on Skandia International and Shorko Films," In <u>Strategic Information Systems: A European Perspective</u>, C. J. Ciborra, ed., John Wiley & Sons., New York, NY, 1994.

[31]   Edvinsson, L., and M. Malone, *Intellectual Capital: Realizing Your Company's True Value by Finding Its Hidden Brain Power*. Harper Business, New York, 1997.

[32]   Eisenhardt, K. M., and B. N. Tabrizi, "Accelerating Adaptive Processes: Product Innovation in the Global Computer Industry," *Administrative Science Quarterly,* 1(40), 1995, pp. 84–110.

[33]   Epple, D., L. Argote, and R. Devadas, "An Empirical Investigation of the Microstructure of Knowledge Acquisition and Transfer Through Learning By Doing," *Operations Research,* 1(44), 1991, pp. 77–86.

[34]   Epple, D., L. Argote, and R. Devadas, "Organizational Learning Curves," *Organization Science,* 2(1), 1991, pp. 58–70.

[35]   Fayyad, U., *Advance In Knowledge Discovery and Data Mining*. AAAI Press, Menlo Park, CA, 1995.

[36]   Frawley, W. J., G. Piatetsky-Shapiro, and C. J. Matheus, "Knowledge Discovery in Databases: An Overview," W. J. Frawley and G. Piatetsky-Shapiro, ed., MIT Press, Cambridge, MA, 1991.

[37]   Grant, R. M., "Prospering in Dynamically-Competitive Environments: Organizational Capability as Knowledge Integration," *Organization Science,* 4(7), 1996, pp. 375–387.

[38]   Grant, R. M., "Toward a Knowledge-Based Theory of the Firm," *Strategic Management Journal,* 17, 1996, pp. 109–122.

[39]   Hebeler, J. W., and D. C. Van Doren, "Unfettered Leverage: The Ascendancy of Knowledge-Rich Products and Processes," *Business Horizons,* July–August), 1997, pp. 2–10.

[40]   Heibler, R. J., "Benchmarking Knowledge Management," *Strategy & Leadership,* March/April), 1996, pp. 22–29.

[41]   Henderson, R. M., "Technological Change and the Management of Architectural Knowledge," in <u>Transforming Education</u>, T. A. Kochan and M. Useem, ed. 1992, Sloan School of Management, Boston, MA, 1992.

[42]   Hu, J., K. T. Huang, K. Kuse, G. Su, and K. Wang, "Customer Information Quality and Knowledge Management: A Case Study Using Knowledge Cockpit," *Journal of Knowledge Management,* 1(3), 1998, pp. 225–236.

[43]   Huang, K. T., "Creating and Exploiting Organizational Knowledge to Speed up Business Growth," in *IBM Internal Report*, North Tarrytown, NY: IBM, 1996.

[44]   Huang, K. T., "Industry Guide to Management of Asset Based Solutions," in *IBM Internal Report* Tarrytown, N.Y, IBM, 1996.

[45]  Huang, K. T., "Capitalizing, Collective Knowledge for Winning, Execution, and Teamwork," *Journal of Knowledge Management,* 1(2), 1997, pp. 149–156.

[46]  Huang, K. T. Knowledge Is Power: So Use It or Lose It. IBM, 1998 <http://www.ibm.com/services/articles/inttelcapsum.html>.

[47]  Huang, K. T., "Capitalizing on Intellectual Assets, not Infrastructure," *IBM Systems Journal,* Forthcoming.

[48]  Iansiti, M., and J. West, "Technology Integration: Turning Great Research into Great Products," *Harvard Business Review,* 75(3), 1997, pp. 69–79.

[49]  IBM, "IBM's Planning Guidelines of Leveraging Asset Use in Solutions and Services," in *IBM Internal Report,* 1996.

[50]  IBM, *The Learning Organizations: Managing Knowledge for Business Success.* IBM Consulting Group, North Tarrytown, NY, 1996.

[51]  *IBM Annual Report.* IBM, 1997 <http://www.ibm.com/AnnualReport/1997>.

[52]  IBM "Kasparov beats Deep Blue 4-2," IBM, 1997 <http://www.chess.ibm.park.org>.

[53]  IBM "Global Services Wins Top Honor For Its Knowledge Management Innovations," IBM, 1998 <http://www.ibm.com/services/pressrel/pr.889566539.html>.

[54]  Jensen, M. C., and W. H. Meckling, " Specific and General Knowledge, and Organizational Structure," *Journal of Applied Corporate Finance,* 8(2), 1995, pp. 4–18.

[55]  Keller, R., and R. R. Chinta, " International Technology Transfer: Strategies for Success," *Academy of Management Executive,* 4(2), 1990, pp. 33–43.

[56]  Knights, D., Murray, F., and H. Willmot, "Networking as Knowledge Work: A Study of Strategic Interorganizational Development in the Financial Services Industry," *Journal of Management Studies,* 30(6), 1993, pp. 975–995.

[57]  Kogut, B., and U. Zander, "Knowledge of the Firm Combinative Capabilities, and the Replication of Technology," *Organization Science,* 3(3), 1992, pp. 383–397.

[58]  Lee, Y., *Collective Knowledge: An Institutional Learning Perspective.* Cambridge Research Group, Cambridge, MA, 1997.

[59]  Lee, Y., *Quality Information, Organizational Knowledge, and Core Competency.* Cambridge Research Group, Cambridge, MA, 1997.

[60]  Lee, Y. W., "Why "Know Why" Knowledge is Useful for Solving Information Quality Problems," In *Proceedings of Americas Conference on Information Systems.* Phoenix, AZ, 1996, pp. 200–202.

[61]     Leonard-Barton, D., *Wellsprings of Knowledge: Building and Sustaining the Sources of Innovation*. Harvard Business School Press, Boston, MA, 1995.

[62]     Lloyd, T., "ESS: Technical Architecture Project—Stage 1 Technical Report," in *IBM Internal Report*, 1996.

[63]     Long, C. and M. Vickers-Koch, "Using Core Capabilities to Create Competitive Advantage," *Organizational Dynamics* (24), 1995, pp. 7–20.

[64]     Lotus "A vision for Knowledge Management," Lotus, 1998
        <http://www.lotus.com>.

[65]     Lyles, M. A. and C. R. Schwenk, "Top Management, Strategy and Organizational Knowledge Structures," *Journal of Management Studies,* 29(2), 1992, pp. 155–174.

[66]     Mann, M., R. Rudman, T. Jenckes and B. McNurlin, "EPRINET: Leveraging Knowledge in the Electric Utility Industry," *MIS Quarterly,* 15(3), 1991, pp. 403–421.

[67]     Miles, R. E., C. C. Snow, J. A. Mathew, G. Miles and H. J. J. Coleman, "Organizing in the Knowledge Age: Anticipating the Cellular Form," *Academy of Management Executive,* 4(11), 1997, pp. 7–19.

[68]     Monachino, M. "The Solution Optimization Process," in *IBM Internal Report*, IBM, 1995.

[69]     Nass, C., "Knowledge or Skills: Which Do Administrators Learn from Experience?," *Organizational Science,* 4(6), 1994, pp. 38–50.

[70]     Nielsen, L., O. Von Malaise and K. Riley, "Solution Business Management," in IBM, 1996.

[71]     Nonaka, I., "The Knowledge-Creating Company," *Harvard Business Review,* 69(6), 1991, pp. 96–104.

[72]     Nonaka, I. and H. Takeuchi, *The Knowledge-Creating Company: How Japanese Companies Create the Dynamics of Innovation*. Oxford University Press, New York, NY, 1995.

[73]     New York Times, <http://www.nytimes.com/library/cyber/week/071397vacation.html>.

[74]     Orr, J. E., "Sharing Knowledge, Celebrating Identity," in Collective Remembering, D. S. Middleton and D. Edwards, ed. 1990, Sage, Newbury Park, CA, 1990.

[75]     Pine, B. J. I., *Mass Customization: the New Frontier in Business Competition*. Harvard Business School Press, Boston, MA, 1993.

[76]     Pisano, G. P., "Knowledge, Integration, and the Locus of Learning: An Empirical Analysis of Process Development," *Stategic Management Journal,* 15, 1994, pp. 85–100.

[77]     Polanyi, M., *The Tacit Dimension*. Doubleday, Garden City, NY, 1966.

[78]     Popper, K. P., *Objective Knowledge*. Clarendon Press, Oxford, 1972.

[79]     Porter, M. E., *Competitive Advantage*. Free Press, New York, 1985.

[80]  Prahalad, C. K., and G. Kamel, "The Core Competence of the Corporation," *Harvard Business Review,* May–June), 1990, pp. 79–91.

[81]  Quinn, J. B., *Intellegence Enterprise.* The Free Press, New York, 1992.

[82]  Quinn, J. B., P. Anderson, and S. Finkelstein, "Managing Professional Intellect: Making the Most of the Best," *Harvard Business Review,* 2(74), 1996, pp. 71–80.

[83]  Quinn, J. B., J. J. Baruch, and K. A. Zien, *Innovation Explosion: Using Intellect and Software to Revolutionize Growth Strategies.* The Free Press, New York, NY, 1997.

[84]  Reich, R., *The Work of Nations.* Alfred A. Knopf, New York, NY, 1991.

[85]  Ren, S., and K. T. Huang, "The Automotive Industry and its Newest Recruit: the NetDealerships," *IBM Intranet Webpage Report,* 1997.

[86]  Rice, R. E., and E. Rogers, "Reinvention in the Innovation Process," *Knowledge,* 1(4), 1980, pp. 499–514.

[87]  Saint-Onge, H., "Tacit Knowledge: The Key to Strategic Alignment," *Strategy & Leadership,* March/April, 1996, pp. 10–14.

[88]  Sanchez, R., and A. Heene, *Strategic Learning & Knowledge Management.* John Wiley, Chicester, 1997.

[89]  Sanchez, R., and J. T. Mahoney, "Modularity, Flexibility, and Knowledge Management in Product and Organization Design," *Strategic Management Journal,* 17(Winter), 1996, pp. 63-76.

[90]  Sandberg, J. " At Thousands of Web Sites, Time Stands Still: Many Web Sites Need Updating," *The Wall Street Journal,* March 11, 1997 p. B1.

[91]  Schön, D., *Educating the Reflective Practitioner.* Jossey Bass, San Francisco, CA, 1990.

[92]  Simonin, B. L., "The Importance of Collaborative Know-How: An Empirical Test of the Learning Organization," *Academy of Management Journal,* 5(40), 1997, pp. 1150–1174.

[93]  SPC, "Reuse Adoption Guidebook," in *Software Productivity Consortium Services Corporation,* 1993.

[94]  SPC, "Reuse-Driven Software Processes Guidebook," in *Software Productivity Consortium Services Corporation,* 1993.

[95]  Spender, J. C., "Making Knowledge the Basis of a Dynamic Theory of the Firm," *Strategic Management Journal,* 17(Winter), 1996, pp. 45–62.

[96]  Starbuck, W. H., "Learning by Knowledge-Intensive Firms," *Journal of Management Studies,* 29(6), 1992, pp. 713–740.

[97]  Wang, R. Y., Y. L. Lee, L. Pipino, and D. M. Strong, "Manage Your Information as a Product," *Sloan Management Review,* 39(4), 1998, pp. 95–105.

[98]    WARIA , *WARIA and Giga Information Group Announce the Finalists of 1998 Giga Excellence Awards for Excellence in Document /Knowledge Management and Workflow/Process Management in North America*. WARIA, 1998 <http://www.waria.com/awards98.html>.

[99]    Weick, K. E., "Collective Mind in Organizations: Heedful Interrelating on Flight Decks," *Administative Science Quarterly*, 3(38), 1993, pp. 357–381.

[100]   Weiss, A. R., and P. Birnbaum, "Technological Infrastructure and the Implementation of Technological Strategies," 35(8), 1989, pp. 1014–1026.

[101]   Wilson, L., "Devil In Your Data," *Information Week*, August 31, p. 1992.

[102]   Wilson, P., "Information Retrieval and Cognitive Authority," in <u>Second Hand Knowledge</u>, Greenwood Publishing Group, Westport, CT, 1983.

[103]   Winch, G. S., E., "Managing the Knowledge-Based Organization: The Case of Architectural Practice," *Journal of Management Studies*, 30(6), 1993, pp. 923–937.

[104]   Winslow, C. D. B., W.L., *FutureWork: Putting Knowledge to Work in the Knowledge Economy*. Free Press, New York, 1994.

[105]   Winter, S. G., "Knowledge and Competence as Strategic Assets," In <u>The Competitive Challenge</u>, D. J. Teece, ed., Ballinger, Cambridge, MA, 1987.

# Glossary

**application-dependent IQ metrics** Measures IQ quality along quantifiable, objective variables that are domain specific. *Chapter 4, Application-Dependent IQ Metrics*

**application-independent metrics** Measures IQ quality along quantifiable, objective variables. *Chapter 4, Objective, Application-Independent Metrics*

**core competency** The end product of combining human capital, processes, intangible assets, and technologies. *Chapter 6, How to Manage Knowledge Assets*

**data deficiency** An unconformity between the view of the real-world system that can be inferred from a representing information system and the view that can be obtained by directly observing the real-world system. *Chapter 3, Data Deficiency*

**data mining** Process of discovering meaningful patterns by analyzing large amounts of data with mathematical techniques. *Chapter 7, Data and Knowledge Mining*

**enhanced product realization** Experimental information system which allows manufacturers to collaborate and cater to customers' needs through an extranet.

**extranet** Semi-public network used by several collaborating parties. *Chapter 8, The Internet, Intranets, and Extranets*

**garbling** When a real-world lawful state is mapped to an information system's lawful state that it should not be mapped to. *Chapter 3, Operation Deficiencies*

**incompleteness** The term used to describe the condition when lawful states of a real-world system cannot all be represented by the information system. *Chapter 3, Design Deficiencies.*

**information consumers** Those who use information products in their work. *Chapter 2, Information Manufacturing Systems*

**information custodians** People who design, develop, or maintain the data and systems infrastructure for the information product. *Chapter 2, Information Manufacturing Systems*

**information manufacturing** A processing system acting on raw data to produce information products. *Chapter 2, From Product to Information Manufacturing*

**information manufacturing system** A system divided into four separate roles (information provider, information custodian, information customer, and information product manager) whose goal is to produce information products. *Chapter 2, Information Manufacturing Systems*

**information product manager** Person responsible for managing the entire information product production process and the information product life cycle. *Chapter 2, Information Manufacturing Systems*

**information providers** People who create or collect data for the information product. *Chapter 2, Information Manufacturing Systems*

**Information Quality Assessment Tool** Software tool that performs dimensional IQ assessment and IQ knowledge assessment. *Chapter 4, IQA Survey Tool*

**information quality dimension** A set of information quality attributes that represent a single aspect or construct of information quality. *Chapter 2, Dimensions of Information Quality*

**Integrity Analyzer** Software tool that utilizes both the TDQM cycle and Codd's five integrity rules in the relational model to analyze the soundness of data. *Chapter 4, Integrity Analyzer*

**intellectual asset** A group of structured knowledge items that are reuseable and have added value to an organization. *Chapter 7, Intellectual Asset and Solution*

**IQ knowledge assessment** Subjective IQ metric used to measure the three types of IQ knowledge, IQ know-what, know-how, and know-why within an organization. *Chapter 4, Analyze IQ*

**knowledge harvesting** Knowledge creation and reuse process. *Chapter 6, How to Manage Knowledge Assets*

**knowledge hunting** Process of collecting knowledge, harvesting the process of filtering, and hardening the process of structuring tacit, useful knowledge into explicit, reuseable knowledge. *Chapter 6, How to Manage Knowledge Assets*

**knowledge management** Organizing and structuring of institutional processes, mechanisms, and infrastructures to create, store, and reuse organizational knowledge; the management of organizational knowledge. *Chapter 6, What is Knowledge Management*

**knowledge management process** Process by which tacit knowledge is identified and converted into structured knowledge.

**knowledge mining** Process for abstracting valid, previously unknown, ultimately comprehensible knowledge from several information sources; one of the three categories of technology that supports knowledge management. *Chapter 7, Data and Knowledge Mining*

**knowledge sourcing** Method of retrieving information from multiple sources and delivering value-added knowledge for customers to solve business problems. *Chapter 6, Ten Strategies for Knowledge Management*

**meaningless states** Term used to describe an information system's lawful states that cannot be mapped back to real-world lawful states. *Chapter 3, Design Deficiencies*

**organizational Alzheimer's disease** The improper use, flow, and articulation of organizational knowledge. *Chapter 1, Organizational Knowledge*

**organizational knowledge** An organization's knowledge of the various processes, products, services, and customers that is the result of the collection of individual employees' knowledge. *Chapter 1, Organizational Knowledge*

**product manufacturing** A processing system that acts on raw materials to produce physical products. *Chapter 2, From Product to Information Manufacturing*

**reuse** The process of taking the work of one project and using it on subsequent projects with the objective of reducing the overall effort required for the projects *Chapter 7, Harvesting and Hardening Assets for Reuse*

**Total Data Quality Management (TDQM) cycle** The TDQM cycle encompasses four components. The *definition* component of the TDQM cycle identifies IQ dimensions, the *measurement* component produces IQ metrics, the *analysis* component identifies root causes for IQ problems and calculates the impacts of poor-quality information, and finally, the *improvement* component provides techniques for improving IQ. *Chapter 2, TDQM Cycle*

# Index

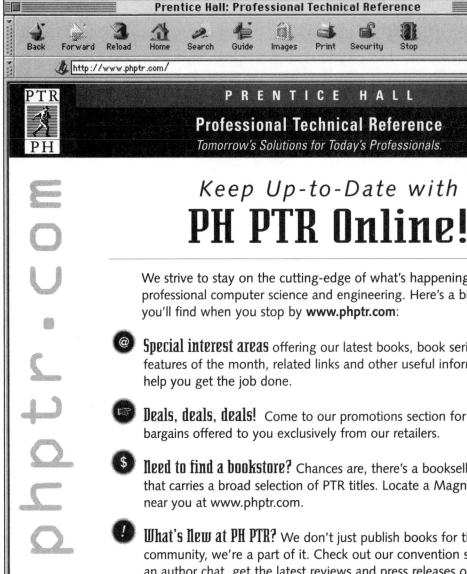

**Prentice Hall: Professional Technical Reference**

http://www.phptr.com/

## PRENTICE HALL
### Professional Technical Reference
*Tomorrow's Solutions for Today's Professionals.*

## Keep Up-to-Date with
# PH PTR Online!

We strive to stay on the cutting-edge of what's happening in professional computer science and engineering. Here's a bit of what you'll find when you stop by **www.phptr.com**:

**Special interest areas** offering our latest books, book series, software, features of the month, related links and other useful information to help you get the job done.

**Deals, deals, deals!** Come to our promotions section for the latest bargains offered to you exclusively from our retailers.

**Need to find a bookstore?** Chances are, there's a bookseller near you that carries a broad selection of PTR titles. Locate a Magnet bookstore near you at www.phptr.com.

**What's New at PH PTR?** We don't just publish books for the professional community, we're a part of it. Check out our convention schedule, join an author chat, get the latest reviews and press releases on topics of interest to you.

**Subscribe Today!** **Join PH PTR's monthly email newsletter!**

Want to be kept up-to-date on your area of interest? Choose a targeted category on our website, and we'll keep you informed of the latest PH PTR products, author events, reviews and conferences in your interest area.

Visit our mailroom to subscribe today! **http://www.phptr.com/mail_lists**